*Praise for* **THE ROAD TO BLAIR MOUNTAIN**

NO LONGER PROPERTY OF
SEATTLE PUBLIC LIBRARY

"Chuck Keeney takes over where his great-grandfather left off a century ago—in a no-holds-barred fight against King Coal and its pursuit of profits over people. Keeney delivers a riveting and propulsive story about a nine-year battle to save sacred ground that was the site of the largest labor uprising in American history. You'll find yourself rooting for Keeney from beginning to end. He unveils a powerful playbook on successful activism that will inspire countless others for generations to come."

> —Eric Eyre, Pulitzer Prize winner and author of *Death in Mud Lick: A Coal Country Fight against the Drug Companies That Delivered the Opioid Epidemic*

"Keeney brings a lifetime of scholarship, family relations, and activism to this twenty-first-century chapter of the epic and ongoing saga of Blair Mountain."

> —Catherine Venable Moore, president, West Virginia Mine Wars Museum

"This book connects to work on twentieth-century labor history, but it is more than that. It is an insider's thoughts on regional identity and activism as well as a reassessment of how people see Appalachia in the popular mind. When Charles Keeney speaks directly to the reader and offers advice, it resonates in a powerful and present way."

> —Steven E. Nash, East Tennessee State University

"Fascinating. . . . Suspenseful to the very end."

> —*Daily Yonder*

D1603712

# THE
# ROAD
# ᴛᴏ BLAIR
# MOUNTAIN

## Saving a
## Mine Wars
## Battlefield from
## King Coal

# CHARLES B. KEENEY

 **West Virginia University Press**
**Morgantown**

Copyright © 2021 by West Virginia University Press
All rights reserved
First edition published 2021 by West Virginia University Press
Printed in the United States of America

ISBN
Cloth 978-1-949199-84-0
Paper 978-1-949199-85-7
Ebook 978-1-949199-86-4

Library of Congress Cataloging-in-Publication Data
Names: Keeney, Charles Belmont, author.
Title: The road to Blair Mountain : saving a Mine Wars battlefield from
king coal / Charles B. Keeney.
Description: First edition. | Morgantown : West Virginia University Press,
2021. | Includes bibliographical references and index.
Identifiers: LCCN 2020022380 | ISBN 9781949199840 (cloth) | ISBN
9781949199857 (paperback) | ISBN 9781949199864 (ebook)
Subjects: LCSH: Historic sites—Conservation and restoration—West
Virginia. | Environmentalism—West Virginia. | Blair Mountain (W. Va.)
Classification: LCC F247.L8 K44 2021 | DDC 975.4—dc23
LC record available at https://lccn.loc.gov/2020022380

Book and cover design by Than Saffel / WVU Press

*For all the Red Necks,*
*past, present, and future.*
*You know who you are.*

# Contents

>>>>>> <<<<<<

# Preface

**A** lump of coal rests atop a red bandana in my home.
The lump of coal is from Blair Mountain. The red
bandana is from a 2011 protest march organized to protect
Blair Mountain from destruction by mountaintop removal
mining. After the protest march, I drove back to Blair and
found the piece of coal about halfway up the southern crest.
Upon returning home, I placed it over the bandana I wore
on the march and put the display atop a bookshelf where
I could see it from anywhere in the room. Its shrine-like
presence served two purposes. First, it reminded me of what
I was fighting for and why I was fighting. Second, I took the
piece of coal because, as I reasoned to myself with a grin,
no matter what happened, the coal companies would not
get all of it.

From 2009 to 2018, a small group of activists fought a successful campaign against three multi-billion-dollar corporations, a state government, and the military-industrial complex
in order to preserve a battlefield. This book is about the significance of that fight and how we won it. On a more personal

level, this is a firsthand account of my own experience in this fight. I am a native West Virginian, have lived here my entire life, and my roots in the region are deep. The Keeney family settled in the Greenbrier Valley of what is now West Virginia in 1751. Frank Keeney, my great-grandfather, played a central role in the West Virginia Mine Wars and the events surrounding the 1921 Battle of Blair Mountain. He spent his life fighting for coal miners and against coal companies. This personal heritage motivated me, in part, to earn a doctorate in history with a specialization in Appalachia. Additionally, without this heritage, I would not have gotten involved in the fight to save Blair Mountain, much less become a central figure in that effort.

Raymond Chafin, a highly successful coalfield politician during the middle of the twentieth century often said, "In West Virginia everything is political except politics, and that's personal."[1] There is a lot of truth to Chafin's statement. The history of West Virginia is also intensely personal. Because of my intimacy with this history, the fight to prevent the destruction of the Blair Mountain Battlefield became almost like a crusade to protect a family member. My hope is that the reader will digest this book with the understanding that I have both the advantage and the liability of my deeply personal connection to the events I describe. That is why this book is a memoir and not strictly an academic enterprise.

That said, I hope readers will be able to glean a number of things from the narrative. As the twenty-first century proceeds, global industrialization and expanding urbanization will continue to threaten valuable natural and historic areas all around the world. Fossil fuel extraction, timbering, and mining threaten areas such as Blair Mountain, the Grand Canyon, and Bear Ears ancestral landscape in Utah. Industrial agriculture, such as the cocoa industry on the Ivory Coast of Africa and palm oil plantations in Indonesia, contribute to mass deforestation and devastating habitat loss in parks and rainforests. Grassroots activists and indigenous people, often in rural areas, find themselves facing enormous odds when protecting sacred landscapes against the financial and political might of major extraction and agricultural industries. Such individuals and groups may find valuable lessons in this book.

Before my involvement in the efforts to save the Blair Mountain Battlefield, I had no experience with activism or protests. Within a year of my initiation, the board of Friends of Blair Mountain (FOBM) elected me their president as we set upon the task of defeating the coal industry on its own turf. There are many things I wish I knew then and this book includes things I wish someone would have told me when the journey began. Writing this book was a means of recording what I have learned about activism and leadership in grassroots organizations—where we succeeded and where we failed. Perhaps those embarking on their own road in their cause will be able to benefit from my experiences and perspective.

My fellow Americans who read this work should view it, for better or worse, as a long, hard look in the mirror. Appalachia is often portrayed as a place separate and apart from the rest of America. Among other things, this allows Americans to absolve themselves of any accountability or relation. But Appalachia is America, even if those who live outside the region do not want to admit it. I suspect that with a close inspection of the region in its proper historical context, Americans would find more of themselves in Appalachia than they care to admit. Take, for example, the tangible manifestation of historical ignorance. Many aspects of contemporary life in Appalachia reflect the consequences of erased history. Most people don't even think about it—how the absence of knowledge and the failure to learn from the past manifests itself in the world around them. Understanding the significance of Blair Mountain, and its relationship to America at large, is to see a portrait of a place where myth battles fact for influence over society. I do not believe Appalachia is unique in this regard.

My theory is that people from different regions of America will find more similarities than differences in the local politics, economic problems, and social issues described in this book. Throughout the course of this narrative, the reader will see examples of what happens on a regional level when Americans learn from their history and what happens when they do not. By consequence, the narrative also contributes to and sometimes contradicts what many others have written about my home.

Nothing is simplistic when it comes to Blair Mountain. That lump of coal and bandana I see as I write these very words remind me of the complexities surrounding the battle and the place. This is a story with many layers. Blair Mountain is about our history, our memory, unions, corporations, environment, culture, politics, and more. Understanding these layers in their historical context became crucial to the success of our activism. I spend a good deal of the narrative placing our activism in the context of regional history and contemporary events. In the end, I hope readers will reach a better understanding of the place I, and so many others, fought to defend, why we took on the fight, and how we won. Blair Mountain is important. If I wrote the book well enough, you will understand why.

Pink Anderson, a southern Appalachian blues guitarist, once recorded a song called "You Don't Know My Mind."

In the song, Anderson sings, "When you see me laugh, I'm laughin' just to keep from cryin'." Throughout the course of our efforts to save Blair Mountain, the lyrics kept resurfacing in my mind and I began to understand more and more what they meant. One of the sources of our resilience in Appalachia is the ability to look into the abyss and smile. This alludes to the second reason I kept a lump of coal from Blair Mountain. If one can look at the many tragedies in West Virginia and manage to grin defiantly in the face of it, it is a step in the right direction. As this book will reveal, there are many steps to take and each one counts.

CHAPTER ONE

# Fighting
# for a Battlefield

>>>>> <<<<<

**T**his was not a place I ever expected to be. It was June
11, 2011, at about 4:00 p.m., sunny, and about ninety
degrees. I sat in the shade on a forested ridgeline near the
southern summit of Blair Mountain by an old dirt road, the
kind you need a four-wheel drive to climb. The road led up
to where a fire tower had once been. The Civilian Conservation Corps (CCC) had built dozens of fire towers throughout
West Virginia during the Depression, and they built one on
the southern summit of Blair. The fire tower itself no longer
existed; Arch Coal had torn it down a few years before.
Now only a dirt road leads to where the tower once stood. A
number of similar roads in West Virginia climb up to empty
spaces where fire towers once stood. On this particular June
afternoon, I sat on the edge of the dirt road while Joe Stanley
and Michael Morrison continued on up to where the fire
tower had once been, still holding their UMWA Local 1440
signs over their heads.

It was nice to have a brief moment alone up there. My legs
dangled over the edge and I looked down the steep, densely

forested slope. Through the trees and down to my left I could
barely see the curve of Route 17 in the distance. In the cracks
between the branches and trees, I caught glimpses of the
mass of people, around 800, with colorful banners and red
bandanas. I faintly heard them singing just above the sound of
the breeze and, although I had no idea what they sang, I still
felt energy coming from the crowd. They ascended a sharp
curve and gathered at a wide spot by the main road where
the old dirt road veered up to the southern summit. I could
not see the gathering from where I sat—I was a little farther
up the ridgeline—but I could hear them cheer followed by
someone giving a speech through a loudspeaker. The CNN
crew, who had followed me up, had returned to the larger
scene, thankfully, and left me alone. I had a moment to sit
quietly and enjoy the view.

Earlier my friend Jason Tackett had sat down with me for
a bit. We have known each other all our lives and Jason had
marched with us on this day and on the Thursday before.
His workload as an ER doctor only allowed him to be with
us those two days, but I was thankful for his presence. It
is always nice to have a familiar face when in strange circumstances. After a while, Jason had gone off to check on
a woman who was slightly dehydrated by the two-mile hike
up the mountain road, but then, satisfied that she was okay,
he came back and sat down again, and we started talking
about the battle.

Long before the CCC built a fire tower at Blair, the
mountain had seen the culmination of West Virginia's Mine
Wars. In 1921, thousands of union coal miners formed an
army and marched south from the state capitol in Charleston
into the southern coalfields. The miners' army intended to
rescue imprisoned striking miners in Mingo County and
bring aid to starving families whose food supply had been

cut off by authorities. The miners also hoped to forcefully end the Mine Guard System—something of an industrial police state—which had permeated throughout the coalfields for nearly three decades. Those who marched south toward Mingo did not take up arms for themselves, but for the sake of their working-class brothers and sisters immersed in a life-and-death struggle along the Tug River. In their minds, they fought for the freedom of others. To make it to Mingo, however, the miners needed to march through Logan County. Don Chafin, the pro-company sheriff of Logan, formed his own army and they were entrenched on hilltops and ridgelines north of Logan town. The coal companies' army and the coal miners' army clashed at Blair Mountain and along a front extending for about twelve miles. The company's men possessed the high ground and the firepower. The miners had the numbers and the will to fight. For five days, the miners and company forces fought in the dense, steep, summer mountains, but the miners were ultimately unable to successfully break through the companies' entrenched defenses. They surrendered to federal troops when they arrived on the scene on September 4, 1921.

Jason and I were sitting near one of the defensive entrenchments on the southern flank of the battlefield. I tried to point it out to him, but it was just out of our sight. A little further up the ridge and above us sat an old machine gun nest used by Don Chafin's defensive forces in the battle. We looked back down the slope and speculated on what the defenders must have seen and heard. Certainly not waving banners and singing. We talked about what it would have been like to have been down below, making your way from tree to tree with a machine gun firing down on you. The slope is very steep and it is easy to see how a defender, well supplied with the right weaponry, could hold this ridge against much larger numbers. Jason and I had never seen any sort of combat; perhaps the closest thing would have been us running around in the woods as kids with BB guns pretending to be soldiers. But we had run up and down many slopes just like the one we were staring down now. We didn't need to discuss how serious a man would have to be to climb this mountain with a machine gun nest right above him. We had known mountains like this our whole lives, but this wasn't any ordinary mountain.

## • KING OF BLAIR MOUNTAIN •

Nearly a century has passed since the 1921 armed uprising at Blair Mountain. The battle has been called America's greatest labor uprising and the largest armed insurrection since the Civil War. The battle was part of a larger wave of revolutions and workers' uprisings that swept across the western world in the wake of World War I. These turbulent years saw revolutions in Russia, Hungary, Ireland, and Mexico; labor revolts in Vienna; the Spartacist uprising in Germany; the Bienno Rosso in Italy; and massive steelworkers and textile strikes in the United States. The West Virginia Mine Wars as a whole have earned a significant place in the annals of American labor and folklore with their dramatic, violent strikes. Some legendary figures in the American pantheon, such as Mother Jones and Sid Hatfield, emerged from these conflicts. The Mine Wars even inspired famous protest songs like "Solidarity Forever" and "We Shall Not Be Moved." And yet, until very recently, the Mine Wars and the Battle of Blair Mountain have been largely unknown chapters in American history.

In the 1980s and early '90s the Mine Wars and Blair Mountain emerged in the regional consciousness. The publication of David Alan Corbin's *Life, Work, and Rebellion in the Coal Fields* in 1981 sparked a decade or so of scholarly and artistic works surrounding the Mine Wars. Denise Giardina's novel *Storming Heaven*, John Sayles's independent film *Matewan*, a local PBS documentary, and a handful of history books brought the story of the West Virginia miners to the general public for the first time. The films and books received little national attention, but they generated a regional buzz. Meanwhile, in Logan County, a local mountaineer began systematically searching the slopes and ridges around Ethel Hollow and along Spruce Fork Ridge—areas associated with the Blair Battlefield—looking for relics and remains of the conflict. The man who sifted through the trees and rocks is a grandson of a miner who fought at Blair Mountain. His name is Kenny King.

The 1921 Battle of Blair Mountain encompassed an area much larger than the mountain itself, which is actually rather typical for battles. The Battle of Bunker Hill, for instance, mostly occurred along neighboring Breed's Hill. The Battle of San Juan Hill, during the Spanish-American War, was also much larger than the hill that gave the battle its name. Such was the case with Blair Mountain. As the miners' army, called the Red Neck Army for the red bandanas they wore, advanced south toward Logan and Mingo Counties, Sheriff Don Chafin decided to make his defensive stand along a series of steep ridgelines and mountains a few miles north of the town of Logan. The defensive positions began at Blair Mountain in the south and stretched northwest along Spruce Fork Ridge for over nearly twelve miles to Mill Creek Gap. The fighting that occurred during the battle took place all along this front. The most intense fighting occurred on the flanks: in the north at Crooked and Mill Creeks and in the south at Blair Mountain. By comparison, the World War I

Battle of Verdun began on an eight-mile front. Thus, the amount of terrain covered in this engagement was very large by any military standards.

Although this particular battlefield held some geographic and strategic similarities to other famous battlefields, it is the unique meaning of the battle that drew Kenny's fascination. In his study of memory and battlefields, Petry J. Raivo states that battlefields are "fundamental parts of the national iconography of modern states."[1] As such, most battlefields represent a nationalistic past and often present a patriotic interpretation of the historic narrative. Places such as Pearl Harbor, Verdun, and Yorktown evoke a sense of patriotism and national pride as well as tragedy, remembrance, and sacrifice. However, the history of the Battle of Blair Mountain does not fit quite so easily into a nationalistic narrative, as it was a conflict not waged by one nation against another, but one that pitted workers against industrialists. The Mine Wars were fought along class and ideological lines that questioned the very idea of liberty in America. Predictably, significant controversy has surrounded the battlefield that may well represent the most potent challenge to the industrial power structure in American history.

Throughout 1990 and 1991, Kenny began exploring this vast area, which no one had really done before. He trekked over miles of Spruce Fork Ridge, locating defensive entrenchments all along the ridgeline. He took a metal detector and found hundreds of shell casings, buried guns, and numerous other artifacts. Kenny retraced the miners' advances along Blair Gap and later explored Crooked Creek Gap in the north. The abundance of artifacts astonished him, even though the thick underbrush, steep slopes, and rock outcroppings made his investigation painstakingly slow and difficult. Nonetheless, Kenny kept searching and what he found revealed an almost completely undisturbed and unexplored archeological site with thousands of artifacts covering thousands of acres that told a forgotten chapter of American history. He had found an archeological gold mine.

Blair Mountain has remained in obscurity for many reasons. One reason is the uprising lacks primary documents from the actual participants. The miners kept to a code of silence about the organization and specifics of the battle and left no written evidence. They were, after all, committing what some would call treason by taking up arms. We do not really know how many people participated in the Armed March, even though 10,000 is the standard number used. Some estimates go as high as 20,000.[2] We also do not know how many people died in the battle. On the defensive side, Don Chafin's forces controlled the local press and remained secretive about their own tactics and strategies. This lack of a written record left a gap in the history that Kenny's findings could help fill.

Kenny was not a professional archeologist or historian, just a local with a family connection to the history who wanted to learn more about it. In this sense, the entire preservation movement surrounding Blair Mountain began as one man's quest for knowledge. Realizing he needed help, Kenny contacted West Virginia University (WVU) and the United Mine Workers of America (UMWA). In 1991, Billy Joe Peyton and Mike Workman, representing the Institute for the History of Technology and Industrial Archaeology at WVU, conducted a cultural resource survey in the West Virginia coalfields; Kenny spent two days with them on the battlefield. Two days only enabled them to view a fragment of the acreage, but in their final report, Peyton and Workman concluded that the battlefield, "maintains a high degree of integrity and would be considered of primary significance to the overall interpretation of the Battle of Blair Mountain."[3]

The report went on to recommend that the area be preserved and possibly developed as a historic park. Peyton and
Workman also recommended the battlefield for inclusion in
the National Register of Historic Places. The UMWA and the
coal companies responded to the increased public interest and
tentatively agreed on an eight-acre park commemorating the
battle on acreage of Blair that would be left over after surface
mining had occurred. As the '90s progressed, however, the
UMWA and the coal companies continued to clash, and any
talk of preserving Blair Mountain faded away.

Kenny felt every acre on the battlefield deserved protection,
not a mere eight. In contrast to industrialists who view the
natural world as a God-given commodity to be exploited for
profit, Kenny viewed Blair Mountain as a sacred landscape,
acreage that no one can measure in monetary value. As talk
of commemorating the battle subsided, Kenny continued his
independent research. Members of the community of Blair,
such as Jimmy Weekley, Charles Bella, and Carlos Gore, supported Kenny's efforts and encouraged him to continue. Even
so, the logistics and size of the battlefield made it difficult for
one man to explore, amateur or not. In his years of exploration, Kenny has only managed to cover about 25 percent of
the battlefield. It was a lifetime's worth of work but Kenny
realized that he might not have a lifetime to complete it. After
all, much of the battlefield area is leased or owned by coal
companies, and they intended to surface mine the area.

Surface mining takes a number of forms. The earliest
surface mines were strip operations that blasted the contour
of a mountain creating a step pyramid or bench effect around
the slopes. In the 1990s, the practice of mountaintop removal
(MTR) became the preferred method of surface mining.
While contour and high-wall surface mining attack the coal
seams from the side of the mountain, MTR blasts the very

mountaintops, removing the rock and minerals like the layers of a cake. Timber is removed with clear-cutting, explosions penetrate the surface, the coal is scooped away, and the rest of the rock is pushed over the side of the mountain into nearby valleys. MTR operations are massive. Some, such as Kayford and Hobet, encompass over 4,000 acres and permanently devastate the landscape.[4] If such mining methods were applied to the Blair Mountain Battlefield, all of the history Kenny King discovered, and everything yet to be discovered, would be lost forever. It was after Kenny learned that the coal companies secured surface mining permits on the battlefield area that he moved to place the battlefield on the National Register of Historic Places.

In 1966, Congress passed the National Historic Preservation Act. This law, now over half a century old, is the single most sweeping legislation to ever deal with historic properties and sites in America. The law created the National Register of Historic Places, the Advisory Council on Historic Preservation (ACHP), and the State Historic Preservation Offices (SHPOs—pronounced *ship-ohs*). The National Register of Historic Places is administered by the National Park Service and is an official list of properties and sites worthy of preservation. The act also recommends some legal protections for these properties. Within each state, SHPO is responsible for keeping an inventory of historic properties, nominating sites for the National Register, and maintaining a statewide preservation plan. If a citizen wishes to include a property on the National Register, he or she must submit a nomination to the SHPO director of the appropriate state. If the SHPO director finds that a site meets with the appropriate criteria of significance, that the site still is largely undisturbed or contains "integrity," and that the property owner or a majority of the owners consents, the director formally submits the nomination to the Keeper of the National Register in Washington, DC. If the Keeper approves, the site is placed on the National Register.[5]

Kenny spent the next several years working to get the battlefield placed on the National Register. He conducted his own research and prepared his own nominations to SHPO. Between 1997 and 2005, Kenny prepared three separate nominations, all of which were turned down by SHPO. Susan Pierce, the director of SHPO and appointed by the governor, refused to acknowledge Kenny's research because he was not a trained archeologist. Undaunted, Kenny enlisted more help. He contacted Regina Hendrix of the West Virginia chapter of the Sierra Club, and Regina put him in contact with Dr. Harvard Ayers, an archeologist from Appalachian State University. Harvard heeded Kenny's call and traveled to West Virginia, where, in the summer of 2006, they conducted a partial survey of the battlefield and, in that small area, identified fifteen complete undisturbed sites. Everything Kenny and Harvard found collectively demonstrated a powerful historic resource in the undisturbed acreage.[6] Afterward, Harvard, assisted by Dr. Barbara Rasmussen, a public historian at WVU, prepared a new nomination for the Blair Battlefield, which included Harvard's groundbreaking study. The process continued to drag on, but, Harvard's and Barbara's nomination was eventually accepted by SHPO and, on March 30, 2009, 1,669 acres of the battlefield area were finally placed on the National Register of Historic Places. Kenny, Harvard, and Barbara could relax and celebrate.

The celebration did not last. Two things happened. First, Don Blankenship, the powerful, antiunion CEO of Massey Energy, and, at the time, the most influential coal operator in West Virginia, allegedly pressured SHPO by threatening to sue each member of their staff. Though staff members employed at SHPO in 2009 would not confirm or deny these allegations, the rumors persisted. Second, Jackson Kelly Inc., a highly influential law firm with a long history of representing the coal industry, approached SHPO. Over the years, Jackson Kelly has represented the industry on a number of issues, most notably, black lung. The firm has successfully prevented thousands of suffering miners from getting aid for dealing with black lung disease, even by withholding medical information from courts. We still do not know how many thousands of miners have died because of the disease. Nonetheless, Jackson Kelly lawyers are held in high esteem by authority figures across West Virginia. In 2018, WVU awarded Jackson Kelly's managing member with its highest honor, the Order of Vandalia, for her great service to the university and the state.[7]

Jackson Kelly lawyers presented a second list of battlefield landowners and challenged the initial list submitted to the Keeper. According to the National Historic Preservation Act, if the majority of private landowners of a nominated area objects to the listing of the property, it cannot be placed on the National Register. When the state submitted the approved nomination of Blair to the Keeper, the majority of property owners consented to the nomination. However, Jackson Kelly later submitted a second list of landowners; more than half of them objected to the nomination. Going against their own regulations, the state accepted the second list and forwarded it to the Keeper of the National Register. On December 30, 2009, Carol Shull, then acting Keeper, delisted the battlefield claiming that there was, "a prejudicial procedural error on the nomination or listing process."[8]

In the nomination process for the National Register, the private landowners of a historic property are given seventy-five days to comment on the nomination. If a private landowner does not want the property on the National Register, he or she can send a notarized statement of objection to SHPO. In 2008, SHPO notified landowners and issued a public notice concerning the nomination. Because the nomination area exceeded 1,600 acres and stretched for over twelve miles, there were many small individual landowners in addition to the major land and coal corporations. Kenny King told me that after SHPO issued its public notice, a company executive and the Logan County commissioner personally visited several landowners and tried to convince them to send an objection. Their efforts only resulted in twenty-two objections among sixty-five landowners in the initial list approved by the Keeper, but Jackson Kelly submitted the second list of landowners, with a majority objecting, a month after Blair Mountain had already been placed on the National Register. By its own regulations, any property list presented to the Keeper for a National Register nomination must be submitted within the ninety days prior to the *intent* to nominate. Jackson Kelly submitted their list months too late. Inexplicably, however, SHPO still forwarded the second list to the Keeper after the nomination was already accepted. Even more baffling, Carol Shull, the Keeper of the National Register, rejected the initial landowner list, opting instead to favor the second list submitted by Jackson Kelly.

Something did not add up. Further investigation into the second list revealed that Jackson Kelly and the corporations relied on inaccurate land records to determine the landowner count. Additionally, they looked into the past for their objectors. Two of the landowners who objected in their list were dead—one of them had been so for over twenty years. When the press contacted SHPO about the discrepancies, Susan Pierce responded, "We cannot confirm or deny that there are no deceased on the SHPO list dated May 21, 2009."[9]

## • A FAMILY HISTORY •

As all this controversy unfolded, I began my first year as a full-time faculty member teaching history, political science, and sociology at Southern West Virginia Community and Technical College in the coalfields after moving to Charleston from Morgantown, where I had been working toward a doctorate in history with a specialization in Appalachia. Southern has four campuses in four counties scattered throughout the coalfields; the main campus is in Logan County. I began my tenure at Southern teaching classes in Boone and Wyoming Counties, but ultimately, I moved to the main campus and began teaching exclusively from Logan.

Logan County is the site of the Battle of Blair Mountain and, for much of the early industrial period, it led the state in coal production. Logan has a long history of antiunionism, and coal and land companies' hold over local government is strong. When the Battle of Blair Mountain occurred, Sheriff Don Chafin ran the county. Sometimes referred to as the "Tsar of Logan," Chafin employed 300 deputies, paid for by the Logan County Coal Operators Association, to keep unions out and miners under control. Former West Virginia Attorney General Howard B. Lee called it the "Kingdom of Logan." Writing about it in the 1960s, Lee observed, "the county was a leer in the face of liberty, a feudal barony defended by soldiers of fortune in the pay of mine owners."[10]

My great-grandfather, along with other union leaders, spent several months in the Logan County Jail after the Battle of Blair Mountain. Don Chafin allowed local residents to go inside, approach Frank Keeney's cell, and harass him and the other prisoners for the cost of 25 cents. Keeney later said that onlookers in Logan threatened to "put a bullet in his back." When T. C. Townsend, the union's attorney, first arrived at the Logan jail to confer with his clients, the jailor handed him the list of prisoners. The list included the prisoners' names and the reason for incarceration. Beside Keeney and the other miners' names, Townsend oddly found the initials "R. N." When Townsend asked the meaning of the letters, the jailer told him it stood for "Red Neck."[11] As I drove from Charleston to Logan to sign my paperwork accepting the position at Southern, I could see the train tracks running alongside the highway and knew it was the same route that Townsend took to meet with Frank Keeney in 1922. I wondered what my great-grandfather would think if he could see his descendant as a professor in Logan, and I wondered how different my reception would be.

Everywhere I go in life, Frank Keeney's story follows me. The first time I heard his name, I was about seven years old, and it was Memorial Day Weekend. My father's side of the family usually hosted an annual family reunion cookout on the Sunday of this holiday weekend. On this particular year, the cookout took place at my great-aunt Georgie's house, which rested on the same hill as my own home in Alum Creek. It was the standard fair, as I recall—hamburgers, cakes, cobblers, pies, potato salad, macaroni salad, hotdogs, coleslaw and chili for the dogs, and more casserole dishes than you could shake a stick at. No booze. Most of the family are fervent Appalachian Protestants. As the youngest in both my immediate and extended family, it seemed like every five minutes or so some old person who I hardly knew came up to me and told me how much I had grown or that they once changed my diapers. In order to avoid the hug-fest, I went behind the house, took out a plastic toy army knife I had brought along, and practiced throwing the toy blade into a patch of moss on the side of the hill. After a few failed attempts—where the knife simply bounced off the moss—I heard a voice behind me.

"You're throwin' it all wrong, son."

The voice belonged to a large man wearing a white cowboy hat and large sunglasses. Even though he was not my father, he called me son, which is typical where I grew up. The man's name was James Jackson, and he was one of Frank Keeney's grandchildren. At the time, I had no idea who he was. He snatched the knife off the grass. "You're holding the handle. You have to hold it by the blade," he said, as he demonstrated the correct throwing motion and handed it back to me. I darted the blade into the moss.

James complimented me on the toss and then said it was good for me to learn how to throw a knife. "You never know," he said, half-joking. "You might have a Baldwin-Felts thug after you one day."

I had no idea what he was talking about and was a little alarmed. What was a Baldwin-Felts thug and why would he be after me? I asked him. James lowered to one knee so that he could look me eye to eye and said, "You're Frank Keeney's great-grandson and you never heard of the mine guards?"

I unleashed a barrage of questions, but the man would not reveal any more details. He simply told me to ask my father, stood up, and walked around to the front of the house. I stayed behind looking up into the woods trying to absorb the information. A minute or two later I found my dad hovering over a grill by the picnic shelter in the backyard. I tugged on his T-shirt and blurted out, "Who was Frank Keeney and what is a mine guard?"

Dad told me that we would talk about it later. From behind, I heard one old lady—I think it was my great aunt Ernie—whisper to another in quiet condemnation, "I bet it was James who told him." Although confused, I knew enough to understand that something had been swept under the rug. As I grew older and learned much more about Frank Keeney and the Mine Wars, I found that a great many things were swept under the rug in Appalachia. The simple question I had posed to my father at that picnic would lead me down a lifelong road of inquiry and personal discovery that would direct the trajectory of my scholarly career and activism. At the time, however, I only sensed that whatever happened with this Frank Keeney had cast something of a shadow over the family. As a kid I only understood the basics—there was a war fought in West Virginia. There were no monuments to this war. No one talked about it. My teachers at school did not know anything about it. But whatever happened, my great-grandfather played a central role in it.

Frank Keeney was born on the Ides of March in 1882, just as West Virginia began its industrial transition and the same year that the world's first coal-fired power plant debuted in New York City.[12] At the time of his birth, the Keeney family collectively owned 3,000 acres along Cabin Creek in Kanawha County, where they operated a sawmill and ran flatboats selling salt down the Kanawha and Ohio Rivers. Frank's father died before he turned two and the family lost their land shortly thereafter. Half of the Keeney lands went to the coal companies whereas the other half became the town of Eskdale. After completing the sixth grade, Frank left school and helped support the family by working as a trap boy in the mines, opening and closing doors for coal carts. He continued working in the mines until 1912, when he became a leader in the bloody Paint Creek–Cabin Creek Strike. Keeney, alongside Fred Mooney, led the miners to victory the following year. Shortly thereafter, Keeney became president of the UMWA in West Virginia and president of the State Federation of Labor. Together, Keeney and Mooney spearheaded the union movement in West

Virginia and became central figures in the events leading up to and following the Battle of Blair Mountain.[13]

For a time, my great-grandfather simultaneously became one of the most loved and hated men in West Virginia. As I discovered his story during my youth, it struck me how friends and foes alike described him in larger-than-life terms. In his autobiography, Fred Mooney wrote, "Keeney was all fire and dynamite. He asked for and showed no quarter." One journalist observed of Keeney, "It is his personality that counts most." Another commented, "He has the hypnotic influence of power." Still another wrote, "Keeney is the embodiment of the union's spirit and purpose in West Virginia."[14] He held a reputation as a hot-tempered fighter and a charismatic, inspiring orator. Writer Robert Shogun observed: "Powerfully built, with large facial features and an open countenance, Keeney commonly wore a broad grin. But the friendly demeanor cloaked an iron will and a quick mind, and a far more supple intelligence than that of most of his colleagues. He could be equally convincing in a blustery harangue to the rank and file or in a sophisticated argument across the bargaining table from the mine owners."[15]

Another journalist, Winthrop Lane, interviewed Keeney in 1920. What follows is his impression:

There is the suggestion of the tiger in Keeney's personality. He seems always ready to spring. This impression contains nothing soft or catlike, but the force and alert watchfulness of the tiger are there. He is constantly trying to figure out your next move while you talk to him. A vehement nature seems gathering itself to reply; you feel in danger of being seized and torn. Keeney is direct rather than subtle. His speech, like his manner, is impetuous. Words roll out of his mouth in torrents; they pile up on themselves. If he were a large man the effect would be Niagara-like.[16]

Keeney possessed a talent for dramatic and inspiring oratory. He exhorted the miners to break the shackles of ignorance and have pride in themselves. "Quit hanging your heads!" he yelled in one speech. "Don't tell me that the miners . . . are all ignorant. Nor tell me that you're all incapable and wouldn't know how to run a coal mine if the boss gave it to you. That's because we tell ourselves we're coal miners and don't know how to do anything but dig coal."[17] Although he had only reached the sixth grade in school, Frank read as many books as he could. In the 1930s, writer Malcolm Ross observed, "Keeney's thought ranges beyond his mountains. He has armed himself with knowledge in every subject touching his own campaigns—with law that he may hinder evictions and get boys out of jail, with politics that he may harass hostile officials, with world labor movements that he may inspire his people with a goal."[18] Upon the completion of my doctorate, my aunt Donna presented me with a book of poetry that Frank kept with him in his tent during the Paint Creek–Cabin Creek Strike. During some of the more tense moments of my tenure as president of Friends of Blair Mountain, I referred to the book and found some encouragement in reading poems Frank had underlined and the notes he had written in the margins. The book is currently on display at the West Virginia Mine Wars Museum.

Frank told the miners to stand up lest they be "crushed like a beetle beneath the golden chariot of the money kings."[19] He urged them to fight on during the bitterest of times: "What does your old age mean to you? You paupers! Your town is full of cripples, products of the industrial system. . . . We've got to have songs, got to have fun, to learn things. Or else what will we have to look back at when we come to die? When you're going through it—living in your tent—it doesn't sound like that. But when you come to the end of life you can say, 'I tried. I suffered. I didn't go back.' "[20]

On August 7, 1921, one week after the murder of Sid Hatfield and three weeks before the Battle of Blair Mountain, Keeney stood on the doorstep of the state capitol building in front of thousands of miners and declared, "The only way you can get your rights is with a high-powered rifle!" He then told the miners to go home and await the call to march.[21]

For his actions, the government and industry labeled Keeney a radical. To this, Keeney responded, "Who made me a radical? I've seen the time when I was refused the right to eat in this state. I've been served with eviction papers and thrown out of my house. I've seen women and children brutally treated in mining camps. I've seen Hell turned loose!"[22] His actions matched his rhetoric. When a coal operator accosted Keeney in downtown Charleston, calling him an outlaw and a criminal, Keeney punched him out and kicked him down the entrance steps of a bank in front of over fifty witnesses.[23] Such incidents both cemented the miners' loyalty and the coal operators' hatred.

After the Battle of Blair Mountain, the state charged Keeney and over 500 others with crimes ranging from treason to murder. The treason trials lingered on until 1924. The state eventually dropped the treason charges against Keeney and the jury acquitted him of murder. But even though Keeney and the miners escaped the hangman's noose, the trials bankrupted the UMWA in West Virginia, and the state continued to be controlled by the industrial elite. John L. Lewis, who had become president of the international UMWA in 1920, privately condemned Keeney and Mooney for their role in the 1921 uprising and forced them to resign from the union two weeks after the end of the trials. Keeney subsequently resigned as president of the State Federation of Labor. Lewis suspended elections for state union officials and began appointing them. Keeney would be the last UMWA president in West Virginia elected by the miners for fifty-two years. Upon his resignation, there were nearly 50,000 UMWA miners in West Virginia. Five years later, as the Great Depression dominated American life, there were less than 1,000.[24]

Amid these desperate conditions, Frank Keeney launched what I feel is the most valiant effort of his life. He reemerged in March 1931 and founded the West Virginia Mine Workers Union and the West Virginia Labor Party. Within a month, 23,000 miners flocked to his banner and joined the new union.[25] His union secured funding from wealthy liberals in the north and from charitable Christian groups, most of which went to feeding and clothing downtrodden miners and their families.[26] While the UMWA and most national labor organizations continued to reel from the strike losses of the previous decade, Keeney's organization kept the union spirit alive in the mountains. More tangible than upholding a "union spirit," however, was the fact that the food and clothing provided by Keeney's union helped keep many impoverished mountaineers alive. Although such an achievement did not alter the course of labor or American history, it certainly meant a great deal to those families in the coalfields who suffered through the Depression.

And some of those miners remembered. Walter Seacrist, a member of Keeney's union from Cabin Creek, wrote a poem called the "Coal Miner's Dream." In it, a Depression-era coal miner witnesses Judgment Day, during which the governor of West Virginia and John L. Lewis are "kicked down the golden stair" for their betrayal of the coal miners. Then, Seacrist writes

> Next came Frank Keeney
> A man we all knew well
> With a West Virginia Coal Miners agreement
> He had followed the coal operators to Hell
> Then grand old Saint Peter
> Looked down the golden stair
> And said, "Come on up higher!
> It's too hot for a union man down there."[27]

In spite of this continued union spirit, the coal operators had no intention of giving an inch to Keeney's new union. After a failed strike in 1931, Keeney organized a hunger march on Charleston. In August of that year, some 600 miners and their families made a twenty-mile march from their coal camps to Charleston. It was a solemn procession. Miners, their wives, and children, slowly put one foot in front of the other, bearing ragged clothes, empty bellies, and signs that read, "Why Should We Starve Quietly?"[28] As they marched into town, the miners, some of whom were African American, began singing an old slave spiritual, "I Shall Not Be Moved," with the lyrics, "Frank Keeney is our leader and we shall not be moved."[29]

The miners marched to the governor's mansion, where they were turned away without help. Over the course of the next year, Keeney led two more hunger marches to Charleston. On the second and third marches, police would not allow the miners into the capitol city. Governor William G. Conley, the mayor of Charleston, and several dozen state police set up a barricade at the city limits. When Keeney and his followers arrived there, the police met them with aimed rifles and tommy guns. The governor turned them away both times— once after giving them a $10 bill and telling Keeney, "This is all I can do."[30]

Later that year, Keeney sold his house in Charleston in order to buy food for the striking miners—a decision which caused great strain within his family.[31] In 1933, with the coming of Franklin Roosevelt's New Deal and the passage of the National Industrial Recovery Act (NIRA), unions suddenly became legal in the United States. Although the Supreme Court later declared the law unconstitutional, the NIRA had an immediate impact on West Virginia. John L. Lewis sent a host of organizers to the Mountain State in the wake of the new law declaring, "The President wants you to join the union." Within a few months, the UMWA transformed from an organization on life support to a serious power player in West Virginia. Keeney disbanded his union and his labor party, encouraging his miners to rejoin the UMWA. Because of his brand as a "dual unionist," however, official UMWA histories diminished Frank's role in helping unionize the state. He would never again be involved with the union he helped build.[32]

Frank spent the rest of his life moving from job to job. He owned a nightclub in downtown Charleston for a few years and ended up as a parking lot attendant in that town. Today, Haddad Riverfront Park sits on the spot where Frank Keeney's parking lot stood. Before I was born, my parents and two sisters parked their car at Frank's lot when they came to town. Dad said that he can still see his grandfather standing in the lot with his cigarette and his Smith & Wesson .38 caliber tucked in his belt buckle. Frank dealt with death threats throughout his life and even kept his handgun with him the last year of his life when he lived in a retirement home. He died in 1970 at the age of eighty-eight, believing himself and the Mine Wars forgotten.

It is difficult to explain what it means to grow up with a

history like this. In recent years, I have been approached a number of times and told, "It must've been great being raised with such a rich history." Growing up, though, I didn't think of it that way. Most of my family did not see my great-grand-father as a hero. Frank Keeney came out on the losing side of the Mine Wars. He led huge, violent armed uprisings and was responsible for killing people. Once an old miner approached my father and said of Frank, "We killed for him." Teachers did not cover the Mine Wars in history class. My eighth grade West Virginia Studies teacher had never even heard of Frank Keeney or the Mine Wars.

On top of his labor and political controversies, Frank lived a rambunctious life with a lot of drinking and at least a little bit of womanizing. Frank's wife Bessie left him after the Mine Wars, in part because she believed he had chosen his miners over his family, and in part because he had cheated on her. All these factors combined to leave bitter feelings within the family. Four of Frank's six children, the exceptions being my grandfather and Frank's eldest daughter, refused to have anything to do with him for the rest of their lives. At Frank's funeral, as dozens of old miners came to pay their respects, only my grandfather and Frank's other grandsons greeted the miners. The rest of the family remained in a side room during the visitation, ashamed of his radical past.

In his later years, Frank often stayed with my grandfather and his family on the weekends. This was in the same house in which I was raised. He rode the bus to Alum Creek from Charleston on Friday evenings. My father says he can still see Frank walking up the hill to the house with a cigarette in his hand. My grandmother didn't like him and often grumbled to herself as he approached the front door. She did not approve of the way he drank and cursed in front of the children. But drink and curse he did, all while sitting on the porch and telling stories about the Mine Wars to my father and aunt. Eventually these stories were passed down to me.

I was a teenager before my family began opening up about who Frank Keeney was and what his life meant. The more I learned, the more his life and the Mine Wars intrigued and perplexed me—a towering figure in a forgotten epic. Although his protestant Christian family frowned upon Frank's lifestyle of drinking, cussing, and leading violent revolts, he gave more of himself to alleviate the suffering and plight of the poor than most of the Christians I have ever met. Keeney's life, and the wars he fought, contradicted the notion of West Virginia as a simple place inhabited by a simple people.

Every year or so as I grew to manhood, strangers approached me and told me or my father a Frank Keeney or a Mine Wars story: *I shook Frank Keeney's hand at a union rally once. I heard Frank Keeney give a speech once. My grandfather fought on Cabin Creek with Keeney.* An elderly man once approached me at the Cultural Center in Charleston, asking me if I was Frank Keeney's great-grandson. When I said yes, he told me that his father had gotten him out of elementary school one day to meet Frank Keeney. He said that he attended school in downtown Charleston and one afternoon his father, who at one time had been a coal miner but had since transitioned to construction work, appeared at his classroom door. His father took him out of school, still in a dirty construction outfit, and walked him a few blocks to a bar. He said that in the bar sat an old man drinking whiskey and smoking a cigarette. The old man, of course, was Frank Keeney. The father introduced his son to Frank. The son, who told me the story many years later, said that Frank smiled, leaned down and shook his hand, said something funny, and then returned to his drink. His father then took him outside.

The son said, "Who was that old man?" His father took him for a walk and told him.

Frank Keeney's life story combined with the obscurity of the history carried a weight with it that I could never seem to shake. The weight followed me to Logan County in 2009. Teaching at Southern, I felt, would be a good way to honor Frank's memory and alleviate the persistent sense of responsibility I felt toward my family history. When I began teaching, most of my students had never heard of Blair Mountain and had no idea that a major battlefield lay only a few miles from campus. The irony did not escape me. It is easy to destroy a battlefield when the younger generation does not know it exists. Make no mistake, my students at Southern understood a great deal about the contemporary coal industry. They were often coal miners or coal miners' wives, daughters, and sons. Some of my students worked the mines at night—called the hoot owl shift—and arrived in class covered in coal dust. They certainly held strong feelings about coal and the politics of coal, and yet they knew so little of its history. If nothing else, I could change that. However, I would soon find myself doing much more than teaching, as my arrival in Logan coincided with the delisting of the Blair Mountain Battlefield.

• **PIGEONROOST HOLLOW** •

As I learned more about the battlefield controversy, my anger and frustration grew. In late 2009, just before the Keeper of the National Register delisted Blair Mountain and a few weeks before my dissertation defense, the Preservation Alliance of West Virginia gave me an opportunity to voice my frustration when they asked me to write an essay on the Blair situation for their newsletter. A few hours after receiving the invitation, I had fleshed out my thoughts. This is an excerpt from what I wrote:

> To strip mine Blair Mountain is to strip us of our own history, and this cannot be allowed. Blair Mountain reminds us of who we are as West Virginians. I believe Frank Keeney summed it up well when he said, "I am a native West Virginian and there are others like me in the mines here. We don't propose to get out of the way when a lot of capitalists from New York and London come down and tell us to get off the earth. They played that game on the American Indian. They gave him the end of a log to sit on and then pushed him off that. We don't propose to be pushed off." Blair Mountain reminds us of a time when West Virginians refused to be pushed off the log.
>
> Blair Mountain also reminds us that the fight is not over. In a speech to a crowd of striking miners, Keeney reassured them that the cause for which they suffered was not in vain. "One day there will be no more tent colonies, no more gunmen, because right now you people are going through what you are." He was right. Today, there are no more tent colonies, and the mine guards are now found only in books or pieces of fiction. But the absence of these things does not signify that the conflict over coal, people, and history in West Virginia has ended. As recent events clearly demonstrate, there are some who would have us forget Blair Mountain. There are those who are fighting to have it taken off the National Register so that the mountain can be open for strip mining. They must be reminded that we will still not be pushed off the log.

A friend of mine once asked me in a joking manner, "You think if Frank Keeney were alive today that he'd have a Friends of Coal bumper sticker?" I responded that Frank Keeney was no Friend of Coal, but he was a friend of coal miners. There is a big difference. If we are to be friends of the miners who stormed Blair Mountain so many years ago, we must keep it on the National Register of Historic Places. If we give up on this fight, then we give up on the ideals of the Red Neck Army of 1921. If Frank Keeney were alive today, I believe he would still be fighting.[33]

After sending it off, I did a little internet research and found an organization called Friends of Blair Mountain (FOBM). Kenny King, Jimmy Weekley, a retired miner from Blair, Harvard Ayers, and Barbara Rasmussen had formed a nonprofit organization intending to preserve and commemorate the history of Blair Mountain. I found Harvard's email address on the website and sent him a quick message introducing myself and offering my services. Harvard responded by telling me that they were promoting a letter-writing campaign to Carol Shull, the Keeper of the National Register, and that he would keep me informed of further developments. I wrote my own letter to the Keeper and encouraged others to do so online, wondering what the fate of the battlefield would be.

A number of months passed before I heard from Harvard again. It was November 9, 2010. I taught six classes that semester and planned to spend what little spare time I had converting my dissertation on West Virginia soldiers in World War II into a book. Things changed when I sat down in my office chair in between classes and checked my email. Harvard wrote,

I have an invite for you. Could you join us at James Weekley's house in Blair this Sunday at 1:00? It's up Pigeonroost
hollow, the only occupied house up that road, I think. It's
only about 1/2 mile off #17 highway. Your contacts, especially locally, could be a great help. We are planning to
re-create the 1921 march on Blair Mountain by the miners.
We want locals to lead the hike and other activities. Please
join us. This is confidential at this stage of planning. I have
so much to tell you, some of which is on our Friends website. Harvard[34]

I probably stared at the email on the computer screen for a
half hour. So, I thought, they wanted to do a protest march.
If they wanted to re-create the entire 1921 march, they'd have
to walk fifty miles and it would take several days. When I
offered Harvard my help, I imagined he would respond by
asking me to write some other letter, or an op-ed piece for
publication, or perhaps give a lecture somewhere. Helping to
re-create a historic march over fifty miles reached an entirely
different level. Never in my life had I even attended a protest
of any kind, much less helped organize one. Granted, in high
school, my friend Shawn Sowards and I led our entire class
on a day-long walkout in support of a teachers' strike. But
we only did it to get out of class for the day and because we
knew the teachers wouldn't stop us. During my freshmen
year of college, three friends and I protested poor cafeteria
food by stealing all the salt shakers (nearly 100) in the college
cafeteria. The next day we left a ransom note threatening,
"If the food does not improve within 72 hours, you'll never
see your salt again. Respectfully yours, The Salt Bandits."
Tragically, our valiant efforts to improve the college dining
experience proved fruitless. The food didn't improve at all
and, a few days later, we returned all the salt unscathed in

a box by the cafeteria door, thinking ourselves quite clever and funny.

A protest march to save the Blair Mountain Battlefield was no joke, however. There is a reason the industry is referred to as King Coal. In the coalfields, the coal companies get their way. Only on rare occasions, like Paint Creek and Cabin Creek in 1913, or with the Black Lung Association in 1969, did the industry give significant ground to its opposition. Blair Mountain, of course, stood as the largest historic example of local resistance to coal company domination. I readily understood why coal operators would want to destroy it. I also understood why it was not taught in schools. But this was King Coal. If the industry wanted to blow up this battlefield it would be hard to stop them. The industry would control the narrative presented to the local public about our protest. And I knew what this narrative would be. The protestors would be painted as environmental extremists trying to take away coal jobs by preventing mining. More personally, if I joined this undertaking, I would be painted in that light.

I have never been one to dwell on what others think of me, but while staring at Harvard's email that afternoon in 2010, I certainly did. If I joined this protest, I would be on the news and the focus of a lot of attention. My family connection to the history and my position as a historian would draw reporters to me. I would be marching past homes of people who were fellow high school students, or people with whom I have attended the same church events, or teammates from high school sports. Many of them would not understand what I was doing or why I was doing it. I could see some of their heads shaking and hear their voices in the back of my mind already. *What on earth happened to him? He went up there to that university and got liberalized by all those lefty professors, that's what happened. Now he's one of those academics*

*with his head up in the clouds and he doesn't get how the real*
*world works. That's what happens. They go up to get all that*
*education and come back with a bunch of crazy theories. I bet*
*he doesn't even read the King James Version.*

The thought of it made me cringe, and I sat in my office
chair and tried to talk myself out of getting involved. Do
I want any part of this fight? Is there any real chance of
success? My great-grandfather fought the coal companies his
whole life and it cost him dearly. It could cost me dearly. My
reputation in my own home would never be the same, for
better or worse. Some in coal country would despise me and
some might even try to cause me physical harm. The governor's wife also happened to be the president of my college. If
I became too controversial or if the march turned out badly, I
could lose my job. I knew that if I joined the protest, it would
follow me the rest of my life.

I read the email again. The meeting was Sunday at 1:00
p.m. It was at least an hour drive from my place in Charleston,
and I already drove two hours in my daily commute during
the week. Did I really feel like making that long drive on
my day off? Maybe they could email me a summary of the
meeting and I could think things over before making any
commitment. Plus, I am a diehard, lifelong Pittsburgh Steelers
fan (a Terrible Towel hangs triumphantly on my office wall),
and autumn Sunday afternoons were reserved for football. I
went online and quickly checked to see who the Steelers were
playing and how important the game might be for the playoff
race. As it turned out, the Steelers were scheduled to play the
primetime game that Sunday and not at 1:00 p.m. I couldn't
use the Black and Gold as an excuse. For two more days I
thought and prayed about it until finally I emailed Harvard
and told him I would be there.

Three days later, under an overcast sky and drizzling rain,

I drove to the community of Blair. I passed by Danville, hit state Route 17, and followed the winding two-lane south. Along the way I passed through the old coal town of Sharples. Once, there had been a high school at Sharples, and I recalled playing basketball there as I drove by. After winning a high school game, our bus was pelted with rocks when it pulled away from the school. When I finished rehashing the incident for my mother later that evening she said, "They need to get those kids under control." I said, "Mom, the parents were the ones throwing the rocks." The Sharples I drove by in 2010 had hardly anyone left to throw any rocks. The community had dwindled to near extinction.

Such was also the case a few miles further on with the community of Blair. Once a thriving coal town with a train station, restaurants, saloons—one early saloon was called "The Bloody Bucket"—and a general store, the Blair of 2010 truly resembled a ghost town. Abandoned houses dotted both sides of the lonely road. There is no cell phone reception. Before reaching the foot of Blair Mountain, I turned left onto Pigeonroost Hollow and found Jimmy Weekley's house. It is a small, one story wooden home with a sizable front porch holding many chairs. After parking and knocking on the door, I was met by a smiling, soft-spoken, mustached gentleman wearing a flannel shirt and ball cap. He introduced himself as Kenny King and invited me in.

Aside from Kenny and myself, seven others attended this meeting. Harvard Ayers, accompanied by a grad student, and Brandon Nida, then a doctoral candidate in archeology at UC Berkeley and another native of Lincoln County, were there. To my knowledge, the protest march originated with Brandon, and at this meeting he appeared to be the most outspoken and enthusiastic supporter of organizing a march.

Like Kenny King, Jimmy Weekley's grandfather also fought

at Blair Mountain. Jimmy also had been a coal miner and was the first person to really bring the practice of MTR to the attention of the rest of America. In 1997, Jimmy refused to sell his land to Arch Coal and started a lawsuit that stopped the company from blasting the mountains around his house, just north of Blair Mountain. Jimmy had been vilified by the coal industry, received death threats for being a so called "job killer," and remained the target of many petty torments by the industry. Jimmy told me that Arch occasionally ran empty haul trucks and heavy machinery back and forth on the dirt road by his house all night long just to keep him awake. He was skin and bones, with silver whiskers, and a heavy coal country accent. Industrialists and journalists alike have taken his appearance as a sign of weakness and his accent as a mark of ignorance. He was neither.

Three young activists also joined us: Katey Lauer, Andrew Munn, and Jasper Conner. Jasper worked with labor organizations whereas Katey and Andrew worked with environmental groups who combatted MTR. The previous September, Katey and Andrew had been heavily involved in a major MTR protest in Washington, DC, called "Appalachia Rising." Everyone at the meeting talked of that protest as having been a major event and a great success. Until they brought it up, though, I had no knowledge that it ever occurred. All of these individuals would play pivotal roles in the success of the protest march to Blair Mountain.

Over the course of a few hours, we agreed to try and organize a march that would take place the following summer. We planned to hold organizational meetings once a month and create committees to handle different aspects of the undertaking, such as fundraising and public outreach. Our protest march would cover the full fifty miles from Marmet (where the miners originally began their march in 1921) to

Blair Mountain. The protesters would march ten miles a day from Monday through Friday, and the march would culminate with a rally at Blair on Saturday. At the end of each day, we planned for the protestors to stop and sleep at one of the numerous campsites in the area. We would need to find campsites, provide food, and provide protection. In 1999, Harvard, Kenny, Jimmy, and about twenty-five others had attempted the same march we were about to try and met with heavy resistance. A few miles south of Marmet, a gathering of angry pro-coal locals met the marchers and threw rotten vegetables and cursed them as they walked. Several men shoved and pushed around the marchers, threatening more violence. Ken Hechler, a World War II veteran, former US Congressman, and speechwriter for Harry Truman, received a cut on his head. The incident put an abrupt end to that protest. If we were to be more successful, we needed to be wary of what might stand in our way. I drove back to Charleston later that afternoon wondering what I had gotten myself into.

## CHAPTER TWO

# Marching into Blair

>>>>>> <<<<<<

**O**f the numerous times I spoke on behalf of the protest march to save Blair Mountain, the press conference on March 9, 2011, publicly announcing the protest, stands out the most in my mind. This day, to me, was my own personal Rubicon. Up until this point, there had been no formal public announcement of our intended protest. After the press conference, however, my name would be in the public forum and associated with the protest in local newspapers and on local television. I knew there would be no turning back.

The organizers who coordinated the press conference placed me as the third speaker on the roster because I had to leave early to teach class. Other speakers followed me, such as documentary filmmaker Mari-Lynn Evans, photographer Paul Corbit Brown, and local activist Wilma Steele, but I left before they spoke. They asked each person to speak for three to five minutes. This was the only time in my life I have been nervous giving a speech. Every other speaker was a highly respected veteran of the mountaintop removal (MTR) movement, none more high profile than Ken Hechler and Denise Giardina, the two I would be following.

Few people have a more impressive resume than Ken Hechler. He served with Army Intelligence during World War II and interviewed key Nazi leaders, including Hermann Göring, creator of the Gestapo and commander of the Luftwaffe, before the Nuremberg Trials. He then served on President Harry Truman's staff and later became a US congressman for the state of West Virginia. During his tenure in Congress, Hechler helped author the Federal Coal Mine Health and Safety Act of 1969, the most significant mine safety and black lung benefits legislation in history. No stranger to protest marches, Hechler was also the only member of the US Congress to march with Martin Luther King Jr. from Selma to Montgomery, Alabama, in March 1965. After his tenure in Congress, Hechler was elected West Virginia Secretary of State and became the only local politician to be an outspoken critic of MTR. Hechler had even been arrested, at the age of ninety-four, at an MTR protest at Marsh Fork Elementary school in 2009.[1] At age ninety-six, Hechler served as the opening speaker at the press conference announcing the March on Blair Mountain. He always seemed to be on the right side of history, and it gave me confidence to see him there supporting the Blair Battlefield. While earning a master's degree at Marshall, I organized the Ken Hechler Collection for the Special Collections division of the university library, and, even though we had only met once before, I felt like I knew him, having read through and filed the manuscript collection spanning his entire career.

Denise Giardina, whom I would also follow to the stage, is one of West Virginia's most beloved novelists. Her enduring piece of Mine Wars fiction, *Storming Heaven*, is the most popular novel ever produced regarding Blair Mountain. Her other novels have earned her a special place in the hearts of many mountaineers, and she has appeared in numerous documentaries concerning West Virginia and Appalachia. In 2000, Denise ran for governor as a candidate for the Mountain Party with an anti-MTR platform. Her campaign put the Mountain Party on the map as a legitimate third party in West Virginia. Giardina's presence and endorsement, along with Hechler, added a level of legitimacy to our march that it may otherwise not have enjoyed. Nonetheless, I had to follow these two in my first ever public statement as an activist. No pressure.

This is also the only time in my adult life I have written a speech word for word. Around fifteen minutes before the press conference began, I pulled into the Public Workers Union building on Washington Street East in downtown Charleston on a rainy morning. I walked in with my speech on a folded-up piece of paper in my sport jacket. Inside the building, I met Mari-Lynn Evans and Paul Corbit Brown for the first time—two individuals with whom I would work extensively in the years to come. I approached Hechler and shook his hand, reminding him that we had met after I organized his manu-script collection. Not only did he remember, he surprised me by commenting on an academic article I had published about the Mine Wars a few years before. I shook my head. In his late nineties, Hechler still kept up with scholarly journals.

I sat beside Denise when the press conference began. Several local television news crews, local print journalists, and the ever-present CNN crew all crammed into a small conference room. When my time came to speak, I read my speech mostly word for word. Because there was no podium, only a microphone stand, I held the speech in my right hand. I had trouble reading the speech because my hand shook with a touch of nervousness. I vividly remember seeing Denise out of the corner of my eye staring directly at my hand and I felt embarrassed.

Regardless, I finished the short speech and made my way out of the room. Before I left the building, I gave a brief interview to the CNN crew, who were filming a documentary on MTR and wanted to focus on our protest. The local FOX television crew followed me out as well and wanted to ask me a few additional questions. I tried to be positive and emphasize the history. Because I taught classes all afternoon and evening that semester, I missed the local television coverage, but some of my students saw it. After my evening class, at around 8:30, I was sitting in my office collecting my things before leaving when one of my students stepped in the doorway. His name was Mike. He had been a surface miner for Massey Energy for a number of years, and he was well over twice my size.

"I saw your press conference," he said.

I asked him what he thought, and Mike said, "I think you'd better watch your back around here."

From then on, after I dismissed the evening class each week, Mike escorted me to my car in order to ensure my safety.

## • RED NECK LEGACIES •

One must understand the complex atmosphere enveloping our efforts to save Blair Mountain. Although the Appalachian environmental movement supported our planned protest, it did not receive public endorsement from the United Mine Workers of America (UMWA), the organization whose very history hinged on the 1921 battle. Only UMWA Local 1440, based in Matewan, supported the protest. The international office withheld its support whereas some other union locals vehemently objected to our efforts. One might wonder why a movement to save a battlefield crucial to coal and union history did not receive more popular support from coal miners and the union representing them. One may further wonder why environmentalists would care so much about a historic site and why their support would be crucial to the success of the protest march. As time progressed, the UMWA would play a more active role in the preservation of Blair Mountain. In 2011, however, the UMWA would not condemn the practice of MTR. Most of our major endorsements came from environmental groups. Many members of these groups also did not trust the UMWA, and some did not even want their support. This may seem contradictory as both unions and environmentalists appeared to exist under the umbrella of the Democratic Party. The two would seem to be natural allies, but they were not.

Part of the explanation lies in the storied past of the UMWA. Since the time of the Mine Wars, the UMWA had been the single greatest opposition to coal company control in West Virginia. By the mid-1930s, nearly all coal miners in West Virginia were unionized and the UMWA became a powerful political and social voice in the state. The UMWA worked against coal company executives and their legal representatives to secure better wages, safer working conditions, and benefits for miners whose bodies were broken down by decades of toil underground and whose lungs were ravaged by years of inhaling the black dust. For fifty years, the UMWA remained strong and seemed to have established itself as firmly embedded into the culture as the industry itself.

Four factors greatly eroded the influence of the UMWA in the waning years of the twentieth century: mine mechanization, surface mining, union corruption and tactics, and the rise of coal executive Don Blankenship. Mine mechanization had been an evolutionary process since the formation of the coal industry. After World War II, new developments in underground mining allowed for machines to do more of the work. Between 1950 and 1985, as machines became more effective, the number of miners in West Virginia slowly diminished from over 100,000 to around 45,000. The late eighties and nineties saw the acceleration of MTR and other surface mining methods that used even larger machines and even fewer employees. Between 1985 and 2005, the number of miners slipped further from 45,000 to just over 15,000 while the amount of coal mined annually reached greater heights than ever before.[2] The implications for the UMWA are obvious. An organization with nearly 100,000 members in a single state can sway elections and push a strong agenda in congress. An organization with less than 15,000 members will have a much greater hill to climb on both fronts. Fewer miners means fewer union members. Fewer union members means less strength. The mechanization of the coal industry also foreshadowed the impact of machines on the American workforce in other industries and the weakening of labor unions in general. Contemporary conservative rhetoric often blames job losses in America on immigrants and government regulation, but the main culprit is often increased mechanization.

As union membership declined, the UMWA sought to organize surface miners. Arch Coal Inc., one of the major coal companies in America, negotiated a contract with the UMWA to organize a number of its MTR sites in West Virginia. When Jimmy Weekley won his MTR court case in 1998, halting Arch Coal's proposed expansion of its MTR site on Pigeonroost Hollow, Arch responded by firing over 300 union workers. This forced the UMWA to publicly defend MTR and its union jobs. The UMWA joined the West Virginia Coal Association in pro-coal protests at the state capitol, denouncing those opposed to MTR as extreme environmentalists who wanted to kill jobs. Jimmy Weekley, a retired UMWA miner, was burned in effigy at one of these demonstrations. Such circumstances meant that if our protest march stood against all MTR operations, we would not get support from the UMWA.[3]

The UMWA's support of MTR created a rift on the political left between grassroots environmentalists and coal miners. This phenomenon, however, extended beyond West Virginia and the coal industry. The rise of climate change as a prominent issue on the political left coincided with the decline of manufacturing and industrial jobs in the United States. The Democratic Party continued to support labor organizations, specifically with pensions, benefits, and safety regulations, but Democratic policies have failed to reinvigorate America's industrial and manufacturing base. Part of this stems from President Bill Clinton's adoption of neoliberalism and promotion of globalization in the 1990s, which resulted in manufacturing jobs moving overseas and lower costs of consumer goods for Americans. Blue-collar jobs that had survived increased mechanization were sacrificed to globalization so that American consumers could shop cheaply at Walmart and elsewhere. In the first decade of this century, Walmart, yet another absentee giant, became the top employer in West Virginia.[4]

But even without neoliberal economics and globalization there is still a conflict of interest between environmentalists and industrial unions. Lowering carbon emissions in hopes of stemming the tide of global warming means transitioning away from fossil fuels, greatly damaging the industries who depend on fossil fuels and the unions who survive on these industries. Union leaders in the United Mine Workers, the United Steel Workers, and the United Auto Workers, to name just a few, will greatly decline in membership and in power as the nation transitions away from fossil fuels, so it is only natural that they would fight such a transition if for no other reason than self-preservation. A perfect example came in 2017 when President Trump issued an executive order approving the controversial Dakota Access Pipeline. Many on the left expressed outrage and decried the action as an assault on the environment. Richard Trumka, president of the AFL-CIO, however, praised the decision, as it potentially meant more blue-collar jobs and could strengthen their union base.[5] The Democratic Party's failure to reconcile the differing agendas of industrial unions and environmentalists has pushed many industrial workers to the political right. West Virginia bore the signs of this political shift as early as the 1990s, had anyone cared enough to pay attention.

Past union corruption and poor strike choices also contributed to union decline. Thirty years removed from the rise of union power in the 1930s found a corrupt, pro-company UMWA led by President Tony Boyle. President Boyle opposed black lung benefits and elections for district presidents and even defended the Consolidation Coal Company's claim that a 1968 mine explosion that killed seventy-eight miners in Farmington, West Virginia, was an "act of God." In 1969, Boyle hired men to kill his rival, union reformer Joseph Yablonski. On December 31, three hitmen murdered Yablonski, his wife, and his daughter as they slept in their home. The murder led to an insurrection within the UMWA, which ousted Boyle, and reestablished district elections.[6] Boyle's administration harmed the union's reputation for many years.

Frivolous wildcat strikes have also undermined the credibility of the UMWA. In the early 1980s, the UMWA adopted a new policy called *selective striking*. Traditionally, all union mines went on strike simultaneously to increase their effectiveness. However, with selective striking, certain union

mines could strike while others continued working. This led
to abuses at times by UMWA locals.[7] The union walkouts in
West Virginia coinciding with deer hunting season serve as a
common example. Deer season is divided into a period when
one can only hunt with a bow and when one is allowed to
hunt with a gun, which is usually two weeks. During these
two weeks, union miners in the 1980s and 1990s would often
"pour their water out" in the mines, signaling a walk out,
only to return when the gun hunting period ended.[8] A number
of retired miners have described these activities to me as the
union shooting itself in the foot. They are correct.

The final straw breaking the union's back came in the
form of Don Blankenship. In the 1980s, Blankenship rose
up through the ranks in Appalachia's largest coal company,
Massey Energy. He built a reputation as a union buster who
micromanaged and increased production levels. In 1984,
Blankenship refused to negotiate a new UMWA contract and
vowed to break the union in West Virginia no matter the cost.
The two sides clashed in a violent strike that lasted over a
year and resulted in a Massey victory.[9] Blankenship himself
ultimately became the CEO of Massey Energy and continued his assault on union workers throughout the eighties and
nineties. Typically, Massey bought out a union operation,
closed it down, laid off the union workers, and reopened
it months later as a nonunion mine. Without union rights,
Massey miners worked longer hours, enjoyed fewer benefits,
and worked in much less safe conditions. If a miner suffered
an injury in a union mine, they could take time off to heal
and retain their job. If a miner suffered an injury in a Massey
mine, they had to keep working. To keep their jobs, many
miners relied on painkillers, and as a result, became addicted
to opioids. Unsafe conditions at Massey eventually culminated
in the Upper Big Branch mining disaster, on April 4, 2010,

which killed twenty-nine miners. When Blair Mountain, the strongest symbol of unionism in the state, was placed on the National Register, none other than Don Blankenship threatened to sue each member of the State Historic Preservation Office to get it removed.[10]

As the voice of the UMWA declined, new voices arose to fill the vacuum. The confluence of Don Blankenship, the West Virginia Coal Association, and the Friends of Coal campaign dominated public discourse. The industry created Friends of Coal in 2002 as a direct response to the coal-truck controversy. Between 2000 and 2002, twelve people perished in car accidents involving coal trucks. Illegally overloaded coal trucks cannot safely navigate the windy, narrow mountain roads and accidents with other vehicles inevitably occur. Responding to local outrage, state delegate Mike Caputo introduced a bill in 2002 to place harsher enforcements on the weight limits for coal trucks. Not only did the coal industry successfully kill the bill, the following year they passed a new bill that raised the restrictions on the weight limit of coal trucks from 80,000 to 120,000 pounds. In short, when the public expressed outrage that the coal industry ignored the safety rules for trucks, they simply changed the rules, even if it meant occasional fatal crashes.[11]

The Friends of Coal endeavored to improve the image of the industry and help gain public support for the controversial new coal truck law. The West Virginia Coal Association hired a public relations firm, Charles Ryan Associates, to handle public messaging and internet services. This firm also handled PR for American Electric Power, Appalachian Power, the American Petroleum Institute, the Independent Oil and Gas Association, and Virginia Is for Lovers. They sponsored sporting events such as the Friends of Coal Bowl between Marshall University and West Virginia University's football teams. They also recruited Don Nehlen and Bobby Pruitt, the popular football coaches of each university, to film promotional commercials and radio ads touting the greatness of coal. The coal industry understood the significance of sports to regional identity and weaponized sports as a propaganda tool. After 2003, leaders in the industry credited the Friends of Coal for the successful passage of the coal truck bill. In the years that followed, the Friends of Coal expanded their agenda.[12]

Residents in coal country found themselves bombarded by propaganda. Friends of Coal bumper stickers and billboards appeared everywhere. Radio and television commercials sang, "Coal is West Virginia!"[13] To a relatively uninformed West Virginian living outside the coal counties, the idea of becoming a "Friend of Coal" implied that one supports coal miners and their families. It also implied that the Coal Association served the interests of blue-collar families. In that sense, who wouldn't want to be a Friend of Coal? It was a brilliant propaganda campaign. In the early years of the twenty-first century, coalfield residents endured an intensified layer of coal company indoctrination, its success nearly rivaling the influence of the original company town system.

The Coal Association also sponsored programs in elementary and middle schools to teach children the benefits of coal, whereas the history of Blair Mountain and the Mine Wars rarely, if ever, found its way into a classroom. Coal company recruiters visited area high schools to encourage youngsters to seek employment with coal immediately after graduation. In true welfare capitalist form, Don Blankenship threw occasional entertainment events for his employees, sponsoring a few concerts and festivals with acts like Ted Nugent, Hank Williams Jr., and Sean Hannity. Massey Energy built a few little league baseball parks in the coalfields and occasionally helped finance work on football fields for local high schools. Each event promised that the company was taking care of everyone.[14] Building a little league field is, of course, a nice thing to do for a community, but such benevolent projects also help deflect legitimate criticism and provide distraction. Bread and Circuses, Appalachian style.

With no real strong union voice, and fewer available jobs due to increased mechanization, companies drove home a persuasive message linking the interests of the industry and the locals. Coal is all you have. Be grateful. Any opposing or critical voices threaten our only economy and our way of life. It became a polarizing environment that painted everyone as either pro-coal or anti-coal. Such language did not exist in the heyday of the UMWA. But in the absence of the UMWA, the Friends of Coal campaign and pro-coal versus anti-coal language allowed the industry to set the conditions of the debate.[15] Very early on in our efforts, a number of us realized that if we stood a chance at saving Blair Mountain, we would need to realign the debate and take control of the public narrative.

The ascendency of environmental activism in Appalachia also coincided with the decline of the UMWA. Groups like the Ohio Valley Environmental Coalition (OVEC), the West Virginia Highlands Conservancy, Coal River Mountain Watch, Keepers of the Mountains, Christians for the Mountains, Kentuckians for the Commonwealth, Mountain Justice, and Radical Action for Mountain People's Survival (RAMPS) began cropping up all over the coalfields. Within Appalachia, environmentalists were, and still are, often perceived as outsiders and hippies. Sometimes the word *hipsterbilly* is applied. But locals actually founded and administered most of these small groups. These locals had personally felt the negative impacts of the industry on their lives. A few, like

Judy Bonds, Maria Gunnoe, and Bo Webb turned to activism after their homes had been directly impacted by polluted water, floods, and blasting. Larry Gibson, the charismatic and colorful leader of Keepers of the Mountains, became an activist to protect his family cemetery from an MTR operation. Julian Martin, my high school chemistry teacher and the grandson of a miner who fought at Blair Mountain, simply felt disgusted by the practice of MTR. Even a handful of retired, underground UMWA miners, like Chuck Nelson and Terry Steele, became environmental activists. Then there were Mary Miller and Pauline Canterberry, two white-haired, conservative-looking old ladies from Whitesville, West Virginia, who seemed as though they fit right at home at a Baptist potluck dinner. They became activists because of the coal dust infiltrating their homes. They filmed themselves wiping the coal dust off their homes and their cars every day. Eventually they won a lawsuit against Massey Energy and managed to get some restrictions placed on a local coal prep plant. People called them the "Dustbusters." [16] When I met Pauline Canterberry at one of the march organizational meetings, she said, "I'm going to fight this until we win or until the good Lord takes me."

Most of these groups operated on very little funding and depended on volunteer work. They organized protests, lobbied politicians, and occasionally used civil disobedience tactics such as tree sits or chaining themselves to mining equipment to halt production on a surface mine site. Protests pitted environmentalists on one side and coal miners, all dressed in their orange-striped uniforms, on the other side with a line of police in between. It is no secret that coal management, particularly Don Blankenship, encouraged miners to intimidate and harass environmental protestors. On a few occasions, protestors endured physical attacks. Every individual

I mentioned earlier has received at least one death threat. A handful, such as Larry Gibson, have been threatened at gunpoint. Such intimidation frightened away most potential activists and silenced locals who might have otherwise been inclined to voice their dissent. Those who endured the intimidation and continued to fight are some of the most mentally tough individuals I have ever known.

I had never really identified as an environmentalist. While I certainly did not approve of MTR, I was not on a personal crusade to end the practice. My motivations revolved around the history I wanted to protect. Nonetheless, if this march was going to have any real chance of success, we needed support from the various environmental groups. In order to get their support, however, the groups insisted that the march be about ending all MTR with an emphasis on Blair Mountain. This didn't make me very happy, as I felt that since we planned to reenact the 1921 march, it should focus exclusively on the battlefield. If we focused only on the battlefield, I argued, we could be less polarizing and win more popular support. I even lobbied, unsuccessfully, for any signs or slogans used on the march to contain the word *battlefield*. I felt it would be harder for locals to argue against destroying a mountain if we emphasized the history with the proper language. Of all those I spoke to, only Jimmy Weekley agreed with this approach. The others wanted to use the march to push for an end to all MTR, and they felt that solely referring to the Blair Battlefield was an ideological compromise they were unwilling to make. In these early months, as a rookie amid a host of seasoned activists, I voiced my opinion but did not press the issue.

One thing we could all agree on was the red bandana. There is a long tradition of the red bandana as a symbol of resistance and solidarity in West Virginia. As early as 1877, strikers in Martinsburg, West Virginia, wore red bandanas around their necks in the great railroad strike of that year. When the Mine Wars began along Paint Creek and Cabin Creek in 1912, miners wearing bandanas on their necks were referred to as Red Necks (two words). By 1921, when 10,000 miners marched toward Blair Mountain, the media and locals called them the Red Neck Army. Union miners would continue to use the red bandana as a symbol for another generation. However, use of the bandana dwindled over time alongside the influence and power of the UMWA.[17] The red bandana began to resurface in the early 2000s, due in large part to the efforts of Wilma Steele, an art teacher and coal miner's wife from Mingo County. Wilma gave bandanas to environmental activists and shared the bandana's meaning as a symbol of resistance. At protests, more and more members of groups like Coal River Mountain Watch and Keepers of the Mountains wore the bandana around their neck, renewing the tradition.

The historic roots of the red bandana tradition are not limited to West Virginia, of course. Populist farmers in the Midwest during the Industrial Age sometimes donned red bandanas and were called Red Necks. Populists often represented the interests of lower-class farmers and industrial workers and mostly pitted themselves against the railroad industry. There are also stories of Scottish and Irish Protestants wearing red bandanas in protest of the Catholic Church in the 1600s. Considering that many preindustrial West Virginians had Scottish and Irish roots, it seems conceivable that their American descendants might carry on that tradition in a different form. There is also speculation that fraternal organizations may have influenced the bandana tradition. Many of the Red Necks in West Virginia during the Mine Wars participated in groups like the Order of Red Men and Knights of Pythias. Historians such as Fred Barkey have speculated on a connection between the two.[18]

The term *red neck* came into popular use around the 1890s in different parts of the world. In colonial South Africa during the Boer War, Afrikaners referred to British soldiers as red necks. During the same period, Midwestern populists and industrial strikers in West Virginia were donning red bandanas as symbols of their movements. Meanwhile, red necks also came to be associated with poor, rural whites whose sunburned necks revealed their labor in the fields. Some southern politicians embraced the term, such as South Carolina's Ben Tillman and Mississippi's James Vardaman, who bragged about his "long red neck" and once entered a political rally riding an ox. They used the term as a type of white, Southern pride.[19] Industrialists used the term to marginalize families who lived above huge seams of coal, or whose farms stood in the way of an intended railroad. All the while, the miners conceptualized the term and the bandana as a symbol of their organized resistance. Regardless of its wider origins and use, the bandana tradition has remained something of a scarlet thread throughout West Virginia history that continues to the present day. In early 2018, when West Virginia teachers went on strike, many of them wore red bandanas.

All of our organizers agreed that the bandana should be a symbol of the protest. Not only did our marchers wear them, we had bandanas made and sold for five dollars each to raise funds for the march. I began to recognize the bandana and the fight to preserve the battlefield as symbols by which Appalachians could reclaim their identity. Certainly most Americans did not think of Blair Mountain when they heard *redneck* in its contemporary one-word form. Perhaps, I hoped, our efforts could have an impact on that stereotypical perception. But before identities could be reclaimed, a protest march had to be organized and effectively executed. Nothing would come easy in the coalfields.

•  **YEAR OF THE PROTEST**  •

A couple of weeks or so after the meeting at Jimmy Weekley's house, Rob Howell, a producer from CNN, called me at my office on campus. He explained that CNN planned to produce a story of some kind on MTR and, while researching, he and cameraman Dave Tmko had stumbled upon the Blair Mountain story. Brandon Nida referred them to me and Rob wanted to know if they could stop by on campus to film a quick, "fifteen-minute-or-so" interview about Blair Mountain. I said yes, assuming CNN's curiosity would result in nothing more than a five-minute segment on a prime-time news show about MTR and I might get fifteen seconds of air time. When the time came, however, the fifteen-minute interview turned into a much longer conversation. Afterward, Rob Howell explained that he and Dave were a part of Soledad O'Brien's team at CNN and they planned to produce an hour-long documentary on MTR. The Blair Mountain protest sparked their interest and they wanted to cover every aspect of the protest march from its inception to fruition. Because of my personal connection to the history, they wanted to focus on me as one of the main "characters" in their documentary.

I didn't really know how to take this request and felt uneasy about my initiation to activism being documented on film. I brought this to the attention of the other organizers, and they agreed that I should function as a public face of the march. I made a final decision to say yes a few days later when Rob and Dave accompanied Kenny King and me to the southern crest of Blair Mountain. After spending a few hours with them, I felt comfortable enough to go ahead and play along. From then on, the CNN crew followed me around. They filmed me speaking in the months leading up to the march. They filmed me teaching at my college. They attended each organizational meeting for the march and, of course, followed me on the march itself. Whenever we took a break from our work or from marching, the CNN crew pulled me aside for a quick interview. In the role of spokesman, I tried to articulate what the protest meant, get our message across clearly, and sway public opinion in our favor. Most of the time, I simply tried to avoid saying something stupid. But the role forced me to confront the issues at hand and put them in a broader and more complete context.

Globally speaking, 2011 appeared to be the year of the protestor. The first major protest movement began when Mohamed Bouazizi, a twenty-six-year-old Tunisian street vendor, stood in front of the provincial capital building, poured paint thinner over his body, and lit himself on fire. In a world before the internet, Bouazizi's shocking act may have gone relatively unnoticed, but nearly one in three Tunisians had internet access in 2011. Word quickly spread online and Bouazizi's death sparked the massive protests known as the Arab Spring. Protests led to revolution in Tunisia, Libya, Egypt, Syria, and Yemen, with profound and continuing impacts in the region. In Europe, six million Spaniards, calling themselves *Los Indignados,* and hundreds of thousands of Greeks protested poor economic conditions and political corruption. Russia and China stamped out large prodemocracy demonstrations in their own countries. Meanwhile, in the United States, the capitol of Wisconsin hosted a flood of labor union protests over proposed right-to-work legislation and, before the autumn leaves fell, protestors in New York were occupying public spaces in lower Manhattan declaring, "We are the 99%." Protestors in other major American cities, most notably Oakland, joined the new Occupy movement. In December, *Time* named "The Protestor" as their Person of the Year for 2011.[20]

Social networks on the internet became a key instrument by which groups organized and kept themselves informed on other movements. In some cases, activists from these various movements communicated with one another online. Brandon Nida and Nick Martin, another march organizer, traveled to one of the rallies in Wisconsin bearing a "Remember Blair Mountain" banner and drew a lot of attention by posting a picture of it online. The internet functioned as both an indispensable tool for organizing and as a means of building momentum. All over the world, activists planned events with emails, promoted them on their own social media pages, shared other posts, encouraged one another, raised money, and spread the word, and on and on it built. Online social networks allowed the protests, including our own, to take form, grow, and feed off one another. Perhaps at no other time in world history have so many protests happened all around the world with the activists all possessing a global awareness of each other. A global revolution did not materialize, of course, but the events of 2011 did indicate that online social networks could make a global revolution or movement—of any kind—more plausible than ever before.

Global protests aside, the regional climate intensified. In March, a federal judge upheld the EPA's ruling that the Spruce No. 1 surface mine violated the Clean Water Act. Jimmy Weekley had fought this operation since 1997. Environmentalists celebrated a big victory while coal miners and their families feared layoffs. Local politicians and the industry spoke of President Obama's "War on Coal," and claimed he destroyed livelihoods for the myth of climate change.[21] A month later, Don Blankenship suddenly retired from Massey Energy as a result of growing controversy surrounding the 2010 Upper Big Branch mining disaster. His retirement proved fortuitous, for had Blankenship, known for his heavy-handed tactics, still been the CEO of an independent Massey Energy when our march occurred, I have no doubt events would have transpired quite differently.

Soon after Blankenship retired, Alpha Natural Resources acquired Massey Energy. With holdings in the western United States, Appalachia, and Australia, Alpha aspired to swallow up an even larger share of the market in West Virginia. The year 2011 actually saw major coal companies expanding and taking on large acquisitions, and with it, huge debt. Arch Coal expanded along with Alpha, acquiring the International Coal Group for $3.4 billion. Peabody Energy swallowed up Australia's Macarthur Coal. Alpha, Arch's, and Peabody's financed acquisitions placed huge debt burdens on the corporations; but the expectations for profit were equally huge, as the major coal producers in America looked to China's industrial consumption as its golden goose. This, of course, leads one to question the validity of coal company rhetoric. If they truly believed President Obama threatened the future of coal, why did three of the largest coal corporations embark on massive expansions? Regardless, both corporations failed to predict China's economic downturn and the rapid rise of natural gas consumption. Within a few short years, the debt they accumulated in this expansion came back to haunt them.[22] Of course, no one knew this at the time and, in 2011, coal looked as strong as ever. Upon their new purchase, Alpha immediately launched a public relations campaign promising to be an improvement from Massey. Their slogan was "Running Right Way."

We decided on June 6–11, 2011, as the dates for the march, the same week Alpha's acquisition of Massey became official. We planned to retrace the route coal miners took in 1921 from Marmet, a town just outside Charleston, the state capitol, to Blair Mountain in Logan County. We intended to march about ten miles a day, stopping at designated camp-sites each night until we reached the community of Blair on Friday. The last day's itinerary consisted of a rally of some sort at the campsite in Blair, followed by everyone ascending the final two miles along Route 17 to the southern crest of Blair Mountain. The various groups involved in the planning process decided to call the event March on Blair Mountain: Appalachia's Rising. Our official mission statement read, "We march to preserve Blair Mountain, abolish mountain-top removal in Appalachia, strengthen labor rights, and invest in sustainable job creation for all Appalachian communities."

The statement was an ambitious one, but one meant to appeal to—and appease—a broad range of groups. Success depended on cooperation between multiple activist groups and the broad nature of our objectives connected to everyone's agenda in one way or another. Brandon Nida, Katey Lauer, Andrew Munn, Jasper Conner, Catherine Moore, and a few other college-aged volunteers formed the organizational core. Many of them had helped organize the Appalachia Rising event in September 2010 and used their experience in putting this protest into motion. We created various committees such as a steering, finance, outreach, and media, each working on a different, but vital part of the protest. We held organizational meetings in Logan, Whitesville, Appalachia—a small town in Virginia—and Charleston. During these meetings, usually orchestrated by Katey Lauer, the committees came together to report on their progress and everyone discussed strategies, approaches, and decisions. We made decisions such as where we would camp, how we planned to feed everyone, how to ensure safety, how to promote the event, and on it went. While many of the older activists such as Maria Gunnoe, Larry Gibson, Harvard Ayers, and Mari-Lynn Evans, and others provided valuable guidance and a lot of work as well, the core group of young organizers sacrificed countless hours to make the protest an organized and efficient event from beginning to end.

For my part, I worked in a few committees, went to the organizational meetings, sat in on numerous conference calls, and adapted to my role as a spokesman for the protest. I spent time in between classes educating myself on MTR and the issues at hand and learning statistics and facts to use in speeches and interviews. I hastily put together a speaking tour to build public support that included a lecture at West Virginia University (WVU) with Harvard Ayers on February 24. Brandon Nida and I spoke at West Virginia Wesleyan College on March 25 and again at Marshall University on April 8. On April 15, I found myself speaking before local politicians and businessmen at the Madison Rotary Club, after which two state senators wished me "the best of luck" in saving Blair Mountain but offered no public support.

On April 21, Harvard and I returned to the campus of West Virginia University for Earth Day. Doug Gilburt, a student at WVU and head of the campus Sierra Club chapter, secured a booth for us at the last minute so we could sell bandanas on the lawn behind the Mountainlair on the downtown campus. A good friend from Senegal, Kiva Fall, happened to be a drummer in a band of international students performing on the lawn that day. Throughout the show, they plugged the march and the need to save Blair Mountain. Watching a band of international students playing a reggae version of John Denver's "Country Roads" while wearing red bandanas remains one of the more memorable images of the whole experience.

Perhaps the most significant event leading up to the march occurred in Matewan, West Virginia. Situated along the Tug River, which separates West Virginia from Kentucky, the little town of Matewan became a center of activity during the Mine Wars and, before then, the area hosted many of the events surrounding the famous Hatfield-McCoy Feud. Today Matewan looks and feels almost like an old western town in the green mountains. The union tradition is still strong in this area and the town is home to UMWA Local 1440, the largest UMWA local in America. Local 1440 allowed a number of protest organizers and supporters to come and speak to their membership a month before the march. Many of the organizers attended, as well as reps from the Sierra Club and other environmental groups. Larry Gibson, whom I met for the first time at Matewan, told me that this was the first time he experienced environmentalists and coal miners in the same room, and they were getting along. Blair Mountain, it seemed, provided the common ground. At the end of the evening, Local 1440 declared its support of our efforts to save Blair Mountain, although they stopped short of condemning the practice of MTR. They gave us UMWA signs to carry during the protest and donated $500. Joe Stanley, a retired UMWA miner carried one of those signs the entire length of the protest march. Support from the largest UMWA local in America gave our protest a layer of legitimacy we would not have otherwise enjoyed because the international UMWA did not endorse the protest. That night in Matewan also provided a foundation for working with the union and town of Matewan in the coming years.

From the meeting at Jimmy Weekley's house until the march felt like a crash course in Activism 101. The world of environmental activism, in which I found myself suddenly immersed, is a subculture all its own. My initial realization of this came at our first public organizing meeting in January at the Logan Public Library. The previous night, I had attended the playoff game at Heinz Field between the Pittsburgh Steelers and Baltimore Ravens. In perhaps the most exciting game I've seen in Pittsburgh, the Steelers came from behind in a dramatic fashion to beat the Ravens and advance to the AFC Championship. The next day I arrived at the meeting still pumped about the game. I strode into the conference room and said hello to Harvard, Brandon, and a few others standing around. They asked me how I was and I said, "Great! I was at the playoff game last night and it was incredible!"

They all just looked at me until someone finally said, "What game?" The group went on to explain that many of them had attended Judy Bonds's funeral the day before. Judy Bonds had been one of the more prominent anti-MTR activists and the environmental community held her in high esteem. She died of cancer. But while others in the room revered her, I knew nothing about her.

Despite my rookie status, most of the activists welcomed me into their ranks. I found that I instantly got on well with the local activists. The bulk of the movement consisted of millennials between the ages of 18 and 25. A handful seemed to look at me as though I was the physical embodiment of everything they hated about high school. I tried to be friendly and not overstep my bounds as the new guy. Still, I some-times found it hard to relate. Some of the activists subscribed to anarchist theory and identified themselves as such, which I most certainly did not. Members of the movement ranged from well-informed citizens who shared concerns about water and air quality to those whose activism had become their religion. I also think that a handful of others simply sought their place in society and found one within a cause.

I must admit to a bit of early wariness concerning the

activists who hailed from outside the state. While grateful for their support, I still felt a touch uneasy around them. During a break at the organizational meeting in Whitesville, I noticed several of these activists squatting on the sidewalk outside with a banjo and a guitar attempting to play something resembling traditional mountain music. I did not really know how to take it. Growing up, I hated the sound of a banjo. Every time the national media, or movies, or television shows featured West Virginia, the editors felt the need to play banjo music in the background. My mind could not separate these insultingly derogatory media portrayals with banjo music. Make no mistake; I grew up immersed in strong musical traditions. My grandfather on my mother's side played in old-timey bands for much of his youth. In 1937, he played in a group with country music legend Grandpa Jones. I cherish vivid memories of him, my uncles, aunts, and cousins singing and playing traditional and gospel songs. No one played a banjo. No one I knew played a banjo. When I told the CNN producers that I played guitar, their eyes lit up and Rob Howell immediately asked, "Do you play bluegrass? Can you also play a banjo? We would love to film you playing a banjo." I offered to play them some Pink Floyd or Pearl Jam instead. They quickly lost interest. While the symbol of the red bandana fell well within my comfort zone, I have often felt conflicted about the banjo as a symbol of identity and culture in relation to my home. Like the rest of Appalachia, it is filled with irony—an African instrument synonymous with white trash in the American popular consciousness. Watching kids from other states come to my home and pick up a banjo with the intention of immersing themselves in mountain culture further complicated this irony in my mind.

In spite of my early misgivings, one "outsider" gave me a superb window into this activist world and helped break my own stereotypical preconceptions. About two months before the protest, I met Jordan Freeman, a filmmaker who had moved to West Virginia from California. He had long hair, a bushy beard, wore sandals, had a mild, soft voice, and an affinity for wearing greens and browns. Jordan handed me a DVD rough cut of his new film about the anti-MTR movement called *Low Coal*. My expectations were not high. Fortunately, Jordan proved me wrong. A film with no narration, *Low Coal* is a raw, unique portrait of the coalfields. I even loved the music, which surprisingly included banjos. Much of the scrappy documentary focuses on the reflections of activist Larry Gibson, and by the time I finished watching, I felt as though I had a much better handle on the environmental movement in the coalfields. Although Jordan and Mari-Lynn Evans would go on to make the award-winning film *Blood on the Mountain*, Jordan's little-known *Low Coal* provided me with inspiration in those early months. After all, if a California-bred, bearded hipsterbilly could make a Lincoln County boy enjoy banjo music, anything was possible.

### • THE 2011 MARCH •

On Friday, June 3, 2011, I drove to Marmet, just outside of the capitol city of Charleston. In 1921, coal miners began assembling at Marmet in late August and used the spot as the launching pad for the Armed March on Logan. We began there as well. The organizers rented a small warehouse in Marmet to serve as the protest headquarters. Over a hundred protestors had already arrived and the inside of the warehouse resembled Santa's workshop the night before Christmas Eve. Groups painted signs and banners in one area while volunteers compiled and stacked camp gear. Protestors registered at tables in the front. In a side room, Jasper Conner conducted a class on proper behavior during the protest. The protestors needed to prepare for the inevitable shouts and insults of locals as well as for possible violent attacks. Jasper instructed and schooled everyone not to fight back, not to return shouts, and not to say or do anything provocative. To risk the cliché, we intended to let our walking do the talking.

Behavior concerned all the organizers. Everyone took great pains to ensure that the protest went smoothly. Alcohol and drugs were strictly forbidden. We planned no civil disobedience during the week of the march. We restricted protesters to the warehouse grounds in Marmet. As protestors registered in the warehouse, they read signs with messages like "YOU STAND OUT! DO NOT WANDER AROUND THE COMMUNITY!" We did not want activists mistaken for unruly troublemakers and we felt justifiable concern for the safety of the protestors who, if they came across the wrong sort in the coalfields, could find themselves in a world of trouble.

By Sunday night, around 250 individuals had arrived. As something of a grand finale event before Monday, Mari-Lynn Evans organized a benefit concert for the protest at the Cultural Center in Charleston. Unfortunately, Hazel Dickens, the original headliner for the show, died a month before the concert, so the event evolved into a memorial show to honor Hazel Dickens with labor songs performed by various artists. The event went well in spite of a sense of uneasiness among many of the organizers. I had been informed that dozens of West Virginia State Police troops were assembling in force outside and that they intended "to arrest everyone on the march and do whatever else is necessary if anyone steps out of line."

Maria Gunnoe heard the rumor as well. She and I spoke about it at length in the lobby of the Cultural Center before the concert. I could not help but think of all the historical connections. Governor Ephraim F. Morgan created the State Police in 1919 specifically to function as strikebreakers in the Mine Wars. State Police fought alongside mine guards at Blair Mountain, using tommy guns to shoot at attacking miners. Throughout the twentieth century, state troopers repeatedly defended coal company interests—in the name of property rights—during strikes. During the Massey/UMWA strikes of the 1980s, some local restaurants and gas stations refused to serve state troopers because of their heavy-handed tactics against union miners. As environmental activism rose, state troopers protected coal company property and arrested protestors. Some protestors were beaten. At Marsh Fork Elementary in 2010, the State Police placed a sniper in plain view atop the elementary school roof to intimidate activists. I returned to my place in Charleston that night anxious about what might occur the next day.

The following week passed like a whirlwind. It began the next morning at a little league baseball field about a hundred yards from the rented warehouse. The protestors gathered around the pitcher's mound and listened to short speeches by Wilma Steele, Brandon Nida, Mari-Lynn Evans, and myself. Media cameras and journalists scurried around documenting and questioning participants. All of the colorful banners and signs held by the protestors made us an impressive sight. The approximately 275 individuals who marched that day were as colorful as the banners they carried. Many wore red bandanas in a variety of ways—around their necks, foreheads, and tied to their belts. A few arrived from as far away as France and Australia to join the protest. A couple of Buddhist monks even arrived, wearing orange robes and beating drums as they walked. A little after 10:00 a.m., we took the first steps out of the ballpark towards Blair. Many of the protestors sang labor songs before we set out. I vividly recall John Hennen, a history professor at Morehead State University, leading a number of folks in a verse of "Frank Keeney Is Our Leader and We Shall Not Be Moved." The excitement and intensity of the moment was something quite unlike I had ever before experienced.

The media attention given to the event on the first day and throughout the week worked in our favor. Our media team, headquartered at the warehouse in Marmet, worked diligently to get the word out on the protest and update the online community of our progress. Dozens of online news sites from across the country covered the protest or picked up AP stories about it. Most of the national press focused on the issue of MTR. A few took the angle that the history behind Blair Mountain could bring labor unions and environmentalists together in a common cause.

It seemed to me as though I gave an interview about every fifteen minutes over the course of the week. The other organizers asked me to stay in Marmet on Monday and Wednesday for the sole purpose of conducting interviews. Even while I marched with the other activists, I felt bombarded. Every time we stopped for a break, a journalist or filmmaker of some kind stuck a microphone or camera in my face. On Thursday, Soledad O'Brien interviewed me just before our march reached the Logan County line. She had interviewed me a couple of months earlier by the road at Blair Mountain. I'm glad she conducted our second interview late in the week because by Thursday I had become more comfortable in my role as a spokesman. As with all the other interviews, I tried to sound optimistic, clear, and persuasive. More specifically, I veered the conversation toward the history we were trying to protect whenever possible. However, most of the interviewers, Soledad included, wanted to talk about MTR and the environment. When I explained to one journalist on Friday that I wanted to emphasize the history more, the journalist said that the environment is sexier than history and if I wanted to talk about the history, I should write a book. Very well then.

We received daily coverage on local television and newspapers. Paul Nyden, an award-winning journalist from the *Charleston Gazette,* wrote about us throughout the week. Although I expected bad press, the newspapers allowed us to get our message across to anyone who wanted to take the time to read. I tailored my comments to fit the specific publication. When Zach Harold of the *Charleston Daily Mail,* the state's most popular conservative newspaper, approached me on Monday and asked about the battlefield, I responded with a statement I knew only a West Virginian could comprehend. "I don't understand why any West Virginian would want our history destroyed," I said. "If you want to destroy Blair Mountain, change your name to Rodriguez and move to Michigan."[23] As I expected, this statement received a bigger reaction than anything else I said the entire week.

Rich Rodriguez had been the head coach of West Virginia University's football team. The WVU Mountaineer football program is the premier team in a small state with no professional major league teams and, as a cultural phenomenon, Mountaineer football is an important part of state identity. Because of all the media negativity associated with West Virginia, mountaineers eagerly applaud anyone or anything that casts the state in a positive light, such as successful sports teams and athletes. WVU football also gives locals a reason to cheer amid not so cheerful hard times. So when Rich Rodriguez led the Mountaineers to an upset victory over SEC Champion Georgia in the 2006 Sugar Bowl, West Virginians all across the state were elated. Rodriguez himself became a nearly heroic figure overnight; a local boy, not an outsider, who promised to bring greatness to Mountaineer Nation. In 2007, WVU won its first ten games and only lacked one more victory against archrival Pitt to earn a spot in the National Championship.

Then we choked. In what many call the most disappointing loss in Mountaineer history, Pitt beat WVU in our own stadium and ruined our national championship hopes. Just a few days later, Rich Rodriguez announced his retirement from WVU to accept the head coaching position at the University of Michigan. Rodriguez instantly went from potentially having a statue built in his honor to becoming the most hated man in West Virginia. In the eyes of the Mountaineer faithful, this was betrayal—a local boy turning his back on his home when everyone was at their lowest. A few even bought into a conspiracy theory that Rodriguez purposely threw the game in order to take the Michigan job. His move meant something more than a change in the football program, it was yet another talented mountaineer leaving the state because West Virginia just wasn't good enough or glamorous enough or rich enough. Many locals cheered when Michigan fired Rodriguez a few years later. Students held parties in Morgantown to celebrate, and I even heard a caller say on a Charleston radio show that he would not be satisfied until Rodriguez was living in a cardboard box underneath the Patrick Street Bridge. To West Virginians, the name Rodriguez meant traitor, and I wanted to link betrayal with the threat to Blair Mountain. Those who wish to destroy Blair Mountain have betrayed West Virginia, just as Rodriguez did.

Conflict can be educational. Lou Martin, a friend and history professor who hails from the northern part of the state, traveled south to take part in the protest and wrote about what he learned. Lou stated,

True power does not have to defend itself. We go through our daily lives not questioning it, not challenging it, and so it does nothing while we do its bidding . . . in peacefully walking along the road and announcing that we intended to end mountaintop removal, we forced power to come out of its cave and defend itself. I had studied the power of companies to shape the course of history, and now I was seeing firsthand the power that coal companies possessed to suppress dissent in the coalfields.[24]

Lou is correct. During our protest, power did come out of its cave. Police shadowed our every move. They instructed us to march single file on the left side of the road outside of the white line. Those who walked on the wrong side of the white line risked arrest. Curiously, for significant stretches along the march route, someone had recently repainted the white lines to make the road wider and the space beside the road smaller. Dozens of State Police cars and vans accompanied us on Monday, filming the protestors and keeping a close watch. Fortunately, no strong-arm tactics or arrests materialized, and the State Police actually provided a measure of security during the protest. As fortune would have it, I knew the two state troopers in charge, Tony Cummings and Dave Nelson. The lead state trooper, Tony Cummings, is the younger brother of my brother-in-law, and I had known him for over twenty-five years. Whenever we took a break from marching, and I could escape reporters, I would cross the road to where the State Police cars were parked and joke around a bit with Tony and the other troopers, attempting to ease any possible tensions.

By the end of the evening on Monday, I received word that everyone had safely arrived at the first campsite in the little town of Racine. I went home Monday evening expecting to meet up with the marchers in Racine and begin day two. To my great surprise, I arrived at headquarters in Marmet the next morning to find all of the marchers asleep on the floor of the warehouse. Something had gone very wrong.

As I returned home the night before, the marchers ran into trouble in Racine. A few local residents spent the evening hurling verbal insults and threats at the activists as they set up camp. The local volunteer fire department drove its trucks back and forth blaring their sirens for several hours into the night. At around 10:00, the Boone County Commissioner, accompanied by the county police, arrived on the scene. Although the organizers had previously secured permission from State Police to stay at the park, the State Police were suddenly nowhere to be found. The county police gave the protestors the option to disperse or be arrested. The organizers decided to shuttle everyone in cars back to Marmet. Getting everyone back with the limited number of vehicles we possessed took several trips and several hours. Even worse, the next morning all of the campsites we had reserved for the rest of the week separately called march headquarters and told us we could no longer stay at their sites.

The only option available to us was to shuttle everyone back and forth all week. Each morning we could begin where we ended the day before, walk as usual to the regularly scheduled stopping point, bring everyone back to Marmet, and start the process over the next day. But in addition to this being horribly cumbersome, we lacked the funds necessary to pay for the gasoline throughout the week. Around fifty protestors gave up and went home overnight. Another fifty or so left in the morning. Cars began transporting the one hundred and twenty or so remaining marchers to Racine to begin day two while Larry Gibson and I drove to see Ken Hechler. We convinced him to donate $500 to help us pay for gasoline and then joined the marchers. That evening, at the request of the media team, I returned home and wrote an urgent appeal to people to donate to the protest so we could pay for gas. The next morning, the media team distributed my and a few other hastily written appeals for help across the internet and raised enough money to pay our gas expenses. The marchers continued.

Among other things, the march to Blair Mountain was a walking conversation. People were talking in the coal-fields, office workers in Charleston chatted about the march at the water cooler, individuals posted comments on social media, and families argued about it over dinner. The march encouraged people to take a side, and it made the issues we presented inescapable. A conversation also existed between the marchers and the communities in Boone and Logan Counties. Those who believed we marched to end their jobs voiced their displeasure by giving us the middle finger as they drove by, yelling and screaming from the other side of the street, or by displaying homemade signs in yards. On Thursday, as we neared the border of Logan County, the signs appeared more frequently. I saw a little girl holding a sign that read, "Tree Huggers Suck." A pair of miner's boots rested in front of a poster board sign that read, "Walk a mile in these shoes." A sign on someone's front door proclaimed, "Mountaintop Removal paid for this house." Several signs, meaning to be either funny or provocative, quipped, "Strip Mining Prevents Forest Fires." A man in a pickup truck slowed beside my friend Jason Tackett, who joined us on Thursday, pointed at him and screamed, "Get a job, hippie!" Jason is a doctor of osteopathic medicine and, at the time, he worked around sixty hours a week. The look on his face was priceless.

Tension continued to build all day and reached a climax when we passed through the town of Sharples in the late afternoon. Viewing things through historical lenses as I tend to do, I thought a lot about the role Sharples played in the 1921 miners' uprising. When the first wave of the Red Neck Army entered Sharples in 1921, they found a company mess hall. The company had divided the mess into separate rooms for blacks, whites, and management. The Red Necks took over the mess hall and forced the cooks to serve everyone together in the management section.[25] Today, the term *redneck* is often closely associated with racism. In 1921, the actual Red Necks were practicing their own brand of desegregation all along the march route a generation before it became law.

Nothing could have been more terrifying to the power establishment than to see hillbillies, blacks, and immigrants armed and working together in a common cause. As one coal operator put it, "At any point you were liable to butt into a colored man with a rifle. . . . It is impossible to describe the terrorism that prevailed."[26] This is the kind of history that turns stereotypes on their heads and redefines identity. It's the kind of history I wanted to protect and share. Others wish to destroy this history precisely because of the elements I wanted to celebrate. Industrialists and politicians have spent generations working to incite divisions between immigrants, African Americans, and poor whites. It often works. Blair Mountain gives us the briefest glimpse of what is possible when these groups join forces.

Hours after the miners shared their meal in 1921, Captain J. R. Brockus and a force of 290 state troopers and mine guards crossed Blair Mountain on a horse trail in the darkness and moved toward Sharples. Just before dawn, Brockus and his men confronted the miners. A heated verbal exchange led to a gunfight that killed several men. When the shooting stopped, Brockus and his men fled south, back over Blair

Mountain. By the end of the day, word of the gunfight had spread throughout the coalfields. The Red Neck Army, which nearly abandoned the march after threats of federal military intervention, pressed toward Blair Mountain with renewed fervor.[27]

I tried to process all of the history as it became juxtaposed with what we experienced as we marched. Scores of pro-coal advocates gathered at various spots on the right side of the road. They held signs and screamed at us. One or two spit at us. I wondered how many of the residents of Sharples knew about Captain Brockus or the dinner in the company mess hall. One of ladies across the road yelled out, "Don't you know the miners back then were marching for coal?" Her question answered mine. Fortunately, no one behaved violently on either side. The marchers behaved magnificently. They took the insults and the screaming and no one responded. We simply kept walking.

Although we had all prepared ourselves to deal with the inevitable negativity, many locals surprised me with encouragement over the course of the week. On Monday, just outside of Marmet, a man put a sign on his four-wheeler which simply read, "Thank You." A few others actually handed out flowers to marchers. Several old ladies gave cans of soda to marchers as we passed their homes. Some families stepped out on their porches, applauded for a brief moment, and hurried back inside. I saw a few applauding from their windows. While many drivers hurled insults and middle fingers, some gave us a thumbs up as they passed. On Thursday, an elderly woman invited us all to have lunch in her backyard. We accepted the invitation and she told us that her grandmother had lived in the same house and had fed the 1921 marchers when they went by. She wanted to honor that history. Such bits of encouragement kept the protestors moving forward as much as anything else, and we began to realize that our march gave a voice to individuals who may have been too intimidated or discouraged to speak out for themselves.

We marched into the community of Blair on Friday, where many of the residents welcomed our arrival. Jimmy Weekley awaited us at the mouth of Pigeonroost Hollow wearing his red bandana. We were even able to secure a campsite at the foot of Blair Mountain for the final night. As everyone crossed the road into the campsite area, completing the five-day hike, I stood by and either shook hands, high fived, or fist bumped each marcher as they filed by me. The marchers had endured a week of obstacles, had walked underneath a searing sun with a consistent temperature in the mid-nineties, and had overcome exhaustion to reach Blair Mountain. The entire organizational crew pulled through with flying colors and made the march a success. From the cooks who somehow managed to prepare and deliver three good meals a day, to the crews who worked security and delivered water, to the organizers who stayed up well into each night making nuts and bolts decisions, everyone worked together to see it through. The protestors cheered for quite a while when they reached the campground on Friday.

With one minor exception, Saturday felt like a celebration. A little over 1,100 people attended a rally at the campsite. Nearly every prominent name in the local environmental movement gave a speech. I spent the day meandering about the crowd, talking to people, and conducting a few final interviews. In the afternoon, we hiked the final two miles along the main road up to the southern summit of Blair Mountain. About fifteen minutes before we began the last leg of the protest, one of the other march organizers approached me. She said that a group of around a dozen activists had separated themselves from the rest of the group and they planned to conduct some type of civil disobedience action once everyone reached the southern summit.

The organizers uniformly opposed civil disobedience during the march. In discussions with the media throughout the week, I repeatedly emphasized the marchers' good behavior and obedience to the law. Each evening when I returned home, I monitored Facebook and Twitter to get a sense of local opinion. Most of those skeptical of our efforts opined that we were all hippies who planned some outlandish action once we reached Blair Mountain. I strongly felt that any civil disobedience would play into a narrative that favored the coal industry and would be to the detriment of the overall goal of saving the battlefield. As a group, the protestors held several late-night discussions about the possibility of civil disobedience and the vast majority agreed to follow the lead of the organizers. About a dozen, however, disagreed and resolved to go rogue on Saturday. Because I went home each night, I missed these debates. Thus, when another organizer made me aware of the situation a few minutes before we left the campsite at Blair, I asked her to point out these activists. She did and I approached them. They explained that even though the organizers did not want them to use civil disobedience, such an act was important to them and their own personal stance against the coal industry. The idea that a handful of activists would hurt our larger objectives for their own individual motives upset me. The fact that I did not recognize a number of these individuals from earlier in the week further heightened my suspicions. I assumed that law enforcement or the coal industry—possibly both—employed at least one undercover person among our ranks. Such a person or persons could try to lead a number of activists astray and into an action that would harm us more than help us. I did not know whether any of the individuals in front of me were undercover coal operatives or law enforcement, but I did not intend to let them potentially ruin the progress our march had made. I offered them an alternative view and, admittedly, was not very nice about it. After a short discussion, they backed down and agreed to abandon their action.

With the issue of civil disobedience temporarily resolved, we ascended the final two miles. One could feel the celebration in the air. My friend Jason and I positioned ourselves close to the front of the procession, which stretched about two hundred yards behind us. Larry Gibson marched right ahead of us. He seemed to skip up the sloped roadway, exhorting everyone behind him. "The harder the climb, the sweeter the summit!" he kept saying.

In a final act of spite, someone placed dozens of boulders on the side of the road the entire two miles to the southern summit and covered each one with grease. None of these boulders had been there a few days before, and it would have taken heavy machinery to place them there. The boulders could not prevent our progress, of course, but someone simply wanted to make our path up the mountain a little more inconvenient.

I declined the offer to give a talk at the top. The marchers had already heard me give several speeches throughout the week and I didn't really feel as though I had anything left to say. Besides, quite a few others wanted to give speeches at the top of the mountain. I have come to learn that, with protests, there are no shortages of willing speakers. I was tired of talking and simply wanted to go up on the ridgeline and enjoy the moment.

I have never been one for pep rallies. As everyone celebrated and cheered, I said goodbye to a few people, and Jason and I began walking back toward the campground and our cars. I wanted to go home, rest, and think about what happened and what would happen next. We hadn't made it far down the road when I glanced behind me and caught Rob Howell from CNN running after us with his camera. He pointed it at me, looking for that one last good soundbite, and asked, "Has the march exceeded your expectations?" I think he expected a beaming statement from me. Instead I said, "We haven't saved the mountain yet, so no, it hasn't."

Jason and I kept walking. The further away we went from the cheering the more the reality of what I had said began to sink in. As we descended, I kept glancing at the boulders placed on the side of the road. Whomever had placed them there would have possessed the power to shut down a lane of traffic, bring in heavy equipment, and transport the boulders. It was a great deal of effort in the name of spite. The truth set in on me like the weight of those boulders. Those grease-covered rocks revealed the vindictive, stubborn nature of the executives and politicians who wanted to destroy the battlefield. We had made a gargantuan effort, saw it through to a rousing conclusion, and yet the battlefield remained threatened. There were so many steps yet to take.

## CHAPTER THREE

# Camp Branch

>>>>>> <<<<<<

*Mr. Stanley*: So, we get there. Mr. Campbell is there. Paul
and Jeff are with me. Others start to arrive, and we're
waiting for Mr. King, who was the last to arrive.
Dennis Stottlemeyer was there and Jonathan was
there and John was there. Harold Ward eventually
came, and we're all waiting, and Kenny comes up and
his sister—it looked like—was driving his vehicle and
they dropped him off, and—but prior to him getting
there, there was this guy in a green uniform accompanying a gentleman by the name of Greg Wooten,
who is a landowner, or a representative of Natural
Resource Partners. I assume he—and from what I
understand, he works for Natural Resource Partners,
and why he was there, I would have no clue, but he
was accompanied by a person in similar clothing to
the people that—the West Virginia DEP had on, with
no markings on it, but he was carrying a gun.

Two years removed from the protest march found me
as president of Friends of Blair Mountain (FOBM), the

battlefield still unprotected, and my board members being intimidated by an armed guard. The excerpt above is from Joe Stanley's testimony on December 9, 2013, before the West Virginia Surface Mine Board (SMB) hearing. His testimony concerned a citizens' site inspection conducted by FOBM accompanied by representatives of the West Virginia Department of Environmental Protection (WVDEP) on September 10 of that same year. Joe continued:

> *Mr. Stanley*: And him and Mr. Wooten came up the road, came across the highway directly in front of us and went up the steps at the guard shack and stayed up there several minutes, and there were coal miners that were waiting to get paid because the miners had—while we were standing there discussing this stuff with Mr. Campbell, the miners were going up there and asking the guard guy if the check—if the money was there. So we waited for them to come. Then they came down out of the guard shack, went around the building and went and separated theirselves about thirty foot from where Mr. Campbell, Dennis Stottlemeyer—I think John was standing there. I think Jonathan was also. Paul Corbit was standing there. I was standing there and Jeff Bosley was standing there.
>
> And as soon as Kenny arrived, Mr. Wooten and this guy in the—the green khakis started hollering at him saying, "Hey come over here. Come over here. Come over here." So Kenny says, "Well guys,"—Kenny had two bottles of water I think in his hand. He reached me—he said, "Joe, you need a bottle of water." It was 91 degrees when we got there, and Kenny went over there and started talking to them

and, man, they were brow beating him because you could hear the voices and the fingers and—this guy had a gun on him. It looked like a Glock automatic to me. Now, I'm just—hey you asked me to—

*Mr. Wandling*: I'd just like to object . . .

The objection was overruled. Mary Anne Maul, our attorney, continued her questioning:

*Ms. Maul*: So, Mr. Stanley, what was the result on you of the presence of this person in green with a weapon on him? What was the effect?

*Mr. Stanley*: I was intimidated and I was threatened with either deadly force—definitely bodily force or deadly force. Because he looked at me after one o'clock—after this inspection had turned, and I said, "Kenny, do you need a witness over there?" And I said, "That guy has a gun." And he put the—he had turned around immediately, put his hand on that gun, and he said, "Yes, I do. And I am qualified and certified to use it, and I have the right to use it when I see fit."

And I didn't say anything, and I said, "Well, Kenny looks like he's getting browbeat over there." And he said, "I told you to shut the f**k up. You're on private f**king property and I will throw your f**king ass off."

He started towards me and he said, "You better back off, Red." Benny Campbell stood up and said, "We don't want no trouble here. Joe, go up these stairs and get your training."

Now let me ask you folks, how would you feel under a government protected site visit, as a citizen, who is concerned about destruction of West Virginia history to be threatened by somebody with a gun?

*Ms. Maul*: You can answer that question for us? How did you feel?

*Mr. Stanley*: I was intimidated. Hell, I was shaking.

The following is Kenny King's testimony of the same event:

*Mr. King*: Well, when I first arrived, I was riding with my sister—she gave me a ride up there—dropped me off. As soon as I opened the door, somebody hollered, "I know a troublemaker when I see one. I need to talk to you over here."

I don't know who said—I believe it was the—the armed—whoever the armed guard or state police. He never did identify his self. So I went over and talked to Greg Wooten and the person with the gun. We discussed a matter for several—probably fifteen minutes or so and then after that was settled we went upstairs to do the safety hazard training and . . .

*Ms. Maul*: Well did that have anything to do with the site visit?

*Mr. King*: No. Nothing whatsoever, but I felt—I mean, was really intimidated by this armed person, you know, and, you know, and Greg Wooten.[1]

On the day of the incident described in this testimony, I went through my day teaching classes in Logan. After classes, I went to the local Bob Evans restaurant to meet Paul Corbit Brown, Joe Stanley, and Jeff Bosley to hear their account of how everything had gone wrong. Kenny was in the hospital with a broken ankle. As Joe and the others related the story to me, my mind kept returning to something Frank Keeney had said. Speaking before striking miners at a tent colony along Cabin Creek, Keeney told them, "One day there will be no more gunmen. No more tent colonies. Because of what you people are going through right now." Although the tent colonies no longer exist, the occasional gunmen still linger in the coalfields, protecting company interests. Apparently, someone desperately wanted to put a stop to our efforts. But why?

On March 9, 2009, the Blair Mountain Battlefield was placed on the National Register of Historic Places. On December 30 of that same year, it was delisted. This much I have already related, as well as the details concerning the landowners and the inexplicable actions of the Keeper of the National Register. Nonetheless, the battlefield spent nearly ten months of 2009 listed on the National Register. During those months, the Camp Branch surface mine witnessed some very interesting activity.

Three surface mines threatened the Blair Mountain Battlefield: Adkins Fork, Bumbo No. 2, and Camp Branch. Adkins Fork is located at Blair Mountain, Bumbo No. 2 is a massive operation located in the north, and Camp Branch is located in the center. Of the three, Camp Branch actually threatened the smallest portion of the battlefield—only about fifty acres, in fact. But, these fifty acres hosted the most intense fighting in our battle to save Blair Mountain.

On October 8, 2009, while the battlefield remained on the National Register, Major General Allan E. Tackett, then serving as adjutant general for West Virginia, wrote a letter to James Jones, then president of Aracoma Coal Company, and Greg Wooten, vice president at Natural Resource Partners (NRP). Aracoma Coal is the same company responsible for the Upper Big Branch mining disaster, which killed twenty-nine men in 2010. Aracoma is also a subsidiary of Alpha Natural Resources, one of the largest coal companies in

America. At the time of this letter, however, the Upper Big Branch disaster had yet to occur, Aracoma remained a subsidiary of Massey Energy, and Don Blankenship reigned as CEO. Based out of Texas, NRP is the second-largest landowning corporation in America, owning land in forty-eight states. NRP is one of the major landowners on the Blair Mountain Battlefield and typically leases their land out to coal companies. On the land encompassed by the Camp Branch Permit, NRP owns the land and Aracoma leases the land to mine it.

General Tackett wrote the following: "The West Virginia National Guard requests your favorable consideration in modifying Camp Branch Surface Mine Permit (S-5013–90) Post Mine Land Use from Forest Land and Fish/Wildlife Habitat to Public Use, for an Adverse Weather Aerial Delivery System (AWADS), Drop Zone (DZ), and Landing Zone (LZ)."

The letter goes on to state that the National Guard intended to build a base and drop zone on the Camp Branch Permit after the completion of mining operations. The base would be a spot for special ops training and drop zones for, according to General Tackett, "C-130s, C-27s, C-23s, and virtually any type of helicopter, just to mention a few." The letter also declares that the plan for the base was "favorably endorsed" by then Governor Joe Manchin and would aid, "in the fight against Global Terrorism."[2]

Less than a month later, on November 4, 2009, Greg Wooten of NRP, wrote a letter to James Jones, president of Aracoma Coal Company: "Discussions continue among WPP [Western Pocahontas Partners Inc.], the Logan County Development Authority, and with the West Virginia Air National Guard to develop a site suitable for an Adverse Weather Aerial Delivery System (AWADS), Drop Zone, and Landing Zone. Mr. Wooten requested that, 'Aracoma seek a variance from the AOC [Army Corps of Engineers] requirement in order to allow for continued discussions of the alternative post mining land use as an AWADS, Drop Zone, and Landing Zone.' "[3]

When a coal company is granted a permit for a surface mine operation, they must submit a post-mining plan to the Army Corps of Engineers. In other words, the company must outline a reclamation plan for what will happen to the land after it has been mined. For most permits, the post-mining plan is simply to mark it as a fish or wildlife habitat. The companies blast a mountain, scoop out the coal, and make a new landscape with what material they have left. Afterward, they usually plant a few trees, proclaim the area a wildlife habitat, and move on. On rare occasions, the post-mining plans are for specific purposes, such as building a prison or school. In this case, the adjutant general of West Virginia and the vice president of a behemoth landowning corporation asked a coal company to change its post-mining plan at Camp Branch from a wildlife habitat to accommodate a National Guard base. A potential problem with this request was that a portion of the Camp Branch surface mine permit area overlaps onto the Blair Mountain Battlefield, which, at the time, was listed on the National Register of Historic Places. The West Virginia State Code forbids surface mining on places listed on the National Register.[4]

One month later, the Keeper delisted Blair Mountain from the National Register of Historic Places.

## • HILLBILLY FIRING SQUAD •

Six months after the 2011 march, I was elected president of FOBM. As the leading organization in the fight to preserve the battlefield, FOBM needed to devise a strategy to win. How do we go about saving a battlefield? Can the governor issue a declaration to protect it? Can the president? Which government agencies are responsible for regulating mining on the battlefield and what role do they play? What are the legal protections for historic sites? Who are the key politicians who may help us? Who are the ones in opposition to our efforts? What about the private landowners and their intentions? How do we deal with the coal companies and, more specifically, the individuals within these companies with the power to make decisions regarding mining on the battlefield? Who are those individuals? How many mining operations threaten the battlefield and which companies own which mining permits? Where on earth do we start?

We needed a unique approach. The 2011 protest march embraced three broad ideals brought about by a huge coalition of groups: labor rights, ending mountaintop removal (MTR), and building a sustainable economy in Appalachia. While these broad objectives are worthwhile causes, our group chose to narrow our focus exclusively on the Blair Mountain Battlefield. In the year that followed the march, FOBM adopted three main strategies to achieve our specific goal of saving Blair Mountain:

1. **Identity Reclamation:** Take control of the public narrative and win the support of the local population. This would require us to build bridges with folks in coal country who held serious biases against environmentalists and who had spent their entire existence living in a company propaganda bubble.

2. **Become Citizen Regulators:** Learn the system and use it to our advantage. In other words, we endeavored to educate ourselves on the government agencies, laws, and regulations, to use our knowledge of regional history, and to find ways to harness all of them to achieve our goals. If coal companies could

rig the system to work for them, we reasoned that we could rig the system to work for us.

3. **Political Maneuvering:** Get in the room with the power players and find a solution. We wanted to approach the executives, politicians, and regulators directly, establish relationships with them, offer an alternative vision to blasting the battlefield, and reach a settlement.

Controlling the narrative around Blair Mountain and the need to preserve it would be our most crucial strategy, as it could influence much more than just the preservation movement. To educate the public meant challenging entrenched regional worldviews and, if we were successful, this would have political, cultural, and economic ramifications. This strategy would also be the most difficult to implement because it would require patience and time. To establish a distinct identity among other activist groups, Joe Stanley came up with an official motto for us—History. Labor. Culture. Much more on this message in chapter five.

Our unique approach meant that we made a conscious decision to move away from strategies that other grassroots and environmental organizations in the region have traditionally used. Namely, we minimized protests and eliminated civil disobedience. For generations, protests have been the go-to tactic of activist groups. Sometimes they produce spectacular results. However, to induce real change, protests usually need big numbers and they must be sustained over time. In the 1960s, for example, West Virginia Governor Arch Moore signed a bill into law recognizing black lung as a disease. But he only did so after thousands of coal miners went on strike and protested at the capitol for weeks. Regarding the Blair Battlefield, it took a broad coalition of groups seven months of planning to make a one-week protest a reality. The protest reached its height on the last day of our march when a little over 1,000 people rallied in Blair and about 800 trekked up to the southern summit that afternoon. After the march, many of the participants returned to their homes across the country and went on with their lives, leaving the remaining locals to continue the push. While the event provided a great start, we knew that we would not be able to get the tens of thousands of activists needed to sway politicians and the company executives into action. This is the dilemma facing many grassroots activist groups in rural areas. Protests usually need big numbers to succeed. In rural, remote areas, big numbers are hard to come by. In the final cost-benefit analysis, we felt that the potential gains of conducting protests simply were not worth the time, energy, and resources we would need to expend when we knew it was unlikely that we could ever get the numbers needed to produce victory. We instead reimagined ourselves as something of an activist version of a special ops force, conducting precise missions behind enemy lines.

The question of civil disobedience became contentious within our organization. A few members felt that acts of civil disobedience made a powerful statement, raised awareness of the issue, and were empowering. In my opinion, however, activists often use the word *empowering* as a feel-good substitute for tangible gains. I have no doubt that many people felt quite empowered after our 2011 protest march, but levels of personal empowerment do not revoke mining permits. I also feel that some activists romanticize civil disobedience. As exemplified by the group of activists at the 2011 march who wanted to break the law and get arrested on the last day, their own personal motivations, and what they symbolized, were more important to them than whether the act itself would actually get us closer to saving the battlefield. This has nothing to do with whether an activist is brave or dedicated, as most are, but, to be blunt, some activists I know participate in civil disobedience so they can wear it as a badge of honor and say they stood up to The Man. I fully understand that this is a hard pill for many activists to swallow. Yet I encourage activists to ask the question, Am I participating in an act of civil disobedience because it will actually work, because I do not know what else to do, or because it will make me feel better about myself? Each tactic utilized in each cause needs to be evaluated and adjusted to fit the specific needs for success within that cause.

Environmental activists in West Virginia have occasionally conducted *tree sits*, where they stay in a tree for a number of days on surface mining sites to halt production. Such actions have succeeded in briefly stalling production, but the companies often retaliated by docking the wages of miners to compensate for loss in production. This can turn more miners and their families against the activists, thus impeding our goal of controlling the public narrative. We wanted the miners and their families to join our side. If we used tree sits or locked ourselves to the door of Arch Coal's headquarters until the police dragged us away, most locals would not differentiate between FOBM and radical environmentalists. I strongly felt that such tactics would hurt us more than help us in the quest for broad local support. More to the point, no mining permits in West Virginia had ever been denied or revoked as a result of civil disobedience tactics. It had never worked in West Virginia. For me, moving away from a tactic that had never worked was a no brainer. Of course, civil disobedience has worked for numerous causes in the past, particularly if very large numbers participate in the acts, but in remote, rural mining operations, large numbers are not an option, thus necessitating creative tactics. Winning was more important to me than making a personal statement, and civil disobedience was not the way to win this specific fight.

It has been pointed out to me that Frank Keeney and the miners who followed him used quite a lot of civil disobedience and direct action in their struggle against the coal companies during the Mine Wars. Why shouldn't FOBM follow suit? While the fight to save Blair Mountain certainly functioned as a continuation of an ongoing struggle in the coalfields, we were fighting a different kind of war. Unlike Frank Keeney, I did not face eviction and life in a tent colony. As our board members wrestled with the question, I consulted a colleague and friend who is a professor of psychology. When I asked him for his thoughts, he responded, "Everyone knows that the coal companies break the law to get what they want. If you break the law to get what you want, what makes you any different from them?" The point struck me. I, and the FOBM members who sided with me, believed that acts of civil disobedience in this specific conflict played into the hands of the coal industry and fed the narrative they wanted to create about us. We also wanted to prove that we could win without breaking the law. And we did.

Not everyone agreed. Within our organization, a few activists felt that to move away from civil disobedience, focus only on Blair Mountain, and minimize talk of abolishing MTR altogether was too much of an ideological compromise. Some felt that we could not win without direct action. For them, aiming for the larger environmental goals and using civil disobedience could spark a social movement similar to Occupy Wall Street. These individuals felt that Blair Mountain could be a rallying point or springboard for an anarchist movement in Appalachia, and they wanted to base FOBM's organization on anarchist principles. Most of the FOBM board did not agree. I, and most of the other FOBM members, wanted to keep the group focused on a single, achievable goal—preserving the battlefield. We felt that the history itself was the foundation upon which we could build common ground with other locals, who, regardless of how much company Kool-Aid they have been drinking, still understood the need to commemorate coal miner history. Blair Mountain could provide the beachhead that, once breached, enabled conversations on other issues, such as MTR or political reform.

Differences of opinion regarding our strategies, goals, and organization emerged right away and erupted into an internal conflict around the Blair Community Center and Museum. Immediately after the 2011 protest, a local who owned a tiny, abandoned church in the community of Blair offered to allow FOBM to rent the space nearly free of charge—$1 a month. Believing we could ill-afford to miss the opportunity, we accepted and leased the church building. Over the summer, we hastily put together a few displays of Kenny's artifacts and, on Labor Day Weekend 2011, opened the Blair Community Center and Museum. We were still reeling with optimism from the success of the protest march and hoped to build on that momentum with this new facility right next to Blair Mountain.

Problems arose immediately. Everything about the project was rushed. The church building was tiny and old, and it had structural problems, a poor septic system, no internet access, bad wiring, and a host of other issues. All of the repairs associated with these problems would take time and money, and we found ourselves consumed with the arduous task of trying to run and fund a full-time facility in the community of Blair while simultaneously moving forward with our other efforts to save the battlefield. In our rush to capitalize on the success of the march, we opened to the public before the building was ready. We also disagreed over the purpose of the facility.

I, and a number of others at FOBM, wanted the space to function exclusively as a museum. Others wanted it to be a hub of activism and community organizing. This led to enormous internal tension within the group.

The facility, nonetheless, remained open for eight months. On my way to campus one afternoon in early 2012, I stopped by to check on things. Although it should have been opened to the public two hours earlier, I found the door locked and had to knock several times before someone I had never met opened the door and let me in. Once inside, I found around eight people lying asleep on the floor. Brandon Nida, FOBM's executive director at the time, oversaw the facility and had been living there for a month. The center's remote location in Blair left it vulnerable to vandalism and Brandon had literally moved into the facility to guard it. The people asleep on the floor belonged to the group Radical Action for Mountain People's Survival (RAMPS). They were doing important organizing work in the community, Brandon told me, and it was necessary for them to stay. I asked how we expected to have a functioning museum when the place was not open to the public on time and there were activists asleep on the floor. Brandon told me that they were planning some kind of direct action on the battlefield that would likely lead to their arrest, though he would not share specific details with me. Our board of directors had no knowledge of these plans. I immediately took this information back to the board and the resulting controversy erupted into a series of conflicts that nearly destroyed our organization. The board stood firm that the Blair Community Center and Museum should not be headquarters for direct action involving environmental groups, particularly when at that precise time, we were engaged in a series of meetings with the UMWA to form an alliance with them. Brandon maintained that the board did not have the authority to dictate actions taken on the ground in Blair. Neither side budged.

Our differences grew so pronounced that on April 3, 2012, the board voted unanimously to part ways with Brandon Nida. On April 5, a number of board members traveled to the community center to give him the news. I did not join them because of a scheduled speaking engagement at Bowdoin College in Maine. As my plane landed in Portland that afternoon, board members called me to say that Brandon refused to leave the community center and demanded that FOBM be reorganized under an anarchist model with a much smaller board of directors. Brandon only wanted to keep three board members and said the rest should resign. Paul Corbit Brown and Mari-Lynn Evans offered me their resignations from the board. I refused to accept them and convinced them to stay on. Our board then split between those who wanted to continue to try to negotiate with Brandon and those who urged me to call the State Police and have him escorted out of the Blair Community Center and Museum. I opted for a different approach—cut our losses and move on. Instead of continuing this fight, FOBM ended our lease of the church building and left it to Brandon to take it over and negotiate his own lease with the owner, which he personally guaranteed me that he could do. After we cut the lease, several board members departed the group, frustrated with the whole scenario. Brandon Nida, meanwhile, formed his own organization, the Blair Heritage Alliance.[5]

The split engendered bitter feelings. As president of FOBM, I felt the brunt of it. I received a number of phone calls during which I was told that I didn't have the stomach to do what was necessary to defeat King Coal; I wasn't worthy of the last name Keeney. Indeed, a few of the individuals who left the group despise me more than the coal executives I have spent years fighting. As president of the organization, I certainly deserved my fair share of the blame. But regardless of personal insults, I refused to support a facility that housed activists who intended to break the law without the knowledge of the board and wanted to launch a movement well beyond the scope of our organization's objectives. My stance, and the stance of the FOBM members who supported me, created a lot of bad blood between our organization and a few other activists. Given the chance to go back, I would have pressed to delay the opening of the facility until we secured adequate funding and properly prepared it for public consumption. However, I do not regret the stance I took against civil disobedience tactics and the need to focus exclusively on the battlefield in order to build a winning strategy. If people hate me for it, so be it.

Joe Stanley referred to our internal disagreements as the hillbilly firing squad. "Instead of focusing our energy on fighting King Coal, we all stand in a circle and shoot," he said. Joe had a point. Grassroots organizations fighting big industries consist of volunteers passionate about their cause. The road to success against such economic and political might is fraught with obstacles and progress is slow. People get frustrated and angry. At times, they take out their frustrations on one another, further hampering their ultimate goals. FOBM experienced a few volleys from the hillbilly firing squad in those early months after the protest march, but we picked ourselves up, dusted ourselves off, and continued moving forward.

Perhaps the desire for direct action and civil disobedience reflected a yearning for a quick resolution. Although I wanted a final resolution for Blair Mountain as much as anyone, we had signed up for a marathon and not a sprint. Anytime one of my fellow FOBM members called me to express their opinion that we were almost across the finish line, I remembered those boulders placed on the side of the road on Blair Mountain. As someone who views the world through historical lenses, I found some inspiration in George Washington's Revolutionary War strategy. Washington himself knew that the Continental Army could not possibly face the British military toe to toe and hope to win. Like the coal companies, Britain was too powerful. Very much like Washington and the Continental Army, we did not have a lot of power or money, we did not have big numbers of activists, and we were making things up as we went. Washington's solution was to outlast the British. Use hit-and-run tactics. Use surprise. Wear them down over time. As long as the Continental Army remained alive and in the field, the revolution lived.

Inspired by Washington's strategy, perseverance and endurance became my mantra in FOBM. There were many rough times as leader of this organization. Not only did we have to deal with King Coal, but the group itself was full of strong personalities who are accomplished and intelligent individuals in their own right. I had to manage clashing personalities and deal with colliding egos on a regular basis. For several years, I spent hours on the phone every day functioning as a sounding board for FOBM members who wanted to vent, spout their ideas, and discuss everything from strategies to heated arguments with other individuals. As captain of the ship, I did my best to keep us focused, on an even keel, and sailing steadily toward our goal in spite of both external and internal storms.

## • AREA B •

One such storm appeared on the horizon in September 2011, just three months removed from the protest march. We began hearing reports from locals in the community of Blair about company activity near the battlefield. The precise nature of this activity is something we did not know; we simply heard reports of trucks hauling machinery, mechanical noises from the forest, and other activity. The land is private and away from the main roads, so we could not simply stroll up to a site and see for ourselves. Additionally, the companies had responded to the protest by increasing security on their properties and by placing No Trespassing signs on trees all over the battlefield. In the wake of the march, it seemed perfectly plausible to all of us that the coal companies might try to destroy portions of the battlefield right under our noses. In response, FOBM arranged for two of us to secure a flight from a local pilot to provide us with some air reconnaissance. On September 13, 2011, Kenny King and Paul Corbit Brown went on the flyover. No one knows the battlefield better than Kenny, and Paul is an award-winning photographer with experience documenting MTR sites.

Kenny and Paul found evidence of fresh surface disturbances on the Camp Branch Permit. As Kenny would inform us, this was not the first such incident at Camp Branch. In 2009, during one of his hikes, Kenny spotted fresh surface disturbances at Camp Branch exactly where he had documented defensive entrenchments related to the battle. During the flyover, Kenny and Paul noted that an additional forested section in this area had been clear-cut, usually a precursor to surface mining. Someone had recently damaged areas of the battlefield, possibly with intent to destroy specific areas where physical evidence of the battle existed. The timing of these disturbances was also auspicious. The 2009 disturbances took place during the battlefield's brief tenure on the National Register. The 2011 disturbances occurred just after a hugely successful protest march to save the battlefield. Both incidents occurred at Camp Branch and nowhere else. We needed answers.

First, we approached the relevant government agencies. Three existing agencies regulate surface mining: the Office of Surface Mining Reclamation and Enforcement (OSMRE), the Army Corps of Engineers (ACOE), and the West Virginia Department of Environmental Protection (WVDEP). The first two are federal agencies. WVDEP is obviously a state agency. These enforcement agencies derive their power from two pieces of legislation—the Clean Water Act of 1972[6] and the Surface Mining Control and Reclamation Act of 1977,[7] also referred to as SMCRA (pronounced *smack-rah*).

SMCRA created OSMRE, a federal agency within the US Department of Interior. OSMRE allows states to develop their own regulatory programs for surface mining and for state departments of environmental protection to enforce these programs. WVDEP issues mining permits and enforces them. OSMRE sets federal guidelines, looks over the shoulder of WVDEP, and only intervenes if they determine the state is not properly enforcing regulations or improperly approving permits. WVDEP, then, has the primary responsibility for issuing and regulating the mining permits.

The Clean Water Act empowers the ACOE, a federal agency within the military, to issue 404 permits. The ACOE is charged with protecting the waterways of the United States. In many surface mine operations, the top or side of a mountain is blasted away to reveal the coal seam. The blasted material, which is not coal and is often called overburden or fill or dredge material, is pushed off the side of the mountain with large machinery. This extra material will often cover streams, sometimes even headwater streams. Headwater streams in Appalachia are incredibly significant because they lay the foundations of numerous river systems in the eastern United

States. If a coal company intends to blast on a mining permit and cover streams or any other body of water, the company must additionally apply to the ACOE for a 404 permit and get it approved before mining can commence. The ACOE is responsible for enforcing the provisions of the 404 permit. Alpha Natural Resources had secured a mining permit and a 404 permit for Camp Branch. Therefore, the two agencies we needed to approach were the ACOE and WVDEP. If these agencies were not doing their job correctly, we could then approach OSMRE.

Even though the battlefield had been delisted from the National Register, it remained eligible for listing on the National Register. This eligibility meant that the National Historic Preservation Act afforded minimal protection for the battlefield. Under the Preservation Act, if a private operation, such as construction or mining, threatens to destroy a property eligible for the National Register, the State Historic Preservation Office (SHPO) must be consulted. SHPO possesses the authority to comment and provide advice on these threatened properties. However, SHPO does not have independent authority to revoke or deny mining permits. They can recommend that a property be preserved or studied and can oversee archeological studies of properties that may delay mining, but they ultimately cannot prevent the destruction of a property not listed on the National Register.[8]

Amid this alphabet soup of agencies and laws, which were forty to fifty years old, we searched for something that would enable us to protect the battlefield. We all readily understood how the coal industry operated in West Virginia. We knew that it skirted regulations and broke the law as much as it could to maximize profits. Whether it be mine safety, pollution, or, in our case, a historic site, companies often ignore legal regulations and work to keep regulatory agencies from enforcing their infractions. On the occasions when the government holds companies accountable for breaking the law, they are usually only required to pay small fines. Executives calculate that paying occasional fines is less expensive than obeying the law.

Based on this knowledge, research became imperative to achieving our goals. We rightly assumed that the companies must have broken or ignored regulations on the battlefield; it was simply a matter of finding the specific infractions and bringing them to light. Benefiting from the Freedom of Information Act (FOIA), we began making requests for all documents from SHPO, ACOE, WVDEP, and OSMRE related to the permits on the battlefield. As the documents kept arriving in the mail, our board members spent months pouring and pondering over letters, permits, and maps, giving special attention to Camp Branch.

Before all the FOIA requests arrived, we needed to take action on the new disturbances. Our board contacted ACOE and WVDEP, notified them of the disturbances, and asked them to inspect Camp Branch. When approaching these agencies, we made it a point not to treat the employees of these agencies as enemies. We wanted to establish positive relationships with the regulators and, therefore, maintained a polite and professional attitude when dealing with them. Both WVDEP and ACOE responded to our concerns, conducted inspections, and noted the disturbances, but took no enforcement action, initially claiming that the companies made no legal violations. We expected this. It is commonly believed that these agencies are heavily influenced, even manipulated, by the coal industry. There is, of course, a certain level of truth to this, but it is complicated. Manipulation is often difficult to prove and one has to look closely to find its nuances. Although rumors persist of regulators and mine inspectors being bribed and/or threatened to ignore violations and approve permits without question, there are more subtle ways of manipulation. The people who work at these agencies are local. They make considerably less money than management in the industry and thus do not enjoy the same social status. Within these counties, they all live in the same communities. Their children attend the same schools and churches. Many individuals on the regulatory and company ends of the spectrum even attended the same schools as children.

Not only are there economic and political pressures to let the industry have its way in the name of jobs, the industry has held sway over the state for so long that to go against the coal industry in any way is to break a social norm. A feisty inspector who does not get with the program could be prodded in a variety of ways. Perhaps the state suddenly audits his family. If bad weather causes the water pipelines to break, perhaps his house is the last one in the holler to get repairs. Perhaps an inspector writes up violations and suddenly his daughter does not make the cheerleading squad or his son is benched on the little league baseball team, or his wife gets shunned at local church events. When the baseball coach is also a mine superintendent, the cheerleading coach is the wife of a surface miner, and each member of the local school board is a stockholder in the companies, pressure can be applied in a variety of small, nearly untraceable ways. No phone calls need to be made. No orders need to be issued. It just happens. I have no evidence that such tactics were specifically applied with Camp Branch, but pressures like the examples given above do happen, not only with regulators but with anyone who rocks the boat and challenges the local good-old-boy system. I have many students in the coalfields and they love to come to my office and talk about it. And, of course, I grew up in southern West Virginia as well. I have seen it all my life.

Understanding the good-old-boy system is crucial. Local politicians with financial ties to the coal industry maintained power and social norms not only with coal jobs, but with state government and secondary school jobs. Outside of the coal industry, school systems are often the largest employers in these counties. By controlling school boards and the jobs connected to them, local industrial elites literally rule counties as their own little political fiefdoms. To get or keep a job in a school system or in a government office, one must act and vote appropriately. If you have a sign on your front lawn promoting the wrong politician, local magistrates are informed and your name goes into a little black book. If you are in the little black book, local court cases will not go your way, or you may get passed up for promotion at your job, or worse.[9] As historian Ronald Eller puts it, "the good old boys who still dominated much of Appalachian economic, cultural, and political life at the end of the twentieth century disdained criticism, innovation, and wider participation in civic life. . . . They continued to use patronage, fear, and prejudice to maintain privilege and power in their modern little kingdoms."[10]

The perpetuation of these little fiefdoms in the coalfields made the region more vulnerable and less able to adapt to changing economic and political circumstances, such as a downturn in the coal industry. As Pulitzer Prize–winning author Jared Diamond demonstrates in his work *Collapse: How Societies Choose to Fail or Succeed*, the historical record is full of examples—from the Maya to the Greenland Norse—where local elites shun innovation and new ideas that threaten their power and prestige and, by doing so, hasten the destruction of their own societies.[11] Such was the case in West Virginia, where our goal of preserving the battlefield challenged the prevailing power structure. Because we all understood the socioeconomic environment and layers of pressure placed on local regulators, we maintained a firm stance in meetings with the agencies yet refrained from treating them like villains.

We also decided to reach out directly to the coal companies and landowners to see if they were willing to negotiate a resolution. Our board appointed Joe Stanley and Mari-Lynn Evans to be the ones at the forefront of these early negotiation efforts. Joe had negotiated union contracts as a local UMWA president and, therefore, had experience dealing with the coal companies. Mari-Lynn used some of her political connections to open doors for us at the governor's office. It began with phone calls. Conversations took place. Joe and Mari-Lynn argued our points to the executives: preserving the battlefield and building a park is great PR for the industry, they knew as well as we did that the majority of the public favored the preservation of Blair. They could donate the land to the state and probably get a huge tax break or subsidy from it. There is plenty of coal elsewhere in West Virginia and, with coal performing poorly in the marketplace, letting go of 1,600 acres would not hurt them financially. We secured a series of meetings with representatives from the landowners and representatives from the governor's office. Unfortunately, the first few meetings bore little fruit or hope that the coal companies would be willing to abandon their mining plans.

While discussions continued, we methodically focused on Camp Branch. In March 2012, WVDEP held a permit hearing for the Camp Branch Permit in Logan. Coal companies usually secure their permits years in advance of mining. A company may get a permit and not touch the property for ten years, sometimes much longer. Getting permits so far in advance of mining enables companies to secure the property solely for resource extraction and prevent any type of alternative development. The companies can then mine whenever the market and labor conditions are most favorable.

Permits only last for a designated period. When that time passes, the companies typically renew the permits. Law requires that with each permit renewal there must be a period of public comment and, upon request, a public hearing for citizens to voice their opinion for or against the permit renewal. Usually, these public hearings are only attended by WVDEP reps and four or five other people. Camp Branch, on the other hand, was a different matter entirely. Not only was this a surface mine, it intruded onto the battlefield.

Many of our members attended this event at the Logan High School Gym, portions of which are included in the 2016 documentary *Blood on the Mountain*. Just before the hearing began, a hundred or so miners, wearing their work uniforms with the neon orange stripes down the sleeves and the sides of their pants, marched into the gym and sat down. Many of the top political bosses from Mingo and Logan Counties were there as well. The local leadership delivered speeches about jobs and coal. They told the crowd that the protesters were tree huggers who did not know anything about our history and were trying to destroy our way of life. Same old song and dance. Wilma Steele gave a passionate and courageous speech about why she was there and why many of the miners should be standing up for their own heritage. After the hearing, Joe Stanley and Mari-Lynn received a number of verbal threats from coal miners. Neither Joe nor Mari-Lynn are ones to cave in to intimidation, but on this evening, they both feared physical assault, as did many of the others who attended. WVDEP renewed the Camp Branch Permit after the hearing.

The tactic of flooding hearings or other public events with uniformed miners originated during Don Blankenship's tenure as CEO of Massey Energy. Usually deployed to intimidate environmental protestors, busloads of miners arrived at protests and at the occasional public hearing. The miners arrived in full uniform and shouted at the protestors, at times standing in formation like soldiers. During a 2009 protest to move the Marsh Fork Elementary School away from a coal slurry impoundment, about a dozen miners arrived on their motorcycles, parked them in a line near the activists who wanted to speak and revved the engines as loud as possible to drown them out.[12] Some say the miners are paid overtime hours to attend these events. Others say that management orders the miners to attend or they will lose their jobs. Some miners, I'm sure, want to be there. Regardless, Blankenship's tactics continued beyond his tenure. As it turned out, the more we delved into Camp Branch, the more the intimidation increased.

In 1991, the same year Kenny King led a team from WVU onto the battlefield for the first time, WVDEP issued the Camp Branch Permit to Aracoma Coal Company. It has been renewed three times. Originally, this surface mine encompassed 916 acres and is located just southwest of the battlefield line. Although this mine was very close to the battlefield, it originally did not go within 1,000 feet of the nomination area. By the time this permit came up for its first renewal in 2006, much of the original 916 acres had been mined, and Aracoma wished to expand its operation. A year before the WVDEP renewal date, Aracoma received a 404 permit from the ACOE. Aracoma intended to expand Camp Branch an additional 207 acres, for which they would need a 404 Permit from the ACOE. This addition, known to the ACOE as Area B, overlapped onto the Blair Battlefield.[13] Looking over Aracoma's 2005 application documents to the ACOE, we found this:

Aracoma Coal Company, Inc. understands that the Battle of Blair Mountain ("Area of Interest") may be partially within the proposed project area of its Camp Branch surface mine and that the site may be nominated for inclusion in the National Register of Historic Places . . .

Because any potential surface impacts to the Area of Interest would not occur for several years, Aracoma Coal Company, Inc. hereby requests that their 404 permit application be approved conditionally, with the understanding that no surface disturbance on Area B will occur until the question of eligibility for inclusion in the National Register of Historic Places for the Area of Interest is resolved.[14]

The ACOE approved the 404 permit for Camp Branch on the additional acreage. A condition to the permit was that no surface disturbances would occur within 1,000 feet of the Blair Mountain Battlefield. This 1,000-foot buffer zone all lay within Area B. This is precisely where Kenny and Paul found the 2009 and 2011 disturbances. Not only did we then know that the company violated the permit conditions, we knew that the ACOE had not enforced their own rules.

Upon learning this information, we once again notified all of the agencies involved and asked for an explanation as to why no one seemed to be enforcing this breach on the 1,000-foot buffer zone. ACOE reps told us that they were not responsible for enforcement and that we should approach WVDEP for answers. Meanwhile WVDEP reps told us that they were not responsible for enforcement and that we should consult the ACOE. In the spring of 2013, Joe and Mari-Lynn presented this information to members of the governor's staff and representatives of the industry in a private meeting. They emerged from this meeting with information and a promise: First, the industry would offer some sort of settlement plan for the battle-field. Second, the Camp Branch Permit would become a National Guard base after mining completed.

I cannot overstress the significance of documentation. With my training in academia, the idea of wading through documents, researching for hours, and analyzing the data left me entirely within my comfort zone. To their great credit, the other FOBM members recognized the importance of documentation. When we notified the relevant agencies of our concerns, we did so in writing. We filled out forms and made formal requests. We kept their responses. We kept making more FOIA requests to any agency we thought might possess useful information. We had weekly conference calls to discuss what we were finding, what it meant, and how to use it. We also understood that by our written efforts, we left a record behind. The 1921 Battle of Blair Mountain was short on written evidence; the Second Battle of Blair Mountain would not be. Although documentation and research are not as exciting as protest songs and marches, they became crucial to our success.

Information became so imperative because our organization did not really have any funds. During 2012, while getting our organization off the ground, we made some early fundraising efforts, with some, but limited, success. It did not take us long to realize that when fighting several multi-billion-dollar corporations simultaneously, we could not compete with their financial resources. Money is their strength. To win, we would test our knowledge and skills against their monetary influence. The strategy posed difficulties, but I liked the fact that we were taking them on without money. The executives of the major fossil fuel companies place their trust and faith in wealth. It is their god. We wanted to show them that their god was not all-powerful.

Wealth is defined in many ways. The average West Virginian often does not define wealth in the same way as a corporate executive. They do not look for wealth in possessions but with a hillside, a campfire with friends, or an evening with family. Journalists and writers who travel here are often surprised with the humor and even happiness they find amid seemingly miserable conditions. Perhaps they are looking for wealth in all the wrong places. At FOBM, we believed the company executives had put their faith in the wrong kind of wealth and it would contribute to their undoing.

Most attorneys, as it turned out, did not agree with our assessment of wealth. Our lack of funds meant that few attorneys would do more than take a phone call from us, and we needed an attorney to represent our interests, particularly with the documentation we had uncovered. By 2013, Mary Anne Maul, a local attorney who believed in our cause, agreed to represent us pro bono. Mary Anne suggested that if we wanted to know more about this National Guard base and what impact it might have on the battlefield, we should just go to them and ask. Thus, in May 2013, Ms. Maul arranged a meeting with Major General James A. Hoyer, adjutant general for the State of West Virginia, to find more answers.

During the 1921 March on Logan, which culminated in the Battle of Blair Mountain, my great-grandfather also met with a general. As thousands of angry miners marched towards Blair, President Warren Harding dispatched Brigadier General H. H. Bandholtz to West Virginia to appraise the situation and determine whether the US Army should intervene. Bandholtz summoned Keeney and Fred Mooney to the governor's office in the middle of the night and warned them if they did not call off the march, the military would use force to stop it. Keeney and Mooney then rushed off to Madison to intercept the miners before they reached Blair Mountain.[15]

Ninety-two years later, General Hoyer and I discussed the same real estate as Frank Keeney and General Bandholtz had done before, albeit under different circumstances. We met with General Hoyer on May 3 and again on August 14 that summer. Our first meeting took place on a Friday at the state's National Guard headquarters in Charleston. The previous two days I had been very ill and was still running a high fever on the morning of our meeting. I took some medicine, and my fever broke just as our meeting was about to begin at 1:00 p.m. When I walked into the general's office to shake his hand, I did so with sweat pouring down my face. I wore a tie and sport jacket, and the T-shirt I had on underneath was stuck to my chest and back because of all the sweat. I thought, *he must think I'm a nervous wreck*. I'm sure General Hoyer noticed, but he didn't say a word.

Brigadier General David Buckalew accompanied Hoyer at the meeting. I broke the ice by spending a few minutes talking military history with them. My dissertation dealt with World War II soldiers from West Virginia, so it was easy to slip into a conversation about war and soldiers. Early experiences taught me that a confrontational approach avails no one; do not treat them as enemies, even if they deserve it. Hoyer is a native West Virginian, I found him easy to speak with, smart, and eager to listen. Over the course of two meetings, he explained the National Guard's position regarding Blair Mountain. The National Guard, he said, would not build a base on the battlefield nor would they be directly responsible for destroying any portion of the nomination area. The military wanted an isolated base to land aircraft and train special forces. Why the military would build a base next to a major historic site when they sought isolation was never properly explained. Nonetheless, the National Guard planned for a drop zone with two crisscrossing runways: one 4,000 feet long and one 7,000 feet long. The 4,000-foot runway had already been constructed on Area A of Camp Branch. The National Guard signed a thirty-five-year lease with Natural Resource Partners (NRP), the landowner, to construct the base on their property. Aracoma Coal had agreed to build the 7,000-foot runway. The problem, of course, was that Aracoma intended to blast part of the battlefield in order to get the material to construct the runway. Once the facilities were completed, it would be the largest drop zone/base of its kind east of the Mississippi River, according to General Hoyer.

Technically speaking, then, the National Guard was not constructing a base on the battlefield. They wanted a base next to the battlefield and Aracoma Coal would build the 7,000-foot runway with rock overburden taken from the blasted battlefield. Hoyer did tell me that he supported the idea of a historic park at Blair Mountain, and we discussed at length how a park and the base could work together in the area. In all, we learned important information. The coal companies' call to destroy at least part of the battlefield for the sake of coal mining jobs was a farce, if not an outright lie. At the Camp Branch public hearing, politicians and business leaders told a hundred or so miners that this permit was essential to saving their jobs. The truth was that the permit was essential to build a military base. We could add the military-industrial complex to the list of impediments to saving Blair Mountain.

This information also revealed that someone—or a select handful of individuals—potentially stood to make a tremendous amount of money on defense contracts related to this base. We did not know exactly who or how much, but the potential profit from a military base certainly served as another possible motive.

Kenny King told me a very interesting story after our first meeting with the general. In April 2008, when Joe Manchin served as the state's governor, he spoke to a few residents at a small gathering at the 317 Club in downtown Logan. Kenny King attended the talk. After Manchin made his remarks, he followed the Logan County Commissioner Art Kirkendall to a back room in the restaurant. Kenny wanted to ask Manchin about preserving the battlefield and followed them. Kenny told me that Manchin and Kirkendall entered a room where several coal executives from Massey Energy along with Greg Wooten and Chuck Preston, executives at NRP, awaited them. Kenny was not allowed to enter the room but could look inside through a glass window. Inside, Greg Wooten gave a PowerPoint presentation. Each slide contained the Massey Coal emblem in the corner and the slides showed sketches of runways on the Camp Branch Permit. No one answered Kenny's questions that day about the battlefield, but our new information coincided with what Kenny had seen at the 317 Club several years before. This base had been in the works for years and, corroborating with the 2009 letter from General Allan Tackett to Greg Wooten, had the full support of the governor's office. Blair Mountain's inclusion on the National Register in 2009 had interfered with these plans. As mentioned before, West Virginia State Code forbids surface mining when any such activity "will adversely affect any publicly owned park or places included in the national register of historic sites."[16] If Blair remained on the National Register, Aracoma Coal could not build the 7,000-foot runway for the National Guard with material from the battlefield.

• **THE SITE VISIT** •

The 2009 and 2011 disturbances we found on the battlefield at Camp Branch demanded our attention more than ever. In order for a site to be listed on the National Register of Historic

Places, it must possess *integrity*, meaning that the area must be left intact enough to allow for study and potential visitors. It appeared plausible that someone had disturbed these areas of the battlefield in order to ruin its historical integrity and pave the way for a military base. We wanted to get a closer look at Camp Branch. After written requests from Kenny and Joe, WVDEP granted us a citizen's site inspection of the Camp Branch Permit Area B on September 10, 2013. I could not attend because of my teaching schedule, but four of our board members attended including Joe Stanley, Kenny King, Paul Corbit Brown, and Jeff Bosley. A longtime local activist, Jeff Bosley had recently joined FOBM and had quickly established himself as an intelligent, analytical voice of reason within the group. Because of those traits, he was an excellent choice to join the others, particularly in light of what happened.

Everything about this site visit went wrong. Aside from four of our members, several WVDEP officials and Sammy Pugh, an inspector from OSMRE, also attended. During a state or federal site inspection the company or companies being inspected are not supposed to be informed. Yet someone informed the companies ahead of time. Two executives of Natural Resource Partners, Greg Wooten and Chuck Preston, arrived on site to accompany the inspection. They were the same two executives Kenny King saw at the 317 Club in Logan with Joe Manchin in 2008. Mr. Wooten, as mentioned in the quoted testimony at the beginning of this chapter, arrived with an armed man. Mr. Wooten and the armed man pulled Kenny aside when he arrived and proceeded to argue with him. Kenny told me the full details when I visited him in the hospital. When Joe tried to intervene on Kenny's behalf, the armed man threatened Joe with his gun. Benny Campbell, a WVDEP inspector, helped diffuse the situation. But Joe and Kenny were both extremely rattled by the incident.

WVDEP reps later informed us that the armed man was an out-of-uniform state trooper and was supposedly accompanying Mr. Wooten as he delivered payroll checks to miners on the site. Why an out-of-uniform state trooper needed to be with Mr. Wooten as he delivered checks is unclear. It is also unclear why Mr. Wooten, who is an executive at NRP (the landowner), would be delivering payroll to miners employed by Aracoma Coal (the lessee). The armed man did not identify himself and left the scene before the site inspection began. He entered a black car with the license plate number 407 and drove away.

Paul Corbit Brown, who is a professional photographer, attended the site visit specifically because we wanted documentation of the inspection and detailed photos of the disturbances. WVDEP and the governor's office initially agreed to let us document the visit with photos. After the incident between Mr. Wooten, the armed man, Kenny, and Joe, WVDEP would not allow Paul to take any photos because Mr. Wooten and Mr. Preston objected. When Paul and the others protested, the regulators threatened to call off the entire visit if they did not agree to go without cameras. Paul and the others agreed to leave the cameras behind. The entire crew, NRP executives included, then hopped in WVDEP vehicles and drove onto the Camp Branch Permit.

Although the WVDEP reps could have driven to where Area B began, they stopped a quarter of a mile short of Area B and everyone proceeded on foot. Kenny asked why the vehicles had stopped short of where we wanted to go but received no answer. While on the way to Part B, the reps led everyone along a large berm at the edge of sediment ditches. Kenny stepped on some loose rock and fell over the edge, tumbled several feet down the slope, and broke his ankle in the process. An emergency crew arrived and hauled Kenny away on a stretcher. When I visited Kenny in the hospital later, he told me that as he was carried away on the stretcher one WVDEP inspector turned to another and mumbled, "They should make a movie about all this." No one mentioned a book.

The site visit continued to unravel after Kenny's departure. Joe, Paul, and Jeff briefly entered Area B, which encompasses over 200 acres, but when they wished to walk to the areas where the disturbances took place, Mr. Preston, of NRP, objected. The WVDEP reps sided with the company and the inspection ended without us being able to view the disturbances or document anything.

Kenny remained in the hospital for several days. Through a series of conference calls within our organization we put our heads together and tried to decide upon a course of action. We contacted numerous local media outlets, but no one would cover the story of what happened at the Camp Branch site inspection. No regional or national news outlets would touch our information about the National Guard base. We felt as though no one believed us. Two months after the site inspection, Roger Calhoun, the regional director of OSMRE, sent a letter to Joe regarding the site visit and our concerns. In a carefully worded statement, Mr. Calhoun wrote, "You also allege that there was interference and threats issued by the West Virginia State Police at the September 10, 2013 WVDEP citizen inspection. OSMRE attended this site visit and, although our personnel did not hear everything that was said, we did observe that the inspection continued after this incident, so there is no SMCRA violation for OSMRE to review."[17] This was the only written acknowledgement we received regarding the intimidation our members were subjected to at the site visit.

Everyone was upset, some were afraid, and we were all

angry and frustrated. No one wanted to quit. If anything, the events of the site visit strengthened our resolve to assert our rights as citizens. After a number of lengthy and intense discussions, we decided to take our case to the West Virginia Surface Mine Board.

## HISTORY ON TRIAL

The Surface Mine Board (SMB) hears citizen appeals regarding violations of mining permits in West Virginia under the jurisdiction of WVDEP. The board is composed of seven individuals appointed by the governor.[18] The chair of the SMB at the time of our site visit was Mark Schuerger, a coal company executive with Alpha Natural Resources. Aracoma Coal, the company with the permit at Camp Branch, was a subsidiary of Alpha. The odds did not seem to favor us, but we nonetheless filed an appeal to get a second site visit and document the disturbances we knew were on the battlefield. Mary Anne Maul, our pro bono attorney, agreed to represent us in the appeal, which was set for December 9, 2013.

The immediate months following the disastrous site visit included some of the most stressful and intense moments of my life. After Ms. Maul agreed to represent us, Joe and I received mail from her only to find that it had been opened. I posted a picture of one of the tampered with envelopes on my Twitter account. On two occasions, a black SUV followed me as I drove around downtown Charleston. Sometimes county police or state troopers followed me on my way to and from work. Such statements may seem hyperbolic, exaggerated, or even paranoid, but those following me made no attempts at discretion. At times, the police followed directly behind me for as long as twenty miles, typically on Route 119 between Danville and Logan. I did not film them because I feared it would give them an excuse to pull me over for using my phone while driving. Someone followed Mary Anne Maul and Kenny King to a meeting they held at Panera Bread. The man took pictures of them with his phone throughout the meeting. Mari-Lynn and fellow filmmaker Jordan Freeman had their own difficulties on the road as they traveled in and out of the coalfields working with FOBM and on their film, *Blood on the Mountain.* An unmarked black SUV followed them around on a couple of occasions. Jordan filmed a bit of the SUV at least once, but the footage, taken at night, did not turn out well. I actually found myself in a Mexican restaurant in Brooklyn, New York, sitting across from Jordan and Mari-Lynn and saying with all seriousness, "The next time an unmarked SUV trails you guys, get better footage!" This comment even earned a number of strange glances in Brooklyn.

During one of our conference calls, when discussing Camp Branch and the base, our entire board was simultaneously cut off the conference line. Those of us using mobile phones were unable to use them at all for several minutes thereafter. I could not use my smartphone for nearly twenty minutes to call or text anyone. After about a half hour, I managed to get Dr. Mark Myers, our secretary-treasurer, on the line. Myers hailed from Welch, in McDowell County. He and I were graduate students together at West Virginia University where he studied Appalachian and coalfield history. He was yet another welcome, recent addition to our ranks. I personally recruited Myers after the protest march because he is intelligent, understands the coalfields, is dependable, and is easy to work with. When I finally reached him on the phone that night, the first thing he said was, "Intimidation tactics. Doesn't surprise me at all." The next day I began posting many of the FOIA documents on my Twitter account, including the letters referring to the military base. I knew that if someone could disrupt our conference call and phones and follow us around, then surely "they" monitored my Twitter account. I wanted those who tracked us to understand that intimidation tactics did not work on us, and if something bad were to happen to me, people would know why.

It may have sounded like a movie, but we were not entertained. Someone was monitoring us and wanted us to know it. We operated under the assumption that our email accounts, smartphones, and mail were compromised. We began hand-delivering documents and held more face-to-face meetings. I began rendezvousing with our attorney at a local coffee shop in Charleston, where we would transfer documents. A few times, we met in a back room at Taylor Books in Charleston.

On Wednesday morning, November 27, 2013, just twelve days before our scheduled appeal, I received an unexpected email from the West Virginia State Tax Department informing me that FOBM was no longer an organization in "good standing" with the state and was no longer recognized as an organization by the Secretary of State's office. The Tax Department claimed to have found errors in our tax forms from 2010, just before I joined the organization. If the state no longer recognized our organization, our appeal before the SMB would dissolve. Worse still, interveners in an appeal must file their notice of intervention before the SMB at least five business days before the appeal is scheduled. Even worse, I received this notice the day before Thanksgiving, and state offices would be closing for the remainder of the week. Indeed, most state offices would probably shut down well before the end of the business day. If I could not get our organization reinstated by the end of the day, the appeal would be lost and Camp Branch with it.

I grabbed all of our financial information and drove

straight to the state tax offices in downtown Charleston. Luckily I found a nice, older lady willing to sit down with me and hold my hand through the entire process. I filled out the correct forms with her looking over my shoulder, paid the fine, and had FOBM in good standing with the state tax office by 1:00 p.m. I then rushed across town to the Secretary of State's office at the Capitol Complex to meet Mary Anne Maul and get us reinstated. Only one staff member remained at the Secretary of State's office when we arrived. When Ms. Maul and I approached her with our information, she told us that she was closing shop for the day. I turned on as much charm as I could and convinced her to stay another fifteen minutes. A few minutes later, we were reinstated. Ms. Maul then rushed to the SMB, filed our notice of intervention and kept our case alive.

We continued to press forward and prepare as best we could. Ms. Maul was not a specialist in coal mining or historic preservation law. Neither were any of us. We simply learned it together as we went. The day before the hearing, our entire board convened at my place in Charleston, accompanied by Ms. Maul and Rob Goodwin, a paralegal with some experience before the SMB who agreed to help us out. We spent about eight hours honing the entire argument of our case, organized all the documents; we even put on a mock trial with Mark Myers, our secretary-treasurer, acting as opposing council and cross-examining everyone. Late that night, everyone left for their hotels or homes content that we had done all we could do.

The day of truth arrived on December 9. If we won our appeal, we could return to Camp Branch and document the violations we knew existed up there and potentially gain more protection for the battlefield. If we lost, we were pretty much dead in the water. As we arrived at the WVDEP building in Kanawha City, where SMB appeals were held, we learned that three of the seven SMB members, including the SMB Chair, Mr. Schuerger, would be absent. With only four board members present, we would need a unanimous decision to win.

Our argument was this: The conspicuous nature and timing of the disturbances on Camp Branch led us to believe that someone had deliberately disturbed sections of the battlefield with intent to destroy archeological evidence and adversely impact the historical integrity of the site. We requested a citizen's site inspection to see if this was, in fact, what had occurred. However, during the site inspection our members had been intimidated, threatened, not allowed to use photography, and not allowed to see the disturbed areas. Additionally, someone had defied regulatory protocol and informed the companies of the inspection ahead of time. This allowed company officials to restrict the nature of our visit. We believed we were entitled to a second, properly conducted visit.

Ms. Maul called me as her first witness. I testified as to our organization's intentions and objectives as well as the historical significance of the Camp Branch area. My testimony emphasized the absence of a complete archeological study of the area. Among other things, I stated,

If you're studying say, the Battle of Gettysburg, you can look at generals' letters, diaries, letters home from troops—all these kinds of things in order to reconstruct the battle. You don't have that at Blair Mountain because the miners kept to a code of silence. What they were doing was illegal. They were in an uprising, so they didn't talk about what was going on. They didn't leave a paper trail. . . . Because there's no written evidence of the actual fighting, the archeological evidence becomes paramount to understanding what happened. You have to know where people were shooting, where forces were moving, all of that kind of thing. . . . That's why the artifacts and the site itself is important, not just for sentimental value, but scholarship and educational value, also.[19]

Joe Stanley, Kenny King, and Paul Corbit Brown all followed with their own testimony. Kenny hobbled to the witness seat in crutches, still recovering from his injury on the site visit. "I can hardly get around," Kenny told me. "Good," I said. "Make sure you take your time when walking to the stand and don't be afraid to look miserable."

Everyone told the story of what happened on September 10. The state seemed most concerned with absolving its responsibility regarding the incident with the gunman. I sat beside Rob Goodwin and Ms. Maul throughout the entire hearing, sometimes scribbling thoughts or questions on a notepad and sliding them to one of them. Other board members did the same, whispering ideas and strategy back and forth, discussing details over lunch. After eight hours, the SMB deliberated for a time and returned with a unanimous decision. We would be going back to Camp Branch.

December 9, 2013, was one of the most satisfying days in my tenure as president of FOBM, probably our best day as an organization since the Saturday of the 2011 protest march. The entire group had pulled together as a team and had won a hard-fought victory. Granted, the ruling only allowed us to conduct a second site inspection, but it said a lot more than that. It said we would not be intimidated or deterred. They had the money and the power, but we held the moral high ground and the resolve. Aracoma Coal, represented by

Jackson Kelly attempted to intervene on the appeal and challenge the ruling, but the SMB denied their motion to intervene in January.[20] After a number of phone calls and a few
meetings, WVDEP and FOBM agreed on a date for the site
visit and we secured the right to document it with photos
and film.

The second site inspection of Camp Branch Part B occurred
on March 10, 2014. Joe, Jeff, and Kenny were there again.
Rob Goodwin joined us the second time. Mari-Lynn Evans
also came along, accompanied by a cameraman. Phil Smith,
a representative from the UMWA, and Raamie Barker,
Governor Earl Ray Tomblin's senior advisor, attended as well.
Once again, my teaching duties kept me from the battlefield,
but I was happy to let the others go.

This time the group, alongside WVDEP reps, encountered
no company officials, armed guards, or disruptions of any
kind. We took pictures and filmed. The sky was clear and
sunny. The air was cool. We found four areas of disturbance
within the 1,000-foot buffer zone of the nomination area. In
one specific area, on top of the ridgeline, we found an area
that had been scraped with a bulldozer or other large equipment and then timbered. Inexplicably, only this specific area,
on top of the ridgeline, was timbered, with several hundred
acres between the ridgeline and the base of the mountain left
completely untouched. Why was a patch of trees on top of the
ridgeline so valuable that one would bypass over a hundred
acres of trees just to get to these? We failed to notice any real
difference in the size or variance in the tree species on the
entire mountain.

Kenny King, of course, had the answer. He had traversed
these ridgelines numerous times before the coal companies
had put up all the No Trespassing signs and placed guards on
the property. The disturbed area on the ridgeline was exactly

where Kenny had found and documented defensive entrenchments years before. Standing on the ridgeline at Camp Branch,
one could clearly see why defenders would entrench themselves at this particular spot. One could view every approach
from the hollows below and pick the miners apart with rifle
and machine gun fire as they advanced upward. Now the
entrenchments were gone, scraped away, and the area around
them timbered.

All of these efforts resulted in a meeting on May 2, 2014,
with the federal OSMRE, the ACOE, and WVDEP. It was
the only time all three regulatory agencies met in one room
with citizens regarding the Blair Mountain Battlefield. Kenny,
Joe, Mari-Lynn, Paul, Rob Goodwin, Barbara Rassmussen,
and I all crammed into a packed conference room at WVDEP
headquarters and listened to what the agencies planned to do.

First, we learned that WVDEP would not punish the companies for the violations that occurred on the battlefield. Once
again, the companies would slip through the regulatory nets.
An all too familiar story in West Virginia.

However, our efforts still bore significant fruit. OSMRE
had opened up a federal investigation into the disturbances
on Camp Branch after our first site visit.[21] The investigation
by the feds combined with our own investigation compelled
WVDEP to act. OSMRE, who oversees WVDEP, found that
the state mining permit was not consistent with the federally issued ACOE 404 permit, which enforced a 1,000-foot
buffer zone around the battlefield. WVDEP corrected this
mistake by ordering Aracoma Coal to modify their mining
permit to respect the buffer zone. This meant that, although
no one would be punished for the violations, Aracoma Coal
would not be allowed to mine on Part B.[22] If Aracoma wanted
to build a 7,000-foot runway for the National Guard, they
could still do so, but they would have to get the material to

build the runway from someplace other than the battlefield. We had stopped them at Camp Branch.

We nonetheless left the meeting with mixed emotions. On one hand, we had stopped the coal companies on one of the three surface mines threatening the battlefield. WVDEP, OSMRE, and ACOE promised to work together and communicate more effectively with us and with one another on enforcement with the other two surface mining permits. The agencies and companies alike now understood that we were watching them and regulatory enforcement very closely. They would not be able to get away with the same kind of damage they had inflicted on Camp Branch. We also had broken new ground by getting state and federal agencies together in one room to discuss preserving the battlefield and by getting the state agency to go against coal company wishes, a rare occurrence indeed. These were all tangible and significant wins in our overall quest to preserve the battlefield.

On the other hand, we still had a long way to go. We burned an enormous amount of energy and time working exclusively on one permit. There were still unanswered questions with Camp Branch. All of the evidence seemed to confirm a link between the delisting of the battlefield and the implementation of this National Guard base. Kenny witnessed Joe Manchin at the 317 Club in 2008 and Manchin served as governor when the battlefield was delisted. In 2008, before Alpha Natural Resources had bought them out, Massey Energy owned Aracoma Coal. No evidence directly connected Don Blankenship, then CEO of Massey Energy, to the base on Camp Branch, although it is difficult to imagine a micromanager like Blankenship not being aware of these plans. Indeed, Blankenship threatening to sue each staff member at SHPO after Blair's inclusion on the National Register shows that he was certainly cognizant of the battlefield and wanted it delisted. Mr. Wooten and Mr. Preston were seen at both the 2008 meeting at the 317 Club in Logan and at the first site inspection that went so disastrously wrong. This amounted to a great deal of circumstantial evidence.

Aside from Camp Branch, two more permits still threatened the battlefield. Additionally, there was no guarantee of preserving the parts of the battlefield not yet covered by mining permits. Although we had fought the companies hard at Camp Branch and pushed them back, we still needed to do more.

A mountaintop removal operation in southern West Virginia and the potential fate of the Blair Mountain Battlefield. (Courtesy of Paul Corbit Brown)

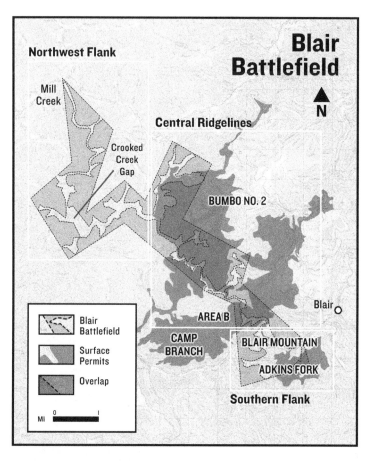

Map of the Blair Mountain Battlefield showing surface permits and the Northwest Flank, Central Ridgelines, and Southern Flank designations. (Map by Than Saffel)

Surface disturbance on Camp Branch Area B. Friends of Blair Mountain documented such violations by Aracoma Coal that destroyed defensive entrenchments and other potential archeological sites on the battlefield. (Courtesy of author's collection)

Kenny King spent years exploring the battlefield. The handgun and bullets seen here are among his many discoveries. (Photo by Kenny King, courtesy of author's collection)

Frank Keeney circa 1931. My family connection to Mine Wars history played a crucial role in my activism. (Courtesy of author's collection)

Me giving a talk to the marchers just before entering our campsite on Friday, June 10, 2011. (Courtesy of author's collection)

Wilma Steele sharing the story of the Red Bandana tradition to visiting students at the Mine Wars Museum. Spreading the story of Blair Mountain to new generations is key to the success of Identity Reclamation. (Courtesy of the West Virginia Mine Wars Museum)

The Mine Wars Museum crew in front of our original space in October 2019. *Top row left to right*: Shaun Slifer, Lou Martin, and Catherine Moore. *Bottom row left to right*: Wilma Steele, Francine Jones, Barbara Ellen Smith, Kim McCoy, Chuck Keeney, Kenzie New, and Courtney Boyd. (Courtesy of the West Virginia Mine Wars Museum)

## CHAPTER FOUR

# The Northwest
# Flank

A bout a week after our May 2, 2014, meeting with all
the regulatory agencies, I took one of my large maps
of the battlefield and spread it out on the kitchen table in my
apartment. The map showed the boundaries of the nomination area, the boundaries of each of the surface mine permits,
and where they overlapped onto the battlefield. I stared at it
in the way I imagine a general might when surveying a map
to decide where best to strike. Friends of Blair Mountain's
(FOBM's) work over the previous three years had demonstrated that there was no magic bullet or home run hit to
this problem. Preserving the battlefield would have to be
done piecemeal with a variety of solutions. A tremendous
amount of energy had been expended in our assault on Camp
Branch, but it was only one of the battlefield permits and
only impacted around fifty acres of the entire nomination
area. Now we needed to decide our next move. I reflected
on Sun Tzu's *The Art of War*, where one is told to attack the
enemy where he is unprepared and appear where you are not
expected.

The Red Neck Army faced a similar strategic dilemma in 1921. As I stared at this huge map of the battlefield on my kitchen table, I thought of their attack plan and how it unfolded. The main thrusts of the miners' offensives occurred at the far southern edge of the defensive positions at Blair Mountain and at the far edge of the northern positions, between ten to twelve miles to the northwest. The layout, in fact, slightly resembles that of Gettysburg, only this time, the union had the low ground. We do know that the miners made some attempts to move on the ridgelines in the center of the battlefield, but there isn't sufficient evidence at this time to know the full extent of the fighting. All current evidence points to the most heated fighting taking place at Blair Mountain and at the Mill Creek and Crooked Creek Gaps. With this in mind, I divided the battlefield into three distinct sections on the map: (1) the Southern Flank, with the community of Blair and Blair Mountain itself; (2) the Central Ridgelines, which stretched for six miles or so along Spruce Fork Ridge; and (3) the Northwest Flank, which included the fighting at Crooked Creek and Mill Creek.

Of all the places on the battlefield, the miners came the closest to a major breakthrough in the section I was by then calling the Northwest Flank. August 30 and 31 saw intense combat at Mill Creek where miners attempted to outflank two machine gun entrenchments. Groups of miners assaulted the defensive positions on the hilltops, advancing from tree to tree and firing as they went. Among the Red Necks were several World War I veterans who later likened the assault to fighting at the Ardennes Forest in France. Machine gun fire cut down two veterans when they tried to outflank one of the entrenchments on their own. Ultimately, the miners could not roll back the flank because of the terrain and the defenders' firepower.

The miners launched a more intense effort just to the south at Crooked Creek Gap. Ironically, the commanders on this section of the battlefield had fought one another before. Ed Reynolds, a union organizer, and Tony Gaujot, a mine guard, had fought against one another in 1913 at the Battle of Mucklow along Paint Creek. In that fight, striking miners assaulted the coal town from the surrounding hillsides while mine guards in bunkers fired back into the woods. Sixteen men died on that day. The second time these two adversaries met, Gaujot held the high ground and two machine guns. Reynolds commanded several hundred men and possessed a Gatling gun. The assault gained some ground as the miners forced Gaujot and his men to retreat about half a mile south. They dug in a second time, however, and halted the attackers' advance. The miners repositioned themselves and awaited reinforcements.[1]

Nearby, union leader Bill Blizzard came and went from a one-room schoolhouse converted into a command station. Miners kept pouring in and received instruction on where to go. Don Chafin sent his own reinforcements, as well as a plane to drop a few bombs on the approaching forces on the Northwest Flank. According to Early Ball, a schoolteacher and World War I veteran who had joined the Red Neck Army, one plane successfully dropped a bomb on the schoolhouse, but no one was injured. Many of the other bombs failed to explode altogether and the planes could not stop the assault.

As it turned out, federal troops ultimately ended the siege of Crooked Creek Gap. Fighting continued in this area well after miners had surrendered at Blair Mountain. Early Ball, in fact, had been promoted to a commander, and he prepared to assault positions along the gap with nearly 1,000 men. Chafin's men were heavily outnumbered. Ball planned for a dawn attack, but before he gave the green light, they received word that federal troops had arrived. The miners called off the attack and the Battle of Blair Mountain ended.[2]

The miners nearly broke the lines at the Northwest Flank. As I stared at the map, I thought that perhaps we could as well. My mind kept going back to something Roger Calhoun, the regional director of the federal Office of Surface Mining Reclamation and Enforcement (OSMRE) had said to me at the end of our May 2, 2014, meeting. As the meeting ended, Mr. Calhoun hinted to me that perhaps we should reexamine the Lands Unsuitable for Mining Petition (LUMP) and see if there were sections of the battlefield which could, according to state regulations, be blocked off for permanent protection.

## • THE LUMP AGREEMENT •

On June 6, 2011, the same day we began the protest march, FOBM, represented by the Sierra Club Environmental Law Program and the Appalachian Center for the Economy and the Environment, submitted a petition to the West Virginia Department of Environmental Protection (WVDEP) requesting that they declare the 1,669 acres of the battlefield unsuitable for surface mining. According to state regulations, some acreage may be declared off limits to surface mining if it has certain environmental, historic, or economic value. Thus, our LUMP argued that the battlefield was a valuable historic, educational resource with potential for unique economic development in the coalfields. Because surface mining would destroy all this potential, WVDEP should declare it unsuitable for mining. The petition itself was nearly one hundred pages long, with personal statements written by historians and other experts, descriptions of the archeological resources, and a strong legal argument.

WVDEP naturally ignored everything just described and

rejected the proposal. On July 5, 2011, Tom Clarke, then acting director of surface mining for WVDEP, wrote to our legal team with the following response: "I have determined that this petition is frivolous and should be rejected."[3] Clarke went on to state that regulations prohibited him from declaring the battlefield unsuitable for surface mining. According to the regulations, any acreage that has been permitted to a coal company after August 3, 1977—the date when the Surface Mining Control and Reclamation Act (SMCRA) became law—cannot be declared unsuitable for mining. Because WVDEP had already permitted approximately 424 acres of the battlefield, the agency could not retroactively void the permits.

Additionally, Clarke argued that "WVDEP shall not consider a petition for an area which was previously and unsuccessfully proposed for designation which does not present new allegations of facts."[4] In April and June 1991, Kenny King and a few of his early allies, filed two separate LUMP petitions for the battlefield—WVDEP rejected them both. According to Clarke, the previous rejections and supposed lack of new findings relating to the battlefield meant that our petition was frivolous. Although Clarke's statements about no new findings were blatantly false—archeological work by Harvard Ayers and Brandon Nida had found a plethora of new information—this new evidence was, without explanation, ignored. FOBM, Sierra Club, West Virginia Highlands Conservancy, the West Virginia Labor History Association, and the Ohio Valley Environmental Coalition all promptly joined a lawsuit to challenge Clarke's decision. Since that time, the lawsuit has languished in state court with no ruling.

In short, WVDEP argued that because they had previously permitted part of the battlefield acreage, they could not protect any of it. Another regulatory excuse. Once permits are issued, often many years in advance, regulations make it extremely difficult to retract or modify those permits, even if regulatory agencies issued them without due diligence. In my focus on the map itself, I could see that the surface mining permits were all concentrated in the areas I had designated as the Southern Flank and the Central Ridgelines. The area I had designated as the Northwest Flank, however, had no permits issued on it at all. Furthermore, most of Harvard Ayers's recent archeological research focused on this area, bringing new, relevant information to light. The reasons WVDEP used to reject the petition did not apply to this area of the battlefield. If we isolated this acreage and designated it under a revised petition, there would be no regulatory reason for them to reject a proposal for permanent protection. The miners hoped to turn the tide in 1921 by taking the Northwest Flank. Perhaps we could do the same.

With this idea in mind, I began drawing up a detailed plan for how the regulatory agencies could preserve the battlefield. A flaw in our negotiating up to that point, as I saw it, was that we went into meetings with the governor's office and with the executives without details on the process for a solution to the controversy over the battlefield. In other words, we went into these meetings with the strategy of appealing to the government and the executives using the "it's the right thing to do" argument coupled with our general vision for a historic park. The political and business leadership found the moral righteousness of our cause an insufficient motive for action. Politicians and executives will usually only do the right thing if it also benefits them. In the case of the battlefield, we needed to tell the individuals in power to save it, and then show them specifically what they should do to make it happen and how taking such action would be to their benefit.

Of the 1,669 acres of the site, surface permits overlapped onto 424 of these acres. This did not mean that the companies only intended to mine 424 acres. Often, once a company has reached the limit of the permit, they apply for extensions. Therefore, the coal companies would likely apply to extend the acreage of those permits or apply for completely new ones to mine more of the battlefield. For the area I designated as the Northwest Flank, however, no permits existed. Again, this did not mean that the companies did not eventually intend to mine it. A number of private citizens held small residential properties in the Northwest Flank. Coal companies tended to buy everyone out of an area and acquire the land before they sought permits. This opened the door for a quick solution to this area. WVDEP could easily declare the Northwest Flank unsuitable for surface mining, be completely within the regulations, and do so without having to deal with the coal companies, as they had no permits on that area yet.

Over the course of the next few days, I put together a fifteen-page report outlining preservation options for the nomination area. The report divided the battlefield into the three sections mentioned earlier—Southern Flank, Central Ridgelines, and Northwest Flank—and examined each section individually with descriptions of the geography, historic relevance, previous/potential mining impacts, and preservation/development options. While preservation of the Southern Flank and Central Ridgelines would need the cooperation of the landowners and coal companies to complete, the Northwest Flank could be protected in a separate agreement that could be enacted independently by WVDEP. On May 27, 2014, less than four weeks after we achieved victory at Camp Branch, I finished the report, along with accompanying maps, and presented a copy to Harold Ward of WVDEP, Roger Calhoun of OSMRE, and Raamie Barker, the governor's senior advisor.

I did this on my own initiative. After the enormous tussle over Camp Branch, the FOBM board was spent. Most everyone felt disheartened by our May 2 meeting with the regulatory agencies. Many hoped for a broader settlement on the entire battlefield as opposed to the one permit modification WVDEP ordered on Camp Branch. Joe Stanley called me one morning after the meeting and told me, "We are in a fixed fight." He then went on to advise me about my future. "This could go on forever," Joe told me. "You still have a career ahead of you and they can destroy that career. I'm retired. My career is over. They can still get to you if you remain a threat." Joe went on to say that no one would think less of me if I chose to move on with my life.

But I couldn't just move on. Blair Mountain was too important, we had invested too much time, the history was too personal to me and, above all, I simply could not stomach conceding defeat to the coal companies. While we licked our wounds from Camp Branch, I used the time between semesters at the college to try to think of a new approach. After giving WVDEP a week to digest my report, I decided to play a card I had been holding for quite a while. At the time, the director of WVDEP was Randy Huffman. Randy's father and my father graduated high school together and were basketball and football teammates. Moreover, my mother and Randy's mother also graduated high school together and were on the same cheerleading squad. To this point, I had not used this connection, but in the wake of Camp Branch, I felt that I needed to get a one-on-one meeting with Secretary Huffman to make more progress. Up until that time, he had not met with any member of FOBM. I called my Dad and asked for his help. Thirty minutes later, I had a scheduled appointment with Secretary Huffman to discuss my preservation report.

Secretary Huffman and I met privately at his office for

a little over an hour in late June 2014. We discussed the preservation options in my report and I explained at length why WVDEP should immediately declare the Northwest Flank unsuitable for mining. Huffman told me that if he did so, the public would perceive it as an effort to shut down all mountaintop removal. This simply would not do, he explained. A long-standing West Virginia reality faced me yet again; in order to make progress with the Department of Environmental Protection, I needed to disavow any form or appearance of an environmental agenda. After all, we would not want the people of West Virginia to have the impression that the Department of Environmental Protection was protecting the environment. As usual, I focused on the historic value of the property. I showed him pictures of areas on the Northwest Flank and demonstrated how undisturbed this area remained compared with the areas around the battlefield to the south. I delivered a mini-lecture on what happened at Crooked Creek Gap in 1921. I handed him bullet shell casings taken from that very area.

As Huffman examined one of the shell casings between his thumb and index finger, he suggested that perhaps a lawsuit settlement on the LUMP case would be the proper way to proceed. He handed back the shell casing to me and told me to sit tight for a moment. He then briefly left and returned a moment later with one of WVDEP's lawyers. After some discussion, Huffman suggested that if FOBM, the Sierra Club, and the other groups would drop the LUMP lawsuit against WVDEP, they would declare the area I had designated as the Northwest Flank unsuitable for surface mining. A preservation solution for the rest of the battlefield would have to take some other form, but the lawsuit settlement would give permanent protection for approximately one-third of the nomination area.

We shook hands and I left. Phone calls consumed the next few days. Our board discussed the potential deal and decided it worth pursuing. I then called Aaron Isherwood, our lead attorney with the Sierra Club. Although several groups were involved in the LUMP lawsuit, the Sierra Club provided the legal team, the specific members of which were Aaron Isherwood, Peter Morgan, and Derek Teaney. Up until this point, my relationship with the Sierra Club legal team had been minimal. I had not met any of them in person and had only spoken with Aaron Isherwood once or twice on the phone. Over the next two years, he and I would have dozens of chats. Isherwood seemed legitimately surprised when I told him Huffman and WVDEP were interested in a settlement on the LUMP case. Over the next few minutes, the other lawyers joined the phone conversation as I explained my proposal. Although they liked the settlement idea, FOBM was only one group on the lawsuit. All the plaintiffs would have to agree to the plan. The next step would be to have a conference call with each of the groups and convince them to sign on to the plan. Assuming this could be accomplished, I could then meet with WVDEP and hammer out any remaining details. Once agreed upon, the lawyers would handle the rest. We could secure permanent protection for a third of the battle-field without even having to deal with a single coal executive. It seemed so simple and straightforward it just might work.

Six different groups had joined on the lawsuit against WVDEP. They included FOBM, the Sierra Club, West Virginia Highlands Conservancy, the West Virginia Labor History Association, the National Trust for Historic Preservation, and the Ohio Valley Environmental Coalition (OVEC). FOBM needed to convince all of these groups to drop the lawsuit, which would mean abandoning the notion of WVDEP declaring the entire battlefield unsuitable for surface mining, in exchange for permanent protection of a third of the site. The National Trust and the Labor History Association did not concern me at all. Knowing a little about the National Trust's work, I felt they would be realistic as opposed to idealistic and support the settlement. I had worked with the Labor History Association and known many of its members for years. Fred Barkey, the "elder statesman" of West Virginia labor historians, founded the organization. Fred's father-in-law fought at Blair Mountain and Fred owned the original red bandana that he wore on the 1921 march. Barkey also served on my master's thesis committee at Marshall University. One of the other board members, Julian Martin, was my high school chemistry teacher. Gordon Simmons, the current president of the association, helped get the Mine Wars Museum off the ground. Because of all those connections and what I knew of them personally, I felt quite confident in their support.

My worry revolved around the possibility that some of the environmental groups would be hesitant to compromise. Two examples illustrate my point of concern. In 2009, in the early days of the Obama administration, a coalition of environmental groups including the Sierra Club, OVEC, the West Virginia Highlands Conservancy, Appalachian Voices, Coal River Mountain Watch, and others converged on DC and lobbied to end surface mining. Joe Stanley, unaffiliated with any organization and representing himself, joined the lobbyists. Joe accompanied representatives from a few of these groups in several meetings with Senator Robert C. Byrd's staff, Senator Jay Rockefeller of West Virginia, Senator Lamar Alexander of Tennessee, and Senator Benjamin Cardin of Maryland. According to Joe, Alexander and Cardin were willing to promote and introduce legislation that would ban MTR coal mining, although other forms of surface mining, such as contour mining, would still be legal. This bill would

be a "sendoff gift" to Senator Byrd, whose health was dete-
riorating, and who, apparently, wanted to see this happen.
The senators felt confident they could get the votes. Although
Joe fervently supported the plan, the environmental groups
refused to endorse it because the bill would not outlaw all
forms of surface mining. With support withdrawn from the
environmentalists, the bill was aborted and never introduced.

Another example occurred in the autumn of 2011, just a
few months after the protest march. In this instance, Alpha
Natural Resources had invited a variety of groups to Jackson
Kelly headquarters in Charleston to discuss a compromise deal
on the battlefield. This occurred before I became president of
FOBM, so I did not attend. However, Joe Stanley, Mari-Lynn
Evans, and Paul Corbit Brown were there, as were representatives of OVEC, Keepers of the Mountains, West Virginia
Highlands Conservancy, and the Sierra Club. Michael Peelish,
who at the time was Alpha's CFO, offered to donate 240 acres
of Alpha's landholdings on the Blair Battlefield. In return,
Alpha wanted the various groups at the meeting to drop any
legal or other challenges to another MTR operation known
as the Reylass Permit. This permit was not located on the
battlefield. The company served everyone lunch, but a few of
the environmental reps refused to eat. As one of them told
me, "It was beneath me to share a meal with those pigs." At
the end of the day, the groups were unwilling to trade one
mountain for another and refused the offer. Since that time,
Alpha has not offered any other acreage on the battlefield and
WVDEP approved the Reylass Permit.

For these reasons, I worried that one or more of the groups
in the lawsuit would not agree to a settlement. Unlike the
Labor History Association, I did not really know the individuals in these other groups well. Mari-Lynn Evans, however,
had been active with the environmental community for a

number of years and she worked the phones to persuade OVEC, West Virginia Highlands, and the others. In July, each of the groups participated in a conference call where Mari-Lynn and I pitched the settlement to them. Reps from Sierra Club's Beyond Coal Campaign and a few others expressed concerns that a compromise may not be preferable to waiting for a ruling from the court. We countered by pointing out that a court victory did not ensure protection for any acreage. In fact, a court victory only guaranteed that WVDEP would have to reconsider our petition and hold a public hearing. If we compromised, we would protect more acreage than if we actually won the case. Mari-Lynn and I assured the other groups that preservation efforts would not end with the settlement. We would use other methods to preserve the two-thirds of the battlefield not protected by a lands unsuitable declaration. After a few conference calls and a measure of effective pitching, the other groups agreed to pursue a settlement. The assault of the Northwest Flank was on.

## • THE PROBLEMATIC AGREEMENT •

By mid-July, all of the plaintiffs on the LUMP lawsuit agreed to proceed with a negotiated settlement. I notified WVDEP and they agreed to meet with me in August to move forward. Feeling optimistic and needing a break, I went on vacation to South Carolina to lounge on the beach and fish for a week. On Friday, July 25, 2014, my last day at the beach, Kenny King called me. He wasn't happy.

"You won't believe this," he said over the phone.

In the summer of 2013, Mari-Lynn Evans and Joe Stanley concluded a series of meetings with Greg Wooten of Natural Resource Partners (NRP) and Raamie Barker, Governor Earl Ray Tomblin's senior advisor. We hoped the meetings would result in a settlement that everyone could live with. At the last meeting, the coal companies promised to submit a preservation plan via a programmatic agreement through the Army Corps of Engineers (ACOE). According to Section 106 of the National Historical Preservation Act, a *programmatic agreement* can be a method of creating a preservation plan to mitigate any adverse effects of a development project. Wooten and Barker did not really give us any details about what the preservation plan might entail, nor did they give us any timeline on when to expect such a plan. Joe and Mari-Lynn, speaking on behalf of FOBM, told them that we would not endorse any settlement that failed to leave a significant amount of acreage permanently protected. Like it or not, we were told, this was the way the companies planned to proceed. The companies would present a plan to the ACOE. The ACOE would then distribute the plan to various "interested parties," which included groups such as FOBM, the Sierra Club, and others. As interested parties, we could then send suggestions and comments to the ACOE, after which they would make revisions they deemed appropriate based on the comments received. After that, we were unsure what would happen.

No one in FOBM wanted to proceed with a programmatic agreement. Based on the little information given us, our organization would not possess any real influence over the final decisions made regarding the preservation of the battlefield. Agencies from WVDEP to the ACOE often have "comment periods" where groups and citizens can submit their concerns on any given permit or development project. In most cases, the process is a farce, merely a box to check for the regulatory agency. In reality, closed-door agreements often precede many permits and development projects long before the public is even made aware of a so-called comment period. Therefore, we held no real hope that a programmatic agreement would please anyone who wanted to preserve the battlefield. After Wooten's promise to deliver such an agreement, nothing happened for over a year. We simply chalked it up as another empty promise from the industry. Accordingly, in the summer of 2014, I drew up alternative plans for preserving the battlefield, starting the chain of events that led us to a possible agreement on the Northwest Flank.

Kenny called to inform me that he had received a draft of the programmatic agreement in the mail and we were given one month to submit comments to the ACOE.

"Eight and a half acres," he said. "It's the same deal as 1991."

In 1991, the UMWA and the coal industry had made a tentative agreement to preserve eight and a half acres on the top of Blair Mountain upon the completion of surface mining. As part of the deal, Arch Coal's sign agreed to use UMWA miners on some of their operations. Active union miners had already dwindled significantly by the '90s and the UMWA needed every organized miner they could get. By allowing the UMWA to organize workers on a few select surface mines, the union found itself in a position where it had to support surface mining and even live with blasting at Blair Mountain. The deal, of course, never came to fruition due to clashes between the companies and the UMWA during the 1990s. Twenty-three years later, the industry had apparently dusted off the original preservation plan, made a few minor additions, and sent it off to the ACOE for approval. Aside from the eight acres on Adkins Fork, they made no promise to preserve any other acreage on the battlefield. Kenny was beside himself. After listening to his description of what he held, I shared his anger. According to the letter accompanying the programmatic agreement, the ACOE had also mailed copies to the

Sierra Club, the UMWA, and the National Trust for Historic Preservation, among others.

The same day Kenny called me, the *Logan Banner* printed an interesting story. The article, "Logan, WV Surface Mine Turned into National Guard Facility," announced that the National Guard had built an airstrip on the Camp Branch surface mine. The article quoted Brigadier General David Buckalew, who had attended our meetings with General Hoyer. Buckalew boasted, "It is the only one of its kind in the country." The article went on to describe how the landing zone would mimic combat conditions overseas and play a strong role in preparing troops for action to fight terrorism. It went on to mention that units from South Carolina, Missouri, and the British Air Force had already used the facility. In conclusion, the article beamed, "With new interest in this Logan County airstrip, economy is booming. When people come there to train they will usually stay overnight. That means they are staying in Logan hotels, shopping around town, and dining in the area. This project seems to be a win-win for everyone."[5]

One would have to be quite dense not to see the connection here. Over the previous two years, FOBM had uncovered a good deal of circumstantial evidence to suggest that plans for a National Guard base at Camp Branch influenced the delisting of the battlefield. We had failed to fill in all the blanks, but we knew a lot. It is important to note that the National Guard could have built the same kind of base on any number of surface mines in the area, yet they chose a site where rock overburden from an MTR site on the battlefield would form the foundation for one of their runways. According to General Hoyer, the coal industry specifically pushed for the runways to be located at Camp Branch. As we know, the Keeper of the National Register delisted the battlefield as these plans progressed. When we uncovered this evidence, we tried to draw media attention to it, but neither the local nor national media would touch the story. I wrote to President Obama and to the Secretary of Interior and received no response from either. We could not get anyone in the state government to even publicly acknowledge the existence of this base. But on the very day the programmatic agreement arrived in Kenny King's mailbox, *The Logan Banner*, seemingly out of the blue, printed a story on the National Guard base at Camp Branch. They did not mention the battlefield but said the base would be great for the local economy and a "win-win for everybody." I read the article online after Kenny called me—he had also read the article and told me to look it up on their website. It gave me a disgusting feeling in the pit of my stomach. I interpreted the article as an attempt to preempt any public backlash to the programmatic agreement by touting the economic benefits of the base and arousing local feelings of patriotism. The next day, I drove home from Charleston, South Carolina, to Charleston, West Virginia, trying to think of what to do.

When I arrived home the following evening, a package from the Army Corps of Engineers (ACOE) awaited me. The package contained a cover letter from Ginger Mullins representing the Regulatory Division of the ACOE, a memorandum of agreement (MOA) that detailed the preservation and mitigation proposals of the coal companies, and an eight-page document describing the function of the Advisory Council on Historic Preservation (ACHP), which was listed as a signatory to the MOA. The letter stated that FOBM was listed as a consulting party on the Blair Mountain Programmatic Agreement (BMPA) that, when finalized, would "govern the implementation of the Corps' responsibilities under Section 106 of the National Historic Preservation Act."[6] The Blair

Battlefield, while delisted from the National Register, was still listed as eligible for the National Register. This "eligible" status meant that federal agencies, such as the ACOE, were expected to enforce Section 106 of the National Historic Preservation Act. The current eligible status of the battlefield ensured that any mitigation or preservation would be under the exclusive jurisdiction of the ACOE. The letter concluded by informing me that FOBM had thirty days to send any comments on the MOA.

Section 106 of the National Historic Preservation Act requires federal agencies to consider and attempt to mitigate the impact of projects on historic properties. A property only needs to be eligible for listing on the National Register in order to qualify for a Section 106 Review. If a development project will have an adverse or damaging effect on a historic site, then the ACHP will consult with the companies or landowners and the appropriate federal agency. Other interested parties, such as the State Historic Preservation Office (SHPO), various activist groups and, when relevant, Native American tribes, are also consulted to find a reasonable mitigation process. This mitigation plan is formalized in an MOA. Once the specifics of the MOA are finalized, the companies, the appropriate federal agency, and the ACHP sign on to the document, at which point it becomes the blueprint for how the companies and federal agencies proceed. It bears remembering that had the battlefield not been delisted, the Section 106 Review would not have been necessary. Properties listed on the National Register are protected from mountaintop removal by state code, but since the battlefield was only "eligible" for listing, state agencies such as WVDEP were under no legal obligation to enforce the Preservation Act. If the battlefield remained delisted, an MOA through Section

106, enforced by the ACOE, was likely to be the best legal protection we could get for the site.

The companies only agreed to enter into this agreement after years of pressure and, interestingly, the ACOE only moved to conduct a Section 106 Review after the companies gave them the green light. FOBM initially hoped to reach a settlement with the industry independent of the regulatory agencies. We had no shot of such a settlement with this process. It was with much trepidation, then, that I began to examine the details of the MOA.

Lawyers wrote the MOA and, therefore, it was ripe with the mundane legalese one might expect. Nevertheless, several things immediately stood out. First, the MOA made it clear that companies still intended to use MTR to blast the entire acreage on all three of the permits—Adkins Fork, Camp Branch, and Bumbo No 2. Second, the companies claimed that they had already conducted cultural resource surveys on the permit areas to identify any sites of historic significance. Furthermore, the MOA absolved the companies from any other future preservation obligations or regulations. In a passage I found instantly alarming, the MOA stated,

SHPO agrees that this Memorandum of Agreement negates the need for additional review of any future permitting the Proponents may require. . . . SHPO further agrees that this Memorandum of Agreement negates the need for further review of any undertakings relevant to the Proponents' proposed activities that are permitted, funded, licensed, or otherwise assisted, in whole or in part, by the state within the BMBNA, in the APE, or within the view shed of the BMBNA that would normally be subject to review.[7]

The BMBNA stood for the Blair Mountain Battlefield nomination area. APE stood for areas of potential effect, which refers to any company-owned land adjacent to the battlefield acreage. The view shed refers to acreage on permitted areas within 1,000 feet of the battlefield. This passage meant that, once the MOA was signed and made official, the West Virginia State Historic Preservation Office recused themselves from any further regulation or review regarding company activities and historic sites on the battlefield, within 1,000 feet of the battlefield, or within company properties near or adjacent to the battlefield. This also, by consequence, absolved WVDEP and the ACOE of any further regulation. In other words, the coal companies would promise to commemorate the site after mining was completed, and in faith of this promise, the regulatory agencies would never interfere with what the companies wanted to do.

The details of their plan to commemorate the battle after the completion of mining were sketchy at best. The MOA listed several "sites" where plaques or monuments "may" be placed, but no accompanying map to let anyone know where exactly these commemorative sites would be located. Much of the commemoration plan dealt with acreage not even on the battlefield. The companies agreed to erect a "monument or plaque" by the side of the road at Sharples to memorialize a shootout that occurred before the Battle of Blair Mountain began. On company property in the town of Blair, the MOA stated that a spot "is contemplated to be established as a picnic area which may include a suitable information board." At other spots in the town of Blair, historic markers "may be erected at these sites."[8]

The companies planned to donate eight and a half acres of property near the top of Blair Mountain for a "lookout site." The MOA states that "from this viewpoint, visitors will be able to link the past with the future through a combination of signs and photos." After the completion of mining, and the reclamation process, the companies also planned to make two tracts of land available to the public. A 140-acre spot was to be designated as a camping area, and another 100-acre section was to be designated as a recreational area. It must be stressed that these areas were to be made available to the public only after the trees had been clear-cut and the surface had been blasted. In short, once the companies had destroyed the property and the historic sites, taken the coal, and found no further use for the acreage, the public was more than welcome to come on down and set up a tent for the night.

I could not help but notice the use and frequency of the words "may" and "contemplate" as opposed to "will." Indeed, the MOA promised nothing regarding preservation. Of the plan just summarized, the companies only agreed to complete "sufficient portions" of what they had proposed. The MOA only guaranteed that the companies could blast on their permits, mine the coal, commit to producing an unspecified amount of signs and benches, set aside some reclaimed land for camping, and preserve eight and a half acres with a lookout site where visitors could look at pictures that would presumably show what Blair Mountain looked like before it was blasted. In exchange, the regulatory agencies would forever forfeit any claim to interfere with the companies' actions on the battlefield or on their properties near the battlefield. The MOA ended with the statement that the companies "will set aside a 252 acre tract for a runway and drop zone for utilization by the West Virginia Air National Guard."[9] The MOA did not explain what a National Guard facility had to do with the preservation of the battlefield or mitigating mining on a historic site, but it was a clever inclusion.

WVDEP, the ACOE, and West Virginia's SHPO were all signatories on this agreement. The previous year, FOBM had won a victory by getting WVDEP to order the modification to the Camp Branch Permit, protecting the battlefield area on that permit. By making the National Guard facility a part of the MOA, and by having WVDEP as a signatory, the terms allowed the companies to sidestep our victory and blast Camp Branch.

It is no wonder that Kenny King began to refer to this MOA as the Problematic Agreement. With a month to prepare for a response, everyone on our board read the document and discussed it over a few conference calls. After getting everyone's thoughts, I wrote our response, which ended up being seven pages single spaced. Mailed on August 15, 2014, it pointed out the many glaring deficiencies and made a few suggestions. We obviously pointed out that preserving eight and a half acres was completely inadequate as a means of commemorating the Battle of Blair Mountain. We also shared enormous concerns over the historic narrative. The MOA mentions that historic signs and markers would be placed in and around the battlefield. Yet, the MOA did not provide details on where these markers would be, what the content of said markers would be, and who would have control over that content. For over ninety years, the companies have sought to control the narrative of this conflict and we would not let that happen at Blair Mountain. To remedy this, FOBM called for the creation of a committee to oversee the content and placement of any monuments or markers. The companies could each contribute one representative to the committee, but the rest of it must include three academics with terminal degrees in either history, archeology, or another humanities discipline. Kenny King would be guaranteed a spot on that committee. No one had worked on Blair Mountain for longer and harder than Kenny and, as far as I was concerned, he deserved a significant voice in any type of preservation on that site.

A significant portion of our response dealt with cultural resource surveys. When a development project might adversely impact a historic site, the companies or agencies involved in the project must conduct some kind of evaluation of the property to identify artifacts, archeological sites, or anything else of historic significance and assess the impacts of the proposed project. They then submit their evaluation to SHPO, who comments and sends recommendations to the companies and relative regulatory agencies. In this case, the proposed projects were MTR mines and a National Guard base. To meet the legal criteria, the companies hired out a private company called Cultural Resource Analysts Inc. to conduct cultural resource surveys on the permit areas that overlapped onto the battlefield.

An anonymous sympathizer at WVDEP gave FOBM a copy of a cultural survey report submitted to SHPO regarding the battlefield. It was a 102-page document and, as I read through it, several glaring problems were evident. According to the report, the study's objective was to present "the results of an architectural survey." The survey "includes the systematic survey and mapping of all buildings, structures, and objects 50 years of age or over." The researchers examined "architectural characteristics to identify building types and estimate dates of construction." They would then carefully study the "ground plan, the height, and the roof configuration of each structure."[10] In short, the companies hired out a private research firm to examine a rural, mountainous battlefield by having them search for old buildings of historic significance in the woods. When, unsurprisingly, they found no buildings, the private firm concluded that no sites of historic significance would be impacted by surface mining.

A quote from our comment letter spells out our reaction.

This is not an archeological study in order to identify artifacts and potential damage to a battlefield, but rather a
survey of architectural properties within a permit area. The
study admits as much. To be listed on the National Register
of Historic Places a property must, to quote the Cultural
Resource Survey, "be both historically significant and retain
integrity, that is, possess the extant physical characteristics
necessary to convey its significance." In order to determine
historic significance, the National Park Service lists four criteria in its regulations. This study omits applying the most
important criteria; Criterion D—which is a property that
has yielded or may yield information important to our past.
The study itself says, *"NRHP eligibility under Criterion D,
which is typically used to assess archeological sites, was not
applied to aboveground properties for this project."* How
can archeological artifacts be found on a known archeological site when the criteria for assessing archeological sites
under NRHP eligibility is ignored in the Cultural Resource
Survey? Furthermore, one does not go looking specifically
for architectural sites to determine the eligibility of a battlefield. One looks for troop movements, buried weapons,
shell casings, entrenchments, buried objects and potential
human remains. None of this is mentioned in this Cultural
Resource Survey which stretches to 102 pages. "No real
efforts were made to find any of these types of artifacts
known to be historically associated with the Battle of Blair
Mountain. Therefore, the use of a Cultural Resource Survey
is insufficient." [11]

An obvious demand to be made then, regarding this MOA,
was that full archeological surveys, conducted by qualified

personnel, must be conducted before there could be any discussion of mining. The cultural resource surveys were obvious farces, meant to appease minimum legal standards and prevent actual archeologists from finding out exactly how many artifacts and sites existed. Going over the MOA and the cultural resource survey with the fine-toothed comb was tedious work, but we felt it imperative to document and expose how inadequate the MOA truly was and how far the companies would go to cut legal corners to get their way.

This documentation was not only relevant regarding the battlefield, but it demonstrated a pattern within the coal industry. If they were finding loopholes, skirting regulations, and cutting corners with a battlefield, how often did the same crafty negligence apply to how they treated public water, reclaimed land, and polluted air; maintained safe working conditions; or provided healthcare benefits to retired miners? The documentation surrounding our efforts to save Blair Mountain exposed a long-standing pattern of disregard for the law, lack of regulatory enforcement of the law, and collusion by the political establishment to enable continued company negligence.

Industrial and regulatory negligence was on full display just a few months earlier. On January 9, 2014, residents in the Charleston area began to complain of a strange odor resembling licorice in the air and in their water. WVDEP inspectors later found that approximately 7,500 gallons of the chemical 4-methylcyclohexane methanol (MCHM) had leaked from a chemical storage facility into the Elk River. The leak occurred just upstream from West Virginia American Water Company's Charleston water treatment plant. Freedom Industries, the company who owned the chemical storage facility and had not been following state regulations, was not aware of the leak until informed by

WVDEP. In fact, the facility had not even been inspected by regulators for years. Governor Earl Ray Tomblin declared a state of emergency for nine surrounding counties. Schools and businesses shut down. Several individuals were hospitalized. No one could use tap water for a week. Stores soon ran out of bottled water and the National Guard distributed bottled water to residents. The chemical, MCHM, was used for cleaning coal. In his first public statement about the disaster, Governor Tomblin assured West Virginians that it was not the fault of the coal industry. In the coming weeks, Tomblin would caution the state legislature against overreacting to the disaster by placing harsh regulations on the chemical industry.[12]

Industrial disasters such as the Monongah Blast, Hawks Nest, Farmington, Buffalo Creek, and Upper Big Branch have taken lives, ruined homes, and damaged the environment throughout West Virginia's history. The Elk River chemical spill was yet another reminder to West Virginians that a lengthy and ongoing historic pattern of corporate negligence harmed the quality of life for mountaineers. Although the threat to the Blair Mountain Battlefield was no industrial disaster, it served as another example of companies getting away with almost anything in West Virginia and showed that the state political apparatus was designed to enable and protect these companies. Tomblin's statement to the people of West Virginia did not assure them that he had their backs. It demonstrated that he had the backs of the absentee corporations. Learning the lesson of Blair Mountain is more than understanding the way things were, it is about understanding the way things are. With this perspective in mind, and hoping for the best, we sent our comments on the programmatic agreement to the ACOE in August of 2014.

Fortunately, we weren't the only ones sending comments.

A number of other activist and preservation groups had also weighed in on the MOA. Among them were the National Trust for Historic Preservation and the Sierra Club, who issued a joint statement to the ACOE. In their joint comments, they flatly stated, "the agreement is limited to mitigation that would essentially document or interpret the history of the place, but without actually preserving the place where that history happened. In our view, the agreement should prohibit all mining activities within the battlefield." [13] The Sierra Club and the National Trust also shared our trepidation about the historic patterns of illegal activity and lack of enforcement. They wrote, "We are concerned by the many comments submitted by others, including the Friends of Blair Mountain and the West Virginia Chapter of the Sierra Club, who report from direct experience a long history of permit violations by these applicants, lack of enforcement by the state and federal agencies, and unlawful damage to historic resources within the Blair Mountain Battlefield." [14]

Perhaps even more encouraging than the joint comments by the Sierra Club and the National Trust were the comments submitted by the United Mine Workers of America (UMWA). As mentioned earlier, in 1991, the UMWA had tentatively agreed to a programmatic agreement similar to the MOA we received in July 2014. Aside from joining our federal lawsuit challenging the delisting from the National Register, the UMWA had been largely silent on Blair Mountain. The national leadership did not offer any public support or endorse our 2011 protest march. They additionally had been persistent proponents of continued surface mining in Appalachia. However, they slowly changed their tune after 2011. FOBM had made a number of overtures to the UMWA and had met with them on a few occasions. Joe Stanley's past record as a UMWA organizer no doubt helped our efforts.

Additionally, Terry Steele another former UMWA miner, and his wife, Wilma, were indispensable in establishing a positive relationship with UMWA Local 1440, the largest union local in the nation at that time. Local 1440 had endorsed our protest march and, by the summer of 2014, was already working with the Mine Wars Museum crew to help us get that project up and running (more on the museum in the next chapter). Phil Smith, head of public relations for the UMWA, had accompanied FOBM on the 2013 visit to Camp Branch, reporting his findings to UMWA president Cecil Roberts. Perhaps all of these efforts and nurtured relationships combined to embolden the UMWA to take a stronger stand on Blair Mountain. Regardless, they sent a strong statement to the ACOE regarding the proposed MOA. A paragraph on page two of their six pages of comments bears quoting: "The principle objective of the MOA is to provide the Proponents with a framework for avoiding, minimizing, and/or mitigating the damage that their planned mining projects will cause to the BMNA. The only way that the MOA can accomplish this goal and ensure that the BMNA is preserved in a meaningful way is by prohibiting the Proponents from conducting surface mining there." [15]

This statement by the UMWA was, to date, their most forceful and public pronouncement regarding their stance on saving Blair Mountain. We did not yet know how the ACOE and the companies would react to all of our comments, but at least the UMWA, the Sierra Club, the National Trust, and FOBM were all on the same page regarding the battlefield. As I have mentioned before, major environmental organizations and industrial unions have been at odds over many development projects and issues in recent years. The common ground established between the UMWA and the Sierra Club on Blair Mountain represented a big step in the right direction.

## • CAMP BRANCH REVISITED •

Important legal developments immediately followed our submission of comments to the Army Corps. In 2010, the Sierra Club, the National Trust, FOBM, and other groups filed a lawsuit in federal district court to challenge the delisting of the battlefield. However, the court initially granted summary judgment against us, ruling that we lacked standing to challenge the Keeper's decision. Because none of us were landowners on the property nominated for inclusion in the National Register, the court ruled that we could not demonstrate "injury, causation, or redressability" regarding the delisting. We appealed this decision to the US District Court of Appeals and, on August 26, 2014, the appeals court ruled in our favor. Even though we were not landowners, the court ruled that our interests "do not depend upon the legal right to make a physical entry onto the battlefield."[16] The battlefield, in short, had educational and emotional value to the public and to the plaintiffs. We won a 2–1 decision. One of the judges who ruled in our favor was Merrick Garland, President Obama's ill-fated nominee for the US Supreme Court.

The win was an encouraging one. This victory meant that the courts would hear our case regarding the illegal delisting of the battlefield. Aaron Isherwood and his legal team at Sierra Club expressed confidence that they would win the case. Although I had confidence in the legal team, I wondered if we would have enough time. It had taken four years in court for us to establish our legal standing on the delisting case. The actual decision on the delisting could, and as it turned out would, take years. The companies could do a lot of damage in a couple of years while we waited on the courts. We at

FOBM hoped for the best in federal court and plunged ever forward in our own way. We had another date with the West Virginia Surface Mine Board (SMB).

When Harold Ward, WVDEP's director of surface mining, issued his decision to make Aracoma modify the Camp Branch Permit in May 2014, it prohibited any surface mining within 1,000 feet of the battlefield on that permit. The decision encouraged us, but we wanted the companies held accountable for the damage they inflicted on the battlefield. FOBM filed for an appeal on Ward's decision before the SMB. Mary Anne Maul, who represented us pro bono in our first appearance before the SMB, had moved on to represent residents in a lawsuit over the Elk River chemical spill. In her stead, she recommended Morgantown lawyer Brad Stephens as someone who would potentially represent us. Operating without any funds meant that lawyers did not exactly line up to help us, but we found a new ally in Brad. In June 2014, I drove 150 miles from Charleston to Morgantown and met with Brad in his office on High Street. Brad had represented environmental groups before but had not really dealt with coal or historic preservation laws. He was no expert on coal, he explained to me, nor was he fully up to speed on everything regarding Camp Branch, but he believed in our cause and wanted to help in any way he could. He agreed to represent us in our appeal before the SMB if we could take care of his expenses to Charleston and back.

The date of our appeal was set for September 8, 2014, which gave us two months to prepare. We sent Brad all the relevant documents on Camp Branch, our site visits, and our first appearance before the SMB. Brad's work on other cases limited the amount of time he could devote to our case. I assisted by going through the permits and documents to try to help formulate an argument. Rob Goodwin, who accompanied us on our second site inspection, also lent his efforts. Eventually, by putting our collective heads together, a strategy formed.

We believed that the SMB should void Area B from the Camp Branch Permit. Area B, of course, overlapped onto the battlefield and Aracoma wished to use the rock over-burden from Area B to build a 7,000-foot runway for the National Guard. WVDEP approved Area B as an extension to the original permit. In Harold Ward's informal review of Camp Branch, he ordered the modification of the permit, which forbade surface mining in Area B. The federal version of the Camp Branch Permit, the ACOE 404, had already established that mining should not intrude within a 1,000-foot buffer zone of the battlefield until the issue of Blair on the National Register had been resolved, but WVDEP had not recognized this buffer zone when they approved the permit. As such, Ward stated, "it is mandatory that the permits do not conflict," and issued the order to modify the permit.[17] Ward's letter stood as an admission that WVDEP should never have approved Area B in the first place. Therefore, we believed that the SMB should void Area B from the permit.

Our appeal also afforded us the opportunity to argue for archeological studies of the battlefield. Our site inspection in March 2014 revealed that excavators or bulldozers had destroyed defensive entrenchments on the battlefield. The cultural resource surveys administered by the coal compa-nies had failed to identify these entrenchments beforehand. This left the sites unmarked and vulnerable. Within the terms of the Camp Branch Permit, under Special Condition No. 3, workers are required to halt operations if they find areas of archeological or historic significance in the course of their activities. While this condition appears sound on paper, someone operating bulldozers, excavators, and the other heavy equipment associated with surface mining would never be able to identify defensive entrenchments and foxholes nestled in a forested area. We argued that Aracoma Coal violated Special Condition No. 3 of the permit by destroying these sites. In response, the SMB should order an extensive archeological survey to locate and mark all areas of historic significance.

Aracoma Coal, represented by Jackson Kelly, moved to be an intervener in the case and the SMB granted their request. We would not only be up against state attorneys, but coal company attorneys as well. This is a common occurrence in West Virginia. Citizen groups often find themselves on one end of the legal aisle with coal companies and the state together on the other side. Additionally, Mark Schuerger, the head of the SMB, who missed our first hearing, would be present for our second appearance. Despite his history as a coal company executive with Alpha Natural Resources, the owner of Aracoma Coal, Mr. Schuerger did not recuse himself from the case. Things, as usual, did not look promising, but it was important to keep the fight going. As Muhammad Ali once said, "It isn't the mountains ahead to climb that wear you out; it's the pebble in your shoe." We endeavored to be the pebble in King Coal's shoe.

There were times, of course, when I felt like I was the one wearing down. I found myself concerned with legal matters and courtroom proceedings far more than I ever anticipated or desired. The subject of law itself never really fascinated me. I perceived law school as a gauntlet of boredom where one must learn to master the dullest language in the world—legalese. To our great ire, circumstances surrounding Blair Mountain forced us all to spend inordinate amounts of time learning the law and becoming hacks at legalese, like a tourist in a foreign country trying to learn enough of the language to order dinner at a restaurant. Keeping track of all the laws, permits, regulations, lawsuits, agencies, and everything else felt like slashing our way through a dense rainforest. At times it was utterly exhausting, and we were not even getting paid for it. To maintain good spirits, I tried my best never to appear tired, distressed, or frustrated in front of the other FOBM members, even though I often felt all three.

The day before the hearing, which was a Sunday, Joe Stanley, Jeff Bosley, Mark Myers, Kenny King, Rob Goodwin, and Brad Stephens all congregated at my place to go over our strategy and finalize our preparations. Just like the previous experience with the SMB, we prepared questions and went over the necessary documents. We went to Kinkos and made copies of our documents to distribute during the hearing. We did our best.

To strengthen our call for more archeological work on the battlefield, we sought help from Billy Joe Peyton, who participated in the original 1991 cultural heritage survey that looked at Blair Mountain. At the time, Peyton served as the head of the history department at West Virginia State University. I had known Peyton for several years and occasionally served as an adjunct at WV State to supplement my community college salary. When preparing for the hearing, I came across Peyton's name in the permit and found that the companies sited his survey as a guideline for preservation conditions. I called him and read the permit conditions to him over the phone. He said it was preposterous that the company or the regulatory agencies would use his study as a guideline. The 1991 survey looked at potential heritage sights across several counties in the coalfields and they only spent two days at Blair Mountain. They had not studied Camp Branch, nor did they conduct an actual archeological survey. Although Peyton's schedule did not allow him to testify at the hearing, he wrote a letter to FOBM and the SMB clarifying the meaning of his study and delivered a copy of it to me the day before the hearing. He wrote, "The 1991 study was limited to a survey of above-ground cultural resources, and did not include any sub-surface investigations. In fact, it was neither intended, nor purported, to be a comprehensive, systematic archaeological study." [18] As I would testify, and as Peyton would reiterate in his letter, "In the 23 years since we completed the original report, many new methods and technologies have emerged in the field of archaeological investigation. Therefore, I strongly support conducting a Phase III archaeological survey in the Camp Branch area that employs modern techniques in order to recover any artifacts in areas that have yet to be disturbed." [19] We hoped Peyton's letter would give us an edge the next day.

If the first appearance before the SMB was one of our most satisfying days, the second was one of the most frustrating. The SMB struck down the first part of our argument before we could even present it. Mark Schuerger, the Alpha executive who presided over our appeal, would not hear our argument that the SMB should void Area B. Brad moved to enter Harold Ward's informal review ruling as evidence, but the SMB refused to admit it. They chose to ignore a letter, written by the man who approves permits for WVDEP, stating that Area B should not have been approved. The SMB would only hear evidence relating to the surface disturbances viewed on the second site visit. Within the first few minutes of the hearing, half of our argument had been shot down.

For the second part of our argument, we needed to prove that the companies destroyed archeological sites on the battlefield and that the SMB should order an extensive archeological survey to identify remaining sites. While the second site inspection of the permit identified four areas of surface disturbance, the most serious violation occurred on the ridge-line where defensive entrenchments had been destroyed. Kenny had taken photos of the defensive positions while exploring the ridgelines a year or so before they were destroyed. Kenny took the stand and testified to this fact while Brad introduced the necessary before-and-after photographic evidence of the areas destroyed.

Special Condition No. 3 of the Camp Branch Permit states that mining operations must halt if workers discover areas of historical or archaeological interest.[20] In his testimony, Joe Stanley explained that the surface disturbances were examples of clear-cutting that precedes surface mining oper-ations. He further testified that heavy equipment operators on the site would be unable to recognize entrenchments and other archeological sites because they had not been marked or identified.[21] Aracoma Coal failed to document these areas of historic significance, failed to stop operations and notify the regulatory agencies, and thus, destroyed these areas in violation of Special Condition No. 3.

As I would testify, Aracoma Coal never completed an adequate archeological survey of the area to identify such places of significance ahead of time. Special Condition No. 2 of the permit stated, "The permittee shall preserve the areas of historical interest within the permit boundaries as identi-fied in the Phase I Final Report, dated June 7, 1991, prepared by the Institute for History of Technology and Industrial Archaeology and Billy Joe Peyton." In other words, to identify specific archeological sites, Aracoma Coal relied on a survey that did not spend any time surveying Camp Branch. The company then argued that no further archeological inquiries were necessary.

Aracoma's misuse of the 1991 survey and their disregard of Special Condition No. 3 could not stand up to real scrutiny.

The legal team representing them knew it, and they strongly objected when we admitted Peyton's letter as evidence. They first challenged the authenticity of the letter and claimed that it might be forged. I testified that Peyton hand delivered a copy of the letter to me the day before. Peyton also emailed copies of the letter to WVDEP and the SMB separately the morning of the hearing. I even offered to call Peyton and have him verify the letter. After a long, extensive argument, the SMB agreed to allow it as evidence. It may seem insignificant to spar so heavily over a letter, but when the SMB agreed to admit it, we had on record that the scholar who conducted the study upon which the companies relied stated definitively that his study should not be used for that purpose.

Jackson Kelly and the state countered with Greg Wooten's testimony. This was the first time I met Wooten, an executive vice president at Natural Resource Partners, face to face. He introduced himself before the start of the hearing and shook hands with all the others. Wooten is dark haired and tall, about 6'5", with a basketball player's build. He played center for Logan County High many years before. Wooten exhibited a tendency to lean in close to people and hover over them in conversation.

Wooten testified that a legal timber operation caused the surface disturbances on the ridgeline. Aracoma Coal had nothing to do with it. Wooten's attorney presented a timbering notification form submitted to the West Virginia Division of Forestry on May 26, 2009. According to their argument, Special Conditions No. 2 and No. 3 of the surface mining permit did not apply because the permit only regulated coal mining, not timbering.[22] WVDEP and the SMB had no authority to regulate timbering, only mining.

We countered by pointing out that, according to the timbering notification form, the timing of the damage corresponded with Blair Mountain's brief listing on the National Register. We argued that because of the battlefield's listed status at the time, someone should have notified the State Historic Preservation Office before surface disturbances began. To our frustration, the SMB discounted this argument.

The hearing lasted for six hours. At the end of the arguments, Brad moved for briefs to be filed so that we could state our argument on paper before the SMB issued a ruling. Thus, the hearing concluded without immediate resolution. Both sides would present their written arguments in the following months, and the SMB would issue a final ruling afterward. I left feeling angry and cynical.

Putting the hearing behind us nonetheless enabled us to move forward on the LUMP settlement. The programmatic agreement draft submitted by the ACOE over the summer and our SMB hearing in September had stalled progress on the potential deal over the LUMP case. After the hearing, Harold Ward contacted me and we scheduled a meeting for later in the month to try to determine the future of the Northwest Flank. With any luck, I hoped, we might be able to seal the deal before the debut of another project, the Mine Wars Museum.

## CHAPTER FIVE

# Identity Reclamation

I first met Don Blankenship when he visited the West Virginia Mine Wars Museum on Saturday, May 23, 2015. The museum had opened exactly one week before. Originally, the museum was only open on weekends, and for its first weekend after the grand opening, I accompanied our museum staff member, Elijah Hooker, a former student and history major, on his first full day of work in order to ensure things went smoothly. We were sitting by a table near the front entrance when a baby blue 1957 Bel Air convertible pulled up next to the entrance.

"Is that who I think it is?" Elijah said to me.

Indeed it was. The former CEO of Massey Energy wore a baseball cap and flannel shirt as he exited his convertible and walked toward the museum. He had actually stopped by the museum two weeks before when the museum had yet to open. Wilma Steele, one of the museum founders, spoke to him then. She was outside the museum entrance painting the front when he strode up to her, curious about what we were doing. They spoke for a few minutes and then he left. Two weeks later, he arrived to see the inside.

Blankenship spent more than an hour in the museum, taking pictures of the exhibits with his phone and reading every word accompanying each of the displays. As I would observe in later months, guests at the museum spent an average of about fifteen minutes going through the exhibits. Most of them read less than half the text accompanying the artifacts. Not Blankenship. He read everything. Afterward, I asked him if he wanted to sign our guest ledger.

"I'm surprised you want me to," he said. At the time, Blankenship faced various federal charges in connection with the 2010 Upper Big Branch mining disaster. Blankenship's trial, which lasted from October to early December 2015, had yet to begin.

I told him I still wanted him to sign in and he did. We proceeded to have one of the more bizarre conversations of my life. Blankenship did most of the talking. He blamed union pensions for high unemployment. He spoke of the coal towns and told me that "they may have been rough but they must've been better than where those immigrants came from." We talked about convict labor in the mines during the industrial period. He even ranted a bit about China's threat to national security and claimed that Chinese submarines are now faster than ours. Then he reverted the conversation back to the museum. He somehow knew that I had written most of the museum's texts, although this is not mentioned anywhere in the museum and I had said nothing of it in any of the interviews leading up to the museum's grand opening. We also spoke about the origins of the red bandana and the Red Necks.

While some may wonder why a man who had once been the most powerful coal executive in the state and was about to face multiple felony charges would bother with our little museum, it made perfect sense to me. Love him or hate him, Blankenship is no fool. He had grown up within a few miles of our museum, located in Matewan, West Virginia. When he reigned as CEO of Massey Energy, Blankenship funded the construction of a railroad depot replica in Matewan. It stands at the opposite end of the small town from our museum. The Matewan Depot Replica Museum functions as a gift shop and small museum in its own right. This museum is largely a collection of photos about the Hatfield-McCoy Feud, with a few photos relating to the Matewan Massacre, a Mine Wars shootout that occurred in 1920. The railroad depot is a nice facility, but it doesn't tell the story of the Mine Wars. Across town, I sat in the very spot where Sid Hatfield had waited for the mine guards to return to Matewan just before the Matewan Massacre and wondered what Blankenship's visit really meant.

Don Blankenship, of course, had made a number of efforts to prevent the preservation of Blair Mountain. He threatened to sue each staff member of the State Historic Preservation Office (SHPO) when the battlefield was first placed on the National Register. Blankenship had been CEO of Massey Energy when the "timbering disturbances" on the battlefield at Camp Branch had occurred. Before the Blair controversy, Blankenship had worked diligently to destroy the United Mine Workers of America (UMWA) in West Virginia, and had nearly succeeded. But, in the time between our protest march and his visit to the Mine Wars Museum, Blankenship had gone from the most powerful to perhaps one of the most reviled men in West Virginia because of the Upper Big Branch mining disaster. Many locals blamed Blankenship for the disaster, saying that he ignored safety precautions in favor of keeping production high, laying the conditions for the explosion that killed twenty-nine men. In the wake of the disaster, Blankenship had resigned from Massey Energy and faced federal charges. Found guilty or not, his legacy had been damaged. Blankenship, I have no doubt, understands the meaning of legacy and the power of memory in the popular consciousness. That is why I believe he helped build the replica railroad depot in Matewan and why he appeared so interested in our museum. A man whose own public identity is so tightly intertwined with that of King Coal would no doubt be concerned about the legacy of the industry itself. What many fail to understand is that the Second Battle for Blair Mountain is more than coal or jobs or environment or even a military base—it is also a battle over hearts and minds. I believe Don Blankenship understands this perfectly.

## • THE MIND GUARD SYSTEM •

History, as it is interpreted in its varied forms of public memory, can be presented as a carefully crafted self-portrait of a society. Some portraits are intended to broaden understanding, while others are intended to shape it. In public memory, the truth about our past is either illuminated or ignored, exaggerated or politically crafted, deemed significant or irrelevant. Historian Niall Ferguson has gone as far as to state that "at its core, a civilization is the texts that are taught in its schools, learned by its students, and recollected in times of tribulation."[1] Indeed, the texts that are taught in schools and the manner in which they are presented can go a long way toward shaping regional and national identities. Beyond the world of textbooks, how we memorialize the past—the places and relics we deem worthy of preservation or restoration—also reflects political conflict, cultural identity, and, if we are fortunate, valuable lessons learned.

Concerning history in public memory, David W. Blight observed, "As events in world politics, curriculum debates, national and international commemorations and anniversaries have shown, historical memories can be severely controlled, can undergo explosive liberation or redefinition from one generation or even one year to the next."[2] Explosive changes in public memory, such as the recent movement to remove many Confederate monuments across the United States, are more often reflections of contemporary values than of the history itself. Regarding the Mine Wars, the problem lay not so much in what was remembered, but in the absence of memory in public discourse and the classroom. Understanding the significance of this absence and the role of historical memory in society is crucial to comprehending Appalachia itself and the need to preserve the Blair Battlefield.

It is vital to understand that the Mine Wars were not merely about labor, wealth, and violent struggle—this was also an ideological conflict. During the Mine Wars, both sides of the conflict believed their actions to be representative of true American values of liberty. Among other things, this paradox reminds us that there have always been competing visions of liberty in our nation's history. When George Washington and his forces emerged victorious at Yorktown, they secured American independence, but not liberty. The war of ideas over what America is and should become—and in some ways the meaning of liberty itself—really began in Philadelphia with the writing of the Constitution in 1787 and has continued ever since. In this context, the Mine Wars were not merely a labor or regional conflict but a manifestation of the continuing struggle between competing ideological visions of what America should be and to what lengths people will go to make their vision the dominant reality.

Coal barons such as Justus Collins and the middle-class professionals who volunteered in Don Chafin's army at Blair Mountain believed themselves to be as American as apple pie. In their minds, they stood for industrial progress and felt that the capitalist world they were building embodied the principles of the country's founders. Likewise, the miners who toiled underground and the families who suffered in the tent colonies likened their resistance to the Sons of Liberty and the patriots at Valley Forge. It is, of course, no accident that the miners on Paint Creek and Cabin Creek referred to their fighting units as Minute Men. Paint Creek and Cabin Creek were their Lexington and Concord. Such a conflict forces one to ask difficult questions. Is it patriotic to be a union man? Is it un-American to challenge capitalism? Were the miners freedom fighters or terrorists? Are the answers somewhere in between? It depends on who you ask. Independence may have been won by George Washington and his soldiers, but the Mine Wars demonstrate to us that the conflict over liberty in America never really ended.

Well before the first bullets of the Mine Wars were fired, coal companies worked to control information and education in the coalfields. In his study of the nature of power in the coalfields, John Gaventa notes that the power structure within Appalachia functions to "maintain and strengthen the absentee-dominated social and political order which was established during industrialization."[3] Historian David Alan Corbin further argues that the companies, "quickly and ruthlessly destroyed old cultures and stimulated the development of a new one."[4] In maintaining this power structure and creating a pro-corporate culture, industrialists seek to create a common purpose or a oneness of purpose within a community in order to achieve their business goals. This was accomplished in the coalfields, in part, by distorting information and exaggerating the economic and cultural benefits of the industry.[5] Schools in company towns served as an important initial means of establishing and propagating these corporate values. Companies built the schools, usually by docking the miners' wages to pay for them, and hired the teachers themselves. Aside from the workplace, the company school was one of the few institutions that brought the community together. Control over the schools during the industrial era enabled the companies to dictate curriculum and prevent any ideologies perceived as a threat, such as unionism, from being taught, while it simultaneously allowed them to promote their own values.[6]

As coal miners organized, went on strike, and challenged the power structure during the Mine Wars, companies and the state government worked together to shape the public narrative of the rebellion while the conflict waged and worked to erase the memory of the narrative when the violence ended. For example, in the summer of 1913, wildcat strikes along Paint Creek and Cabin Creek threatened to dismantle Governor Henry D. Hatfield's dictated compromise between the UMWA and the coal operators. Governor Hatfield attempted to stifle the wildcat strikes by shutting down two local newspapers and arresting their editors because their publications had covered the brutality of the Mine Guard System and urged the miners to continue the strike.[7]

Less than a decade later at Blair Mountain, Boyden Sparkes, a celebrated World War I journalist, and a few other reporters traveled to the Mountain State and attempted to cover the battle. Sparkes and his colleagues managed to convince a local to guide them close to the fighting, but as they made their way through the woods, Sparkes was shot in the leg by State Police and they were all taken into Logan County Sheriff Don Chafin's custody. Chafin held Sparkes and several other reporters captive for a few days and would not allow them to write any stories without his approval. After Sparkes finished his story, Chafin sent a man to read it and censor anything sympathetic to the miners. As Sparkes himself put it, the powers that be would not allow him to write any "sob stuff for the Red Necks."[8]

Coal industry executives certainly shared Chafin's position. Although the Armed March on Logan had not achieved the success the miners had hoped for, industry and state leaders still feared the ideology of unionism and the radicalism of the miners, and they saw the need to take aggressive steps to control the narrative of the labor conflict in schools and public discourse. Indeed, before the Battle of Blair Mountain ever occurred, coal operators, politicians, and other business leaders of West Virginia joined forces to create the American Constitutional Association (ACA). Around 150 businessmen attended the inaugural meeting of the organization including Governor John J. Cornwell, who served as the ACA's first president; future state governor Howard M. Gore; Edwin Keatley, future speaker of the State House of Delegates; and Phil Conley, who would go on to control the content in West Virginia history textbooks for fifty years.[9]

Founded as an "educational organization," the ACA intended to combat what their leaders saw as the un-American ideology of unionism and the growth of socialism by influencing schools, media, and churches. This, of course, must be understood in the context of the post–World War I Red Scare, and state leaders certainly echoed concerns felt by alarmists all across the country. But Phil Conley and the founders of the ACA desired more than the elimination of the perceived communist threat; they wanted to construct a unified state identity that would support "manufacturing interests, the coal interests, the agricultural interests, the gas

interests, and the oil interests."[10] This was the ideology of
*100% Americanism.* Historian John Hennen, who joined us
on the 2011 protest march, wrote that 100% Americanism
was an ideology formed "to equate loyalty to the nation with
obedience to one's employer, or in a broader sense, to corporate capitalism."[11] According to the ACA, loyalty to the
coal industry was synonymous with patriotism and social
progress.

Ephraim F. Morgan, who followed Cornwell as state
governor, was also concerned that the dangerous ideologies
presumably driving the coal miners to rebellion would seep
their way into state classrooms. Morgan testified against the
coal miners during the treason trials that followed the Battle
of Blair Mountain. Addressing the West Virginia Education
Association before the trials, Morgan told them there would
be no room for dissenting ideas in the classroom. "Only those
who stand ready to combat the dangerous, deceptive, blight-
ing, socialistic, communistic, Bolshevistic doctrines that are
being disseminated throughout the country, striking at every
foundation of our free institutions, should be entrusted with
training the youths of America."[12]

P. H. Penna of the National Coal Association took it a step
further. A year after the Battle of Blair Mountain, he said,
"The greatest menace to the United States of America is the
labor union movement. . . . I would like, if I could, to wipe
out not only the UMWA but all memory of the institution."[13]

That same year, as the miners' treason trials were conducted in Charles Town, Phil Conley wrote an article on Blair
Mountain for the *New York Times* entitled "West Virginia
War." In the sarcastically written article, Conley, a Charleston
native, veteran of World War I, and then managing director
of the ACA, claimed to have volunteered to join Don Chafin's
forces against the miners at Blair Mountain. While on a train,

Conley overheard some coal operators talking about Frank Keeney. Conley wrote, "I inquired who Keeney was, and learned that he led the opposing forces. . . . My imagination went wild. I pictured myself and two companions getting off the train with our guns in readiness for a conflict with Keeney's soldiers." One of the coal operators promised to help Conley get to the thick of the fighting. Once in Blair, Conley states that he was disappointed to only find "some semblance of a battle." In fact, national coverage and interest concerning Blair Mountain was much ado about nothing. Conley claims to have heard that only seven men were killed in the fighting. He ends his article by writing, "Seven men killed in one week's fighting, bah! I decided to go to some city where that many men are killed every few hours." [14]

Other attempts would be made to diminish the significance of the rebellion before the end of the decade. G. T. Swain, a Logan native and close associate of Don Chafin, published his account in 1927 called *The Blair Mountain War: Battle of the Rednecks*. In the book, Swain claims, "Logan field has been subject to much false propaganda from mine union officials and from other coalfields of the nation who are jealous of the prosperity of this rich valley." [15] Regarding labor relations, he wrote, "The treatment accorded the laboring man in this field by the operators has been uniformly courteous and employers have been very generous to their employees." [16] Members of the Armed March on Logan were merely misled by "false propaganda" and amounted to a "lawless mob." After being out of print for over eighty years, Swain's book was reprinted in 2009 in Logan County—the same year that the Blair Mountain Battlefield was temporarily placed on the National Register of Historic Places. [17]

The American Civil Liberties Union (ACLU) did not agree with Swain's assessment of conditions in the West Virginia coalfields. In 1923, Roger Baldwin, then head of the ACLU said, "The conditions that exist in West Virginia are the greatest challenge to civil liberties that exist in America today. There is no law in West Virginia outside the law of the armed gunmen in the employ of the coal operators. The operators control everything in sight."[18] Baldwin's comments received sharp criticism by the ACA. The ACA responded to Baldwin's comments by connecting him with communism, "The statements of this near-Bolshevist comprise a gross insult to every citizen in West Virginia. Baldwin is interested in unionizing southern West Virginia. We are not concerned about that matter."[19]

Aside from his role in the ACA, Phil Conley would go on to write a pro-industry book, *The History of the West Virginia Coal Industry,* in which he calls coal the "magic mineral" and a "wonder substance."[20] Writing the preface for the 1960 edition of Conley's book, then West Virginia Governor Cecil H. Underwood stated that "King Coal is a living, breathing giant of Mountain State progress."[21] Conley would go on to become the most influential individual in shaping the way West Virginia history was taught in secondary schools for much of the twentieth century. To his credit, Conley did push for the inclusion of West Virginia history in public schools and was the originator of a statewide history contest for eighth graders, dubbed the Golden Horseshoe Competition.[22]

By 1930, Conley had written his version of the history of West Virginia and lobbied in the state legislature for state history to be taught in secondary schools and for his book to be used as the text. In 1933, the state legislature did pass a bill to make West Virginia history mandatory in public schools, but conservative democrat Governor Herman Guy Kump vetoed the legislation. In his personal journal, Conley wrote,

"I have seen a spectacle of the governor of the State take a personal interest in working against the teaching of the history of West Virginia in the schools."[23] The state, it appears, was not willing to allow any West Virginia history to be taught, Conley's version or otherwise, much less shed light on a major violent uprising that had occurred just over a decade before.

The state government's unwillingness to allow the Mine Wars to be a part of the historic narrative became most evident in 1939 and 1940 when a controversy arose over the *West Virginia Guide*. As a part of many New Deal programs, President Franklin Roosevelt's administration sponsored and commissioned state guides to be written in each state. When the state guide for West Virginia was written, Governor Homer A. Holt vehemently protested the content of the book and denounced the federally appointed supervisor of the project as "a red and a tool of the CIO."[24]

In January 1940, John D. Newsome, representing the Roosevelt administration, traveled to West Virginia from Washington, DC, to hold a private conference with Governor Holt concerning the book. Holt presented Newsome with a number of specific complaints. The governor protested a photograph of a coal miner on his knees washing coal dust out of his hair. Newsome said that this picture "filled the governor with indignation" because it depicted poor conditions in the coalfields. The governor also objected to the inclusion of steelworkers' strikes in Weirton, West Virginia; the mention of absentee landownership in the guide; and the inclusion of the profits of coal operators compared to the wages of coal miners.[25]

Perhaps more striking than anything else was the governor's denial of the Hawks Nest disaster. In the early thirties, chemical manufacturer Union Carbide used some 5,000 workers to drill a massive hydroelectric water diversion tunnel at Hawks Nest, in Fayette County, West Virginia.

While drilling the tunnel, an estimated 764 men—mostly African Americans—died of silicosis, many of whom were buried in unmarked graves nearby. This is, to date, the deadliest industrial disaster in United States history. Governor Holt would not allow it to be included in the book stating, "the cases diagnosed as silicosis were probably not silicosis at all but tuberculosis."[26] After his term as governor, Holt would become a lead attorney for Union Carbide.[27]

In a memorandum, Newsome summed up his meeting with Governor Holt and wrote the following about the governor's opinion on the Mine Wars and Blair Mountain:

> The manuscript contained three (3) references to the famous Miners' March. All these references were considered in bad taste. Here again we were making heroes out of scalawags. At best the Miners' March, if mentioned at all, was not worth more than two or three lines.
>
> The part played by Mother Jones in organizing the workers was given far too much emphasis. Merely because a page, perhaps, was devoted to her activities, we had "glorified" her. Why not just say that "Mother Jones was in West Virginia."
>
> In other words, the Governor informed me, the manuscript was propaganda from start to finish. I quote his own words. The whole tone of the book was objectionable. It lacked style, it lacked quality, it dealt with the sordid side of life instead of doing justice to the progressive spirit of the people of West Virginia.[28]

Governor Holt informed Mr. Newsome that if all of these details were not omitted from the West Virginia Guide, then the state would cease to cooperate with any Works Progress Administration project from the federal government. *The*

*New Republic* chimed in on the controversy by stating, "Any book on West Virginia that failed to mention Mother Jones, the Logan Armed March, and the Weirton Strikes would not be a guide but a fairy story." [29] Newsome agreed, "I believe Governor Holt is making an issue out of the Guide Book solely for political reasons." [30] Nonetheless, the fairy story prevailed. Federal officials succumbed to Governor Holt's wishes and did not publish the book during his administration. [31] Publication of the Guide Book was postponed until Matthew Neely's term as governor. Neely, a New Deal Democrat, was more receptive to the original text that included labor struggles in the state and allowed for some of the material to be included in the final draft. [32]

By the end of the Depression, the teaching of West Virginia history had become mandatory statewide, and Phil Conley was ready to seize the reigns of control. Well-connected politically, known in state business circles, a shareholder in many of the state's industrial corporations, and a staunch opponent of any leftist ideology, Conley was the perfect choice for business interests. He was considered so loyal to anticommunist sentiment that two US Senators—not from West Virginia—wrote letters to Secretary of State John Foster Dulles recommending that Conley be named US Ambassador to Greece at a time when the Truman Doctrine faced its first test of the Cold War. Although Dulles did not give Conley the appointment, in an amusingly ironic twist, he sent the pro-coal West Virginian on a speaking tour of Greece to lecture the Athenians on the benefits of democracy. [33]

Back in the Mountain State, Conley founded the Education Association of West Virginia, which printed the state history textbooks he authored. His book, *West Virginia Yesterday and Today*, became the standard textbook for West Virginia history across the state until the 1970s. In the various editions of the book, there is no mention at all of the Mine Wars, various mining disasters, or the Hawks Nest disaster. For fifty years following the Battle of Blair Mountain, these events remained completely absent from the classroom.[34] How did Conley deal with the violent years in the coalfields of West Virginia after World War I? By stating, "a period of readjustment was inevitable," but "normal conditions soon prevailed."[35] Meanwhile the steel industry after World War I "added much wealth to our people" and, in 1921, the state began a new road building program.[36]

Not until 1972, when historian Otis K. Rice wrote his own West Virginia history textbook, did the Mine Wars make the cut. Rice devoted one paragraph to the Battle of Blair Mountain.[37] The Hawks Nest disaster did not receive any attention in textbooks until the twenty-first century, when the state textbooks began to be published by an out-of-state company.[38]

During the Industrial Age, companies maintained power over the local populace in large part due to the forceful brutality of the Mine Guard System and the company towns. When the Mine Guard System was abolished during the Great Depression and education came under control of the state, industry leaders simply found new ways to influence the culture and schools. With the aid of Conley, the ACA, and supportive politicians, the public classroom became a means by which a pro-industry narrative could be preached. Events such as Blair Mountain, or any other events or ideologies that may threaten the industrial power structure, were simply omitted as though they had never happened. The industry definition of liberty would prevail in the schools and perpetually reinforce corporate ideals. The Mine Guard System evolved into a Mind Guard System.

The great irony is that industrialists and politicians who

seek to destroy labor unions out of fear of radical ideologies defeat their own purpose. Radicalism and extremism on both the political left and the right flourish in the absence of collective bargaining. Ideologies such as communism and anarchism enjoy their greatest support during the times in American history when labor unions are incredibly weak and the gap between the rich and poor widens. When workers can earn a living wage, enjoy decent benefits, and work in safe conditions, they are not so easily seduced by extremism. Yet corporations fight unions as though organized labor will open the floodgates to radical leftism, when, in fact, the opposite is the reality.

When I asked my eighth-grade teacher when we would cover the Mine Wars in class, I was informed that there were no such plans. When I asked her about Frank Keeney, she shrugged her shoulders. She had never heard of him. In retrospect, this is not surprising. She was, after all, a Spanish teacher who was assigned to teach West Virginia Studies because the school did not have anyone else to do it. Having had the task of teaching the subject suddenly thrown upon her, I cannot really blame her for her lack of knowledge. However, it still did not explain to me why falsehoods were promoted and truths were ignored in our state history classes.

One would expect more attention to be given to labor history after the fall of the Soviet Union in 1991. But this is not what happened in West Virginia, where the coal industry actually expanded its efforts to control school curriculum. Fourth- and eighth-grade students living within the state are currently required to take a West Virginia Studies course. During my eighth-grade experience in 1988, my class learned the counties in alphabetical order and the curriculum highlighted optimistic pieces of state trivia. We were informed of all the celebrities who were born in West Virginia such as

Los Angeles Lakers great Jerry West; comedian Don Knotts; Chuck Yeager, who broke the sound barrier; and Mary Lou Retton, an Olympic gold medalist who was the first woman to appear on a Wheaties cereal box.[39]

We were also treated to a host of strange claims about our state throughout the year. We were told that the American Revolution did not begin at Lexington and Concord but rather in what is now West Virginia at the 1774 Battle of Point Pleasant. Our text falsely claimed that West Virginians were actually responsible for major inventions. James Rumsey was credited with the steamboat instead of Fulton, and Amos Dolbear was favored over Alexander Graham Bell for inventing the telephone.[40] Neither the Mine Wars nor the Hawks Nest disaster were covered. We all took in this information as eighth graders one year before the fall of the Berlin Wall. In social studies the year before, our teacher, Doug Smith, told us that in Communist Russia and China, students were taught a phony history in the classroom, crediting people from their nations with major inventions like the steamboat and the lightbulb while overlooking human rights violations such as Stalin's purges.

The act of rewriting history for political interests is literally as old as the pyramids. Egyptian pharaohs did not hesitate to massage the truth when it came to inscribing the history of their reigns on their tomb walls.[41] In the twentieth century, governments often maintain power over populations, at least in part, by using educational systems. Tyrants from Stalin, Mao, and Hitler to Kim Jun Un have all taught their own versions of history in the classroom in order to indoctrinate their populations.[42] Other times, historic fact is willfully ignored in the classroom for political purposes. The history of the Nazis and the Holocaust remained absent from West German classrooms for decades.[43] On the other side of the

world, many Japanese students never learned of their coun-
try's atrocities in World War II. As late as 1986, the Japanese
Minister of Education, Fujio Masayki, publicly declared the
Rape of Nanjing to be a myth.[44]

Such fiction was not taught in free America, we were told.
And yet in 1988, a year away from winning the Cold War,
our state history courses, in an effort to keep communism at
bay and promote a proud state history, seemed to resemble the
very thing we wanted to defeat. Echoing my own experience
in his research, John C. Hennen observed, "Instilling absolute
submission to institutional authority into 'the plastic mold of
youth' could lead to manifestations of state power similar to
those against which America fought."[45]

As the Cold War came to a close, a few books and films
began to tell the story of the Mine Wars. The late eighties and
the early nineties saw the publication of a few history books,
a novel, and an independent feature film, and the Mine Wars
was included in the 1995 PBS film West Virginia: A History.
All the while, Kenny King had begun his exploration and
preservation efforts on Blair Mountain. But the momentum
of this attention did not seem to spill over to the classroom
in any significant way. By the time I taught in the coalfields
at Southern in 2010, most of my students had never heard
of the Battle of Blair Mountain and the classroom where I
asked the question stood within fifteen miles from the spot
of the battle.

The turn of the twenty-first century saw the West Virginia
Coal Association and the Friends of Coal continue and even
expand industrial influence on school curriculum. The Friends
of Coal Ladies Auxiliary currently sponsors a Coal in the
Classroom campaign where wives and mothers of coal miners
visit secondary classrooms in coal counties to tout the benefits
of the industry. Through their efforts, "coal is presented in its

true form, as a legacy and a future industry for the children of West Virginia." According to the Coal in the Classroom rhetoric, coal—meaning the industry itself—is not simply part of local history, but the defining characteristic of state heritage and culture.[46]

Further efforts to shape public opinion via school curriculum were no longer limited to unionist paranoia but expanded to combat climate science. Climate science and the threat of climate change challenges the use of fossil fuels, most notably coal. In the 1990s and early 2000s, a few Appalachian grass-roots environmentalist groups were formed and became active in the coalfields. To counter the growing environmental movement and the mounting evidence surrounding climate science, the coal industry adapted their efforts accordingly. For example, in the 1990s, high school students in the coal counties of Appalachia were treated to a coal industry produced film called *The Greening of Planet Earth*.[47] This film, used in many coal counties well into the 2000s, does not deny global warming, but rather claims that carbon dioxide emissions and global warming will actually increase vegetation on the earth, leading to an agricultural boom and enabling a more prosperous future.[48]

In 1997, the industry funded the formation of Coal Education Development and Resources (CEDAR), a non-profit corporation functioning in West Virginia, Virginia, and Kentucky, "for the purpose of improving the image of the Coal Industry."[49] In West Virginia, CEDAR specifically focuses its efforts on Logan, Mingo, McDowell, and Wyoming Counties. CEDAR makes classroom materials and grants available to K–12 teachers and sponsors annual coal fairs, during which students present coal-themed projects in the fields of science, history, literature, geography, music, and mathematics. Cash prizes are awarded to the top three winners in each category.[50]

These aggressive efforts to promote the coal industry are not limited to the Appalachian coalfields. The Oklahoma Resources Board, with backing from the oil and gas industries, created a series of children's storybooks for elementary school students. The stories revolve around the cartoon character Petro Pete and the benefits of fracking. The books claim that the activities of fossil fuel companies actually improve the environment and make the world a better place.[51] In 2011, the same year activists marched to support the preservation of the Blair Mountain Battlefield, the National Mining Association and the American Coal Foundation teamed up with Scholastic, the world's largest publisher of children's books, to provide classroom materials to fourth grade teachers themed "The United States of Energy." These materials, called industry propaganda by some scholars, promote the benefits of coal, oil, and natural gas, excluding any talk of environmental damage, pollution, and climate science. The American Coal Foundation distributed materials to some 66,000 fourth-grade teachers nationwide.[52]

Even as the coal industry faced serious decline, the West Virginia Legislature continued to push for a pro-industry narrative in the classroom. In February 2016, the West Virginia House of Delegates voted 73–20 on a measure to exclude teaching climate science in the classroom. Delegate Michel Moffatt stated that teaching climate science would give students the notion that "fossil fuels are bad." Delegate Jim Butler reinforced the concern by stating, "In an energy-producing state, it's a concern to me that we are teaching our kids potentially that we are doing immoral things here in order to make a living in our state."[53]

Those who observe coal country from the outside often wonder why mountaineers cling to a status quo that keeps them poor, damages their environment, and leaves them incapable of adapting to economic changes in the twenty-first century. Jared Diamond, in his study of why societies collapse, notes that people in certain regions will irrationally cling to a bad status quo if adaptation threatens long-standing values of cultural identity.[54] Over the previous century, the coal industry constructed a worldview that tied coal mining with progress, Americanism, and even notions of rugged individualism and masculinity. Many mountaineers, for example, are reluctant to consider jobs in renewable energy because working on a windmill or solar farm is not perceived to be as manly as digging coal. To move away from coal is to threaten the very ideas of manhood, individualism, and progress in the minds of many miners. Therefore, they continually cling to an outdated form of energy production while politicians promise to revive a glorious past that never really existed in the first place.

All of our efforts to preserve the battlefield, therefore, involved much more than simply saving a piece of real estate; they meant challenging the Mind Guard System. A couple of generations had already been robbed of an honest retelling of their past. Thus, the preservation movement grew into a movement to reclaim our historical and cultural identity by providing a more complete historical narrative and spreading the word. This also meant that beyond the money and political interests arrayed against us, we must overcome the regional mentality shaped over generations.

As mentioned before, upon the completion of a surface mining operation, coal companies must go through a process known as reclamation in order to reconstruct the mountain and the vegetation as well as possible. I felt as though this is what our preservation movement had become. Like many local mountaintops, our identity had been blasted, swept away, and reconstructed. Just like a mountain, identity can never be re-created exactly as it was, but it can be reclaimed. Identity Reclamation. This would be both the act of controlling our own historical narrative and how we would use it as a strategy to win.

## • HISTORY. LABOR. CULTURE. •

Within the coalfields, King Coal evolved into a cult of personality of its own, giving locals a belief that the industry is nearly omnipresent. Many West Virginians believe that King Coal influences absolutely everything, except, ironically, the climate. Criticisms are whispered. Colleagues and locals have peeked into my office at college, looked both ways in the hall, whispered that they hope I'm successful with Blair Mountain, and walked away in a hurry before I could even thank them. A few colleagues warned me that because of my activism, I would be blacklisted from four-year colleges and universities in the state. Still others openly speculated that the Coal Association probably bugged my office at the college. King Coal was always listening. Always watching.

There is evidence to encourage this paranoia. After all, someone has opened my mail and the mail of several board members. My computer has been hacked six times. Technicians who have looked at my college-provided laptop have told me that someone outside the college network has monitored my emails and internet activity. Lawyers have told me to assume and behave as though the government or the Coal Association has hacked my smartphone. Board members have been followed by black, unmarked vehicles. One colleague suggested that "they" would plant illegal porn or something on my office computer in the hopes of tarnishing my reputation or getting me fired. Such a claim is not as outrageous as it may seem. In 2012, when environmental activist Maria Gunnoe went to Washington, DC, to testify before the Senate about water pollution in areas around MTR sights, she wanted to use a photo of her daughter trying to take a bath in polluted bathwater. The coal companies tried to have her charged with child pornography.[55]

This description paints a rather bleak portrait of coal country. The irony is that most of the locals live their entire lives without even noticing the dark industrial underbelly of their own culture. Like the morning mist in the mountains, coal dominance subconsciously registers as a natural part of the landscape. It is only when one rises up and challenges the system that one discovers the culture for what it is. For me, the realization that the industry may be constantly watching and persistently plotting made it difficult to stay focused on the task at hand. By the time I had a couple of years of activism in the coalfields under my belt, I learned not to trust anyone except my immediate family and longtime friends. I found myself constantly checking the rearview mirror anytime I drove somewhere. Nearly every time someone entered my office on campus, I assumed they had an ulterior motive. In some ways, it forced me to build a wall around myself and not let anyone get too close. This, of course, plays right into the Mind Guard System. Trust is needed to sustain relationships, and it is an essential element to building successful grassroots organizations. You have to trust one another if you are going to win. You also have to get others to trust you. Again, the historical continuity strikes true. During the Mine Wars, mine guards posed as miners, restaurant owners, and bartenders in order to spy on the population. In Mingo County, some companies built their houses a few feet above the ground so that mine guards could crawl underneath at night and eaves-drop on family conversations.[56] Have things changed so much in a century? Companies don't need to crawl under houses anymore, they can simply use smartphones and the internet. Joseph Stalin only dreamed of such spying capability.

In the public spectrum, the coal companies argued that our efforts to save the battlefield disguised a more sinister leftist plot to destroy jobs and end coal mining. During our second appearance before the SMB, the Jackson Kelly attorney representing the industry, in his closing arguments, claimed that FOBM did not want to save our history, we wanted to kill coal. In 2011, coal companies spread rumors that the protest marchers were paid. Many pro-coal locals believed that the protest marchers knew nothing about the actual history of Blair Mountain. We needed to break this perception and gain the public's trust with a message and a vision. To accomplish this, we adopted a multifaceted approach. First, as mentioned earlier, FOBM worked to establish a clear identity as an organization singularly dedicated to the issue of the battlefield. Additionally, we provided a vision for how the battlefield could benefit the region culturally, educationally, and economically. Finally, we endeavored to promote the actual history. This strategy went far beyond mere efforts to "raise awareness" to save a battlefield. This was about toppling the coalfield mentality promoted by the industry for over a century.

Joe Stanley came up with our slogan—History. Labor. Culture. Simple slogans work best and this one said everything we needed it to say. No one in the coalfields could argue against cherishing our history, appreciating the sacrifices of hard work and labor, and preserving our culture. The slogan bluntly stated what we were all about and allowed us to take the first step in reframing the debate.

It seemed natural to me to counter the "killing jobs" argument with a vision on how preserving Blair Mountain could create jobs. A historic park at Blair Mountain would create different kinds of jobs from coal mining, but these jobs would not end when the coal reserves were depleted. A look at the surface mine permits on the battlefield reveal that the coal companies expected their operations to be in reclamation phase after a maximum of eight years of coal mining.[57] A park revolving around the battlefield could employ foresters, museum workers, construction workers, artists, historians, and landscapers, just to name a few. Many of these positions could last much longer than eight years. A park could bring tourism dollars; it could encourage new small businesses to open in and around the dying community of Blair. A surface mine at Blair Mountain would not revitalize the community as most of the employed workers would not come from Blair and would simply commute to the site. A park could also be an opportunity to recast some of the negative stereotypes about the region by focusing on the real history.

By no means was I the first person to think that there should be a park at Blair Mountain. After the West Virginia Institute of Technology and History's 1991 study, Billy Joe Peyton and Mike Workman recommended a park with monuments and trails. Since then, no one had really articulated what a park might look like or be like in any detail. In the fall of 2011, I authored a brief park proposal that the organization could use to sell a vision to the general public, potential investors, and political leaders. I intended to pitch an overall concept with just enough detail to get people excited about the park's potential. I did not think in practical terms. This did not mean that I intended to put forth an impractical plan, I simply did not want to curtail my imagination by worrying about funding, investment, and local political hindrances.

The ten-page document, which I submitted to the board on September 22, 2011, called for the development of "a fully functioning educational and tourist destination, complete with a visitor center, museum, battlefield tours, monuments, historic markers, a living history coal town, an outdoor amphitheater, lodging, camping, restaurants, and retail shops." I envisioned hiking trails dotted with stone markers that would take visitors to pivotal points on the battlefield, and a huge stone monument on the south crest of Blair Mountain, near where our 2011 protest march ended, and a visitors' center and museum in the town of Blair, built to replicate structures of the period. A living history coal town, located near the community of Blair, would be another potential addition.

All of the developed areas belonged outside of the actual battlefield acreage. The coal town, shops, museum, and other major structures did not belong within 1,000 feet of the battlefield acreage, but on nearby or adjacent properties. State route 17 provided access to the south crest of Blair Mountain, a nice space for a monument. Hiking and ATV trails would provide additional access to other areas of the battlefield. Nearby MTR sites could provide ample room for ATV trails, some of which would lead to the edge of the battlefield boundaries. These areas could link to several existing trails along the ridges, providing opportunities to hike the interior of the battlefield without disturbing the site.

On the educational side, I wanted to see a Mine Wars/Coalfield Archive and Library attached to the museum for scholars and secondary students. Facilities at the park could host academic conferences, secondary school events, and college tours. The proposal called for an outdoor amphitheater for speakers, living history reenactments, plays, and concerts. Graduate and undergrad students from regional colleges could serve internships at the museum or in the archives. I envisioned a park that would develop over time to become a center for regional education, art, music, and scholarship with the story of the Mine Wars as the thematic core.

My efforts focused on the grand vision more than the practicalities of cost and implementation, realizing the park in its grandest form would take millions in investment capital. I had no idea how we would get the money. The proposal spoke of economic benefits in a general sense, obviously highlighting the numerous job opportunities a park could create. I promoted the idea of locally owned retail shops and restaurants. Anything built within the confines of the park would conform to a preapproved historic reconstruction building code as approved by a park board of governors. The park could become an important and permanent part of the local economy. A few parks across the country flourish in this way. Colonial Williamsburg brought in an estimated $500 million to its local economy in 2011. Tourism related to the Gettysburg National Battlefield in Pennsylvania contributed an estimated $180 million to their region that same year.[58] Although a park at Blair Mountain could in no way approach those numbers, it could still make a real difference in the coalfields.

We decided that the best way to introduce the park proposal was with media coverage along with an email sent out to each member of the West Virginia legislature and the governor's office. Before sending the proposal, however, I enlisted the aid of Mark Myers, Lou Martin, and John Hennen to get the proposal's endorsement from the scholarly community. Myers, Martin, and Hennen are all labor historians, as well as friends, who had helped our efforts before. Martin and Hennen participated in the 2011 protest march. Myers and I shared an office as graduate instructors at West Virginia University and he would soon join FOBM's board. The three of them crafted a historians' statement proclaiming Blair Mountain's status as a national treasure and the need for its preservation. The statement also included an endorsement of the park proposal. The final product declared that Blair Mountain "stands at the center of labor history in America," and that memorializing the event would also bring to light the rights won by the labor movement in America as a whole, such as the forty-hour work week, the eight-hour day, holidays, pensions, workplace safety, and child labor laws. The statement concluded by exhorting economic diversification, stating, "We should preserve one of America's most important historic sites and make it the cornerstone of a national battlefield park. West Virginia has the potential to build a more sustainable economy in Logan County." [59]

Within a couple of months, 102 highly regarded labor historians and scholars from around the country endorsed the statement and proposal. Our critics could no longer claim that an environmental agenda drove the movement to save Blair Mountain. We emailed the statement, signatures, and park proposal to the entire West Virginia legislature and the governor's office on June 25, 2012, just over one year after the protest march. Paul Nyden, who had covered our efforts very well in the local press, wrote up a large article on the proposal and the historians' statement. [60] We made a good media push with a number of our members giving interviews for newspapers and talk radio. Although we all felt positive about the message, the vision, and the media coverage, we did not get a single response from anyone in the state legislature, the governor's office, or from the offices of US Senators Joe Manchin or Jay Rockefeller. No politician even thanked us for sending it. No one even bothered to lie to us and say they would think about it and get back to us. Not a word from anyone.

We decided to test the extent of their indifference. For three consecutive legislative sessions (2012–2014), FOBM lobbied for the state House and Senate to adopt a resolution supporting a park at Blair Mountain. I wrote a draft resolution and submitted it to elected officials in the coalfields, all of whom flatly rejected to sponsor the resolution. We finally found an ally with Mike Manypenny, a delegate representing District 42 in the northern part of the state, who agreed to sponsor it. Our board members made phone calls to representatives and a number of us went to the capitol to speak to them in their offices. Many were uncomfortable even talking to us about Blair Mountain. I walked into one office of a double-chinned delegate as he attacked a foot-long sub sandwich. Without even looking up from his sandwich or pausing between bites, he said, "I'm not interested in Blair Mountain." I turned around and left. Most frustrating to me was my visit to Delegate Mike Caputo's office; he refused to support or help our resolution while sitting beneath a framed photograph of my great-grandfather that hung behind his desk. Bill Rainey, head of the West Virginia Coal Association, sat in a chair near the delegate's desk, sipped on a cup of coffee, and grinned at me.

We succeeded in getting over thirty delegates to say they would vote for the resolution, but without support from the coalfield legislators, the resolution stood no chance of making its way out of committee. Industry lobbyists, such as the West Virginia Coal Association, and a few executives ensured that the resolution went nowhere. We tried to enlist the aid of the UMWA, but for some reason, they did not put their weight behind our efforts. For three years, we tried and for three years the resolution failed to make the floor of either the House or the Senate.

These failed efforts, while frustrating, still gave us a chance to go to each legislator face to face and at least force them to say yes or no directly to us. During History Day at the Capitol in 2013, Kenny King and I secured a booth for FOBM. History Day is an annual event at the Capitol Complex. Various reenactment groups, museums, and historic societies set up booths and tables in the area between the Senate and House. Politicians go around and shake hands and talk about the importance of our history. We stationed our booth near the entrance to the House of Delegates and Kenny and I watched numerous delegates quicken their pace and look at the floor when they went by. One delegate did give me a thumbs up while walking by, though he did not stop. Delegate Manypenny stopped for a bit and said hello. Two industry associates stood at the entry to the delegate's chamber and stared at us with their arms crossed. We felt like a pea in a corn patch. But I found myself mildly relishing the role. It is interesting to see elected officials scatter like pigeons on a walk through the park just to avoid us.

The general public gave us a much warmer reception than the officials they voted into office. We spread the word about the history as often as we could with whomever would listen. In the first half of 2012, I lectured on the Mine Wars at Carnegie Hall in Lewisburg, Glenville State College, the Gilmer County Historic Society, Elkins, and even at Bowdoin College in Maine. In some cases, such as in Maine, I spoke to rooms of nearly 200. Other times, I spoke to only a dozen. Other FOBM members made their own speaking engagements. Everywhere we went, whether the audiences were large or small, they appeared genuinely fascinated with the actual history and wanted to see it preserved.

One of the more vivid pictures in my memory is Joe Stanley

at Bridge Day. Bridge Day is held every third Saturday in October at the New River Gorge Bridge in Fayette County. Over 60,000 visitors regularly converge on the area to watch and participate in BASE jumping off the 876-foot-tall bridge into the New River below. There are hundreds of booths and vendors. In 2012, FOBM secured a booth and I accompanied Kate McComas, Paul Corbit Brown, and Joe Stanley. It was a gray, windy, and chilly fall day. As Kate, Paul, and I manned the booth, Joe stood out front with his jacket and gloves on calling out to passersby, "Save Blair Mountain! It's labor's Gettysburg!" Watching him there amid the crowds with the mountains in the background and the strong wind, I was reminded of John the Baptist. A voice crying out in the wilderness. Joe, former miner and salt-of-the-earth guy that he is, would probably have had a lot in common with the fishermen who followed John the Baptist and later, Jesus Christ. But, in this instance, Joe was preaching his own kind of union gospel and Blair Mountain was his pulpit. Slowly but surely, the congregation began to pay attention.

Recognizing the need for literature to distribute, we also created *Blair Mountain Journal*. I had been thinking conceptually about a Mine Wars–themed magazine or journal as early as the 2011 protest march. I envisioned a publication for general audiences and scholars alike, with articles relating to the history, culture, literature, and preservation efforts surrounding Blair Mountain and the Mine Wars. We published our premier issue of the journal in the fall of 2012, just a few weeks before Bridge Day. To put together the premiere issue, I rounded up the usual suspects; Harvard Ayers wrote an article on the archeology of Blair Mountain; Kenny King provided a timeline of all his preservation efforts dating back to 1991; Lou Martin and Mark Myers added articles of their own. I contributed an interview with novelist and activist Denise

Giardina. We even included a poem about Blair Mountain by H. S. Sowards. Paul Corbit Brown and Kenny King contributed photos, Kate McCommas helped edit, and Ann Croz handled our graphic design.

With *Blair Mountain Journal,* we had published and printed a firm manifesto stating our ideals, goals, and the purpose of our organization that we could distribute to the public. This helped to solidify our identity as a historic preservation group and explain our objectives in a clear fashion. It also, of course, was another little brick in the wall of our identity reclamation. *Blair Mountain Journal,* unfortunately, was a one hit wonder. More pressing matters with Camp Branch kept my attention in 2013 and 2014, and I failed to find the time or energy to produce a follow-up issue. The idea of a Mine Wars–themed publication would be reborn in 2016, after the opening of the Mine Wars Museum.

## •   MINE WARS MUSEUM   •

It is amazing what a single coin can reveal. Among the many artifacts we gathered for the West Virginia Mine Wars Museum, scrip was and remains the most abundant. As is well known, coal operators of the industrial period did not pay their workers in American dollars, but with company money, commonly referred to as *scrip.* Mainly issued as coins, scrip varied in design from company to company. Usually, the company name appears on one side with a big number 5, 10, 25, and so on. Other artful impressions are often on the other side. Sometimes not. Nearly every coal mining family in Appalachia has a few pieces of scrip stored away in their attic or in an old hope chest. Well before we even opened the museum, locals were offering to donate their scrip. Many coal miners who stop by at the museum still do.

A week before the museum opened, our exhibit designer Shaun Slifer and I sifted through all the scrip to decide which examples to put on display. We have scrip of all sizes, shapes, and regions, and we tried to find a good variety for visitors who wanted to examine the artifacts up close. One piece, however, stood out among all the others. It was a gold colored coin that said

Good for
ONE
Loaf Bread

In most coal towns, scrip was redeemable only at the company store. Families bought their food, clothes, mining equipment, garden tools, seeds, and even furniture at the company store. This resulted in nearly 100-percent profit and control for the companies. Company stores functioned in similar ways to a contemporary Walmart. Both the company store and Walmart provide one-stop shopping for consumers and, thus, drive local shops out of business. Many mine owners refused to allow independent stores on company property, which stifled both consumer options and upward mobility for locals who might want to start a small business.[61] It also meant that these towns, built for the express purpose of meeting the needs of a single industry, prospered or faltered based on the boom and bust cycles of that industry. Predictably, the demand to be paid in American money and not company money became a principal goal of the miners. This one piece of scrip, however, struck me more than all the others because it went as far as to limit purchasing power to a single, specific item. The miner who received this coin—someone we will never know—was given this on his payday. He couldn't buy a ham or a roast, or milk or cheese.

His option was one loaf of bread. The coin I held explained more acutely why a workers' revolt became an armed rebellion than I could ever do in a lecture or essay. When I think of the purpose of the West Virginia Mine Wars Museum, that specific coin often comes to mind.

Shaun Slifer, noting my fixation on this particular piece of scrip, decided to give it a special place apart from the other coins. One can find it in the first exhibit section, where we begin to tell the chronological story of this conflict in the coalfields. I encourage visitors to come to the museum, look at the coin, think about what it means, and then see what followed.

One evening in 2013 Lou Martin called me and said he was putting together a team to create a museum dedicated to Blair Mountain and the Mine Wars. In order to distance the project from any specific activist group, Lou wanted to create a new nonprofit organization called the West Virginia Mine Wars Museum Association. Lou invited Kenny King and me to be on the board of directors and help make the museum a reality. All my activities with FOBM and, naturally, teaching six to seven classes a semester, kept me rather busy, but I felt this museum needed to happen. The coal industry's unwillingness to compromise on Blair and the perpetually cold reception we received from state politicians told me that any notion of a Blair Mountain Historic Park would be years in the making. A successful museum would allow us to broaden public support for Mine Wars preservation, demonstrate the potential for heritage tourism in the coalfields, and perhaps most importantly, function as a means of identity reclamation.

Lou Martin knew of our failed attempt with the Blair Community Center and Museum when he called me in 2013. This is one reason he wanted the new museum to be operated by a new organization. I completely agreed with

Lou's approach and offered my full support. In the following
months, Lou assembled an impressive team. Gordon Simmons
and the West Virginia Labor History Association sponsored
us until we could get our nonprofit status approved. Katey
Lauer, Andrew Munn, and Catherine Moore, organizers
in the 2011 protest march, lent their formidable skills. The
grants and online fundraising drives they organized enabled
us to get off the ground. Catherine created a great website and
promotional videos for fundraising. Lou recruited architect
and professor Greg Galford to help us with our structural
designs. Shaun Slifer designed our exhibits. Kenny King and
Wilma Steele brought their vast knowledge of the history
and their huge artifact collections on board. Terry Steele,
Wilma's husband and a retired UMWA miner, disavowed any
official position with the museum, though he attended all of
our meetings and volunteered countless hours in the building
process. Charles "Hawkeye" Dixon, another retired miner,
UMWA officer, and active member of Local 1440, rounded
out the original team.

The museum would be located at Matewan in Mingo
County. Matewan stood as a center of activity during
the Mine Wars of 1919–1921. The most famous incident
occurred on May 19, 1920, when Matewan's chief of police,
Sid Hatfield, led local deputies and other union sympathiz-
ers in a shootout with Baldwin-Felts detectives after they
had evicted a number of striking miners' families outside of
town. Ten men, including seven mine guards, two miners,
and Matewan's mayor, Cabell Testerman, all died in the
gunfight. A year later, striking miners, aided by Hatfield and
his deputies, fought a pitched battle against mine guards and
West Virginia State Troopers called the Three Days Battle.
The fight took place on both sides of the Tug River and partly
in the town of Matewan itself. Precise numbers are unknown,

but over thirty people may have died. Because of these incidents, and because of Matewan's further connection to events in the famous Hatfield-McCoy Feud, journalists of the time referred to the county as Bloody Mingo.

Historically, then, Matewan made perfect sense. The strong union presence and heritage in the town created a welcoming environment for us, which we needed. If we would have attempted to build our museum in the town of Logan, by contrast, we may have run into serious opposition from local political leadership, many of whom wanted to see Blair Mountain destroyed. Consistent with its history, Logan remains one of the most staunchly anti-union towns in the coalfields. But Matewan, both during the Mine Wars and today, exists as an island of unionism in a sea of company control. In 1920, Frank Keeney wanted to use Matewan as the launch pad from which the union movement in the southernmost coalfields could spring. It is no accident, then, that UMWA Local 1440, situated in Matewan, remains the largest active union local in the nation. Because of their proud history, the current union membership in Matewan embraced the idea of our museum.

Fortune smiled upon us with the location. Even better, Lou secured a space for the museum in a building connected to the Mine Wars. In 1920, the location was home to Reece Chambers' hardware store. Reece's son, Ed Chambers, served as one of Sid Hatfield's deputies. On May 19, 1920, Hatfield, Chambers, the mayor of Matewan, and the other town deputies waited in the hardware store for a group of mine guards who were evicting miners in a nearby coal camp. Hatfield and the others emerged from the hardware store when the mine guards returned for the evening train. After a heated exchange, the famous gunfight ensued. Many decades later, the Mine Wars Museum would sit in the same spot as the hardware store. Although our building is not the original structure, many of the buildings on our street are. There are still bullet holes from the Battle of Matewan in the outside bricks of some of them.

To be in a place so directly connected to the history added to the weight of the museum. The little town has the feel of stepping back in time. I really love the fact that Matewan is so out of the way, even though it drastically cuts down on visitor numbers. This is the kind of history you need to taste in order to really get. You need to feel the morning mist on your face as a coal train screeches and rumbles through an otherwise silent town. You need to see the bullet holes in the battered brick buildings by the tracks. You need to stand on the banks of the Tug and see where Devil Anse and the Hatfields executed the three McCoy brothers. Its remoteness helps preserve that authenticity and makes it a place of pilgrimage for Appalachians and those with a passion for working-class history.

Taking the road to Matewan is also an important part of the pilgrimage. Because of our remote location, you have to drive through the heart of coal country to get to its history. What you see during the drive preps you for the museum. Winding roads, coal tipples, a few beautiful homes situated right next to several shanties, near abandoned little towns, mutts on front porches, a smattering of pizza places. My hope has always been that our museum helps offer an explanation and greater understanding for what one sees on the road to Matewan. If we did our job correctly, someone driving home from our museum may look out the window at the same places with new lenses.

The great thing about old buildings is that they have a history. The bad thing is that they need work. Chambers Hardware had been demolished after the Battle of Matewan.

The building we now inhabit on the same spot dates to 1925. We rented one half of this building. The building's owner gave us free rent for the first two years on the condition that we improved the interior. Although the location and history couldn't have been better, the interior needed a new floor and better electric wiring, the restroom needed to be restored, improvements needed to be made to the ceiling, everything needed a fresh coat of paint, and so on. Lou, Katey, Andrew, and Catherine set to work writing grants and organizing online fundraisers. Through their efforts, we raised around $50,000 in two years and used funds to put in a new floor, add a wall down the center to aid in the placement of exhibits and artifacts, and buy enough supplies to do the rest of the work ourselves.

We scheduled workdays in Matewan where we gathered, made decisions, and put the museum together one piece at a time. Lou and Terry Steele put their carpentering and electrician expertise on display. We washed walls, painted, gave the exterior a facelift, and completed a thousand other small projects until the space was improved enough to house the exhibits. Because funds were so limited, we did most of this labor ourselves and without pay, which was time consuming but extremely rewarding. I vividly remember the whole crew, paint splattered and ruffled, walking over to one of the two restaurants downtown to share a meal and formulate our vision. To build the museum (at least the interior) with our own hands and on our own terms added immeasurable value to the project.

It would be nearly impossible, and somewhat tedious, to give every detail and comment on every contribution made by the original team in the months leading up to the opening of the museum. Suffice it to say, it took a year and a half of work just to prepare the building and raise funds before we could really consider the details of the exhibits and the narrative of the museum. We wanted the history to be comprehensive and general enough to educate the uninitiated while fresh and detailed enough to enlighten scholars and local history buffs. I sat in my office between teaching classes and hammered out the texts—with some contributions from Lou—used to describe exhibits and narrate the Mine Wars story. Writing museum narratives and artifact descriptions was new to me, but I wanted the museum to be more than an encyclopedia on walls. I crafted a coherent, chronological narrative centering around the artifacts and images available to us.

The limited space of the museum hindered our ability to tell the story as completely as we would have liked. I chose a few significant quotes from figures in the Mine Wars that captured the intensity, drama, and general themes of the struggle—remaining true to the story without romanticizing the conflict. Shaun placed the quotes on the wall in huge letters above specific exhibits. One of my great-grandfather's quotes, "One day there will be no more tent colonies, no more gunmen, because of what you people are going through right now," appeared above a replica tent exhibit in our Paint Creek–Cabin Creek section. In our Blair Mountain section, one could find two replica guns—a tommy gun used by the coal company forces and a rifle model typically used by the miners—pointing at one another. Above the miner's gun appeared the quote, "We'll hang Don Chafin on a sour apple tree," which was a song the miners sang as they marched toward Logan County, where Don Chafin was sheriff. The second quote, over the tommy gun, was from Chafin himself just before the battle when he admonished his men to "Kill all the red necks you can." The gun models represented the different weapons accessible to each side—Chafin's men had the best guns of the time, the miners often wielded hunting rifles.

The quotes above them demonstrate the high stakes and the level of hatred on each side. Together we hoped the guns and quotes would make the conflict tangible and the stakes clear, driving home a concise message in the absence of available space and artifacts to elaborate on details. Catherine Moore contributed audio recordings of a few coalfield oral histories to help add a bit more depth.

The replica tent was Wilma Steele's idea. She proposed that we re-create a tent like the ones the miners and their families lived in while on strike during the Mine Wars. Shaun Slifer, who did a wonderful job for us designing the exhibits, dove into the project and produced a replica tent made from the same materials and constructed in the same manner as many of the tents used during the Mine Wars. Visitors could walk into the tent, see household artifacts from the period, and think about what striking families endured to gain basic constitutional rights. The tent is very popular with kids. We also presented archival newsreel footage of Sid Hatfield and the Battle of Blair Mountain. Kenny King and Wilma Steele collected Mine Wars and coalfield artifacts for decades, and their contributions made up the bulk of our collection.

The Mine Wars Museum opened its doors on May 16, 2015. Around 500 visitors attended the opening and listened to speeches from historian David Alan Corbin and UMWA president Cecil Roberts. The oldest running live music radio show in West Virginia, The Wallace Horn Friendly Neighbor Show, recorded by Jeff and Victoria Bosley, also broadcasted live from our museum and provided some traditional mountain music and labor songs for the guests. Two coal mining historic reenactors traveled from Illinois and entertained visitors outside. The people of Matewan seemed genuinely happy with the opening. Many coal miners and their families attended. I'll always remember one coal miner, with black dust still on his shirt from his most recent shift, hoisting his little boy up to the glass case that held the One Loaf of Bread coin.

Opening the museum was only the beginning, of course. We hired Elijah Hooker, one of my former students who went on to earn his bachelor's in history, to staff the museum through its first summer. For the second year, we hired Kimberly McCoy, a local history enthusiast and descendant from the McCoy family of the famous local feud, while Elijah joined our board. Francine Jones, a Matewan resident and town council member, and a few others also joined our board over the years. In December 2018, we hired Kenzie New, our first executive director.

The museum has stayed active and has grown by hosting a variety of events, from documentary film screenings and visiting lectures to live music performances. In 2012, I envisioned a park at Blair Mountain that would become a center for history, education, and the arts in the coalfields. Seven years later, with no park on the horizon, I can nevertheless see this vision emerging organically in Matewan, with the Mine Wars Museum at the core. Our events feature some of the most influential voices in Appalachia today, such as great traditional musicians like Elaine Purkey, leaders of the 2018 Teachers' Strike, filmmakers John Sayles and Mari-Lynn Evans, and historians Fred Barkey and Paul Rakes. We annually coordinate with the Matewan Drama Group, whose members perform an original play on the Mine Wars in Bloody Mingo. The museum has become Ground Zero for Mine Wars history, but it also functions as a center for artists, musicians, and labor leaders. In 2018, leaders in the West Virginia Teachers' Strike presented at the museum. Although the town of Matewan is rather out of the way—even for West

Virginia—I have been consistently surprised at the great attendance for these events. Student groups have traveled from Indiana, Pennsylvania, Maryland, Virginia, Ohio, Missouri, and a host of local secondary schools to visit our little museum.

Even more rewarding are visits to the museum from descendants of actual participants in the Mine Wars. The family of Fred Mooney who, alongside my great-grandfather, led the miners throughout the Mine Wars, traveled to West Virginia to see the museum, which gave me the opportunity to meet Fred Mooney's three surviving sons and interview them. Other families, such as descendants of miners who fought at Blair Mountain and descendants of union organizers have made the pilgrimage as well. I have taken the opportunity to meet them and interview them. It is satisfying to see that the oral tradition, which has kept the history alive in the first place, continues to expand. One doesn't merely get an appreciation for the men and women behind the struggle, but the toll it took on their psyche and their families. I have listened to Fred Mooney's son tell me about his father's suicide. The Dwyer family told me about union organizer Lawrence "Peggy" Dwyer and the numerous attempts on his life. After Blair Mountain, Dwyer had to move his family to Indiana to keep them safe. Some eighty years later, his family came back to Matewan.

Expanding the narrative is as important to me as telling the existing story. There are always more facts to uncover, more stories to be told. It is in this spirit that the museum board enabled me to resurrect *Blair Mountain Journal* under a new name. Since 2016, we have been producing *In These Hills: The Journal of the West Virginia Mine Wars Museum*, which endeavors to continue the mission I began with *Blair Mountain Journal* in 2012. I enlisted the aid of friend and colleague Bill Clough, a professor of English at West Virginia University Institute of Technology, to help with editing. Bill's wife, Kelsey, agreed to handle the design of the journal, the structure of which is nearly identical to the journal I created with FOBM. With the new publication, we keep the public up to speed on museum happenings and promote it, but we also delve deeper into the Mine Wars and continue to educate with new research, oral histories, critical reviews, original fiction, poetry, and exhibit narratives. Words are difficult to destroy. The larger the body of work we create, the longer Blair Mountain will live and the closer we get to reclaiming our identity. Both the museum and the journal contribute to this body.

Don Blankenship actually complimented us on the museum the day he visited back in May 2015. I told him that our museum is small but big things have small beginnings. He laughed politely and walked out. Elijah and I watched him drive away in his baby blue convertible. I counted his visit to the museum as an indicator of our success. Our presence in Matewan concerned him, and if powerful coal operators are concerned, it means progress. The Mind Guard System has held sway over many West Virginians for a long time, trapping mountaineers in a psychological cage, much like the fabled canary in the coal mine. As long as the canary remains in the cage, it has no future; it can only wait for the toxic gasses to come. So it is with West Virginians who continue to cling to King Coal. I believe that the Mine Wars Museum and our efforts to save Blair Mountain function as a key to opening up the cage and letting the canary fly loose. I do not know if the canary can make it out of the mine in time, but if it is free to fly, it at least has a shot.

## CHAPTER SIX

# The Long Road

>>>>> <<<<<

**T**he Second Battle of Blair Mountain became a conflict of attrition. At times, our efforts resembled the strategic predicaments of the Western Front during World War I. No matter what method we tried, a decisive breakthrough eluded us. Enormous efforts netted small gains. During these years, I spent a lot of time reflecting on Frank Keeney's life after Blair Mountain, when he started his own union and led hunger marches. The Mine Wars never really ended for him, and in certain moments, it felt as though I echoed his footsteps, caught up in another fight without end. Nonetheless, everyone at FOBM kept the faith that our small gains would pile up over time and ultimately break our adversary. In the absence of a singular path to success, we would grind our way to victory, pitting our wit, patience, and determination against their money and political power. It was the longest chess match of our lives.

As the years passed, I waged an internal battle of my own. Waging a war of attrition wears on one's soul. On occasional mornings, the first emotion I experienced upon waking was rage. I felt rage toward everything—the delays in action from

regulators, corrupt politicians who did nothing, smug executives and their lies, activists who allowed pettiness and pride
to impede progress. I felt rage toward well-meaning loved
ones and friends who just did not understand and all the
blissfully ignorant people I encountered each day, clueless of
the forces at work around them. Rage at the years of my life
lost. Before my feet hit the bedroom floor, the internal battle
against anger, frustration, and the inability to will our way to
immediate victory threatened to tear me apart from the inside.
Keeping things in perspective helped. Frank Keeney had it
much worse than I did. Many others throughout history have
had it far worse than I can imagine. With a little perspective
in mind, I could recalibrate my emotions, count my blessings,
and continue forward. After all, no one wins by throwing a
pity party for themselves.

Together we pressed on through the bog with patience,
faith, and endurance. After the dust settled from FOBM's
second appearance before the Surface Mine Board (SMB),
Harold Ward, director of surface mining for the West Virginia
Department of Environmental Protection (WVDEP), and I
met in his office on October 21, 2014, with the purpose of
moving forward on the Lands Unsuitable for Mining Petition
(LUMP) settlement. Harold presented me with a map of
the battlefield and each of the permits. The WVDEP map
divided the battlefield into the three sections in accordance
with the preservation plan I had submitted: Southern Flank,
Central Ridgelines, and Northwest Flank. The Southern
Flank, which included Blair Mountain, equaled 424 acres.
The Central Ridgelines totaled 685 acres and the Northwest
Flank equaled 560 acres. Ward told me that if I could indeed
get the Sierra Club and the other groups to drop the state
lawsuit on the LUMP petition, Secretary Huffman would be
willing to declare the Northwest Flank unsuitable for surface

mining. He also informed me that he could set up a meeting with John McDaniel, an executive at Arch Coal, to discuss and potentially proceed with a larger agreement on the battlefield. Ward thought that due to declining stocks and the threat of bankruptcy, Arch Coal might be ready to make a deal. I should sit down with them, he suggested. After consulting with the rest of FOBM, I agreed. A meeting was set for Friday, November 7, 2014.

Three days after the 2014 midterm elections, I met with John McDaniel, Bill Rainey, and Kevin Craig at the West Virginia Coal Association headquarters in Charleston. As head of the Coal Association and a director of the Friends of Coal, Bill Rainey was the public face of the coal industry in West Virginia. Whenever journalists or documentary filmmakers seek to speak with someone in the industry, they talk to Rainey. When the legislature is in session, Rainey is there, sipping coffee with the elected officials and making small talk with them in their offices. He is a small man with dark hair and a thin mustache. He speaks with an easy-going, folksy West Virginia drawl. He is polite. He does not yell or get in your face. He does not lose his cool and can even appear charming when he wants. Although we had seen one another when I lobbied at the legislature for a resolution on Blair Mountain, this meeting was the first time he and I formally met. When I entered the Coal Association's headquarters, a secretary escorted me to a conference room where I waited for several minutes by myself. Rainey entered the room first, smiled at me, shook my hand, and offered me a bottled water with a Friends of Coal emblem on the side.

"So, you teach at Southern over in Logan," he said.

I told him that I did.

"Well, I'm just tickled pink that you decided to stay in West Virginia and teach. We have too many educated people who leave the state."

I smiled and told him I would sleep better at night knowing that I have tickled him pink.

He laughed and we reflected on the week's election. The Republican victory in 2014 could scarcely have been more complete. Democrat Jay Rockefeller, who served as US Senator from 1984 to 2014, resigned. Republican Shelley Moore Capito, the first woman elected to US Congress in state history, left her seat in the House and successfully ran for Rockefeller's open Senate seat. She became the first Republican to represent West Virginia in the Senate since W. Chapman Revercomb in 1959. Nick Joe Rahall, another long-tenured Democrat, lost the Third Congressional District to Evan Jenkins, who had recently switched from Democrat to Republican. Alex Mooney, a Washington, DC, native who recently moved to Charles Town won the Second Congressional District for the Republicans. With Republican David McKinley winning the First District, all of West Virginia's congressional districts became elected Republicans for the first time since 1921, the year of the Battle of Blair Mountain.[1]

Republican victories at the state level were just as impressive. Democrats entered the election controlling the State Senate with a 24–10 margin. After the election, Republicans controlled the Senate with an 18–16 margin. The elections actually left the Senate at a 17–17 tie until Senator Daniel Hall joined the statewide trend of Democrats switching parties and became a Republican. Democrats also lost control of the House of Delegates, which they had controlled since 1931. Republicans gained 17 seats in 2014 giving them a 64–36 majority. For the first time since the early years of the

Great Depression, Republicans controlled both houses of the legislature.[2]

Rainey loved Republicans. "We don't even have to recruit them," he told me. Rainey explained that the Coal Association must court Democrats to get them to support the coal agenda. During the 2014 election cycle, however, new Republican nominees actively courted the favor of the Coal Association. "They come to us," Rainey said. He went on to brag that new Republican candidates arrived at their headquarters a few months prior to the election and asked what they could do to support coal.

After Rainey and I spoke for a few minutes, John McDaniel and Kevin Craig entered the room. McDaniel, in his sixties, worked as an engineer and executive for Arch Coal. He and I initially met two years before in 2012 when FOBM had its first meeting with WVDEP. He was thin, with gray hair and a mustache. On this day, as on the day we first met, he wore a pair of khakis and a golf shirt. Most of the coal company managers and executives I have met do not typically walk around wearing expensive suits. They dress a little more casually, drive pickup trucks or SUVs, and drink Budweiser or Coors—never a craft beer. I am unsure if they drink Coors and Budweiser to give the impression that they are unpretentious or because they are so cheap. McDaniel struck me as the type who would argue over every penny of a deal with a car dealer even if he could easily afford all the cars on the lot. He did not strike me as a vindictive man. Like Rainey, he was polite and levelheaded. I explained FOBM's hopes for preservation and development of the battlefield. When I told McDaniel that I wasn't there so that I could conduct a drum circle and sing "Kumbaya" on top of Blair Mountain, he nearly fell out of his chair laughing.

Kevin Craig served as a captain in the US Army and, at

the time, held a seat in the WV House of Delegates as a Democrat. He was also an executive with CSX railroads and Natural Resource Partners, one of the major landowners on the battlefield. Craig probably spoke less than twenty words over the course of our ninety-minute meeting.

Before the meeting, I had obviously discussed things thoroughly with everyone else in FOBM. We hoped that Arch Coal might be willing to sell their property at Blair Mountain. FOBM certainly didn't have the money to make the purchase—we didn't have any money at all—but, through the various connections of everyone within the group, we might be able to find wealthy individuals willing to step up to the plate. McDaniel responded by letting me know that Arch Coal didn't actually own the land they intended to mine on the battlefield. Just like Alpha Natural Resources, who leased from Natural Resource Partners, Arch leased from a company called United Affiliates. Until McDaniel mentioned it, I had never heard of the company. An internet search after the meeting revealed next to nothing. Regardless, McDaniel told me that they would not be willing to sell any of their holdings "at this time."

We went on to discuss the Army Corps of Engineers' (ACOE's) proposed programmatic agreement. I told them the settlement plan, as drawn up, was completely unacceptable. The very notion of only leaving eight and a half acres on top of Blair Mountain untouched could not be taken seriously. McDaniel said Arch would be willing to increase the acreage. I asked how much. He didn't give me a straight answer and said he would have to discuss that with the shareholders. Rainey said that the Coal Association would go along with whatever the companies decided. Kevin Craig didn't say a word.

We moved on to archeology. Again, bringing up the pro-grammatic agreement, I spent a few minutes deconstructing the validity of their cultural resource surveys. I asked for a complete archeological study and suggested that the coal companies pay for it. Given the difficult terrain and heavily forested area, the best way to begin was with a LiDAR scan of the entire nomination area. LiDAR uses lasers to survey terrain and reveal detailed, precise, three-dimensional maps of a surface. A scanner is attached to an airplane, helicopter, or drone and flown over the appropriate area one wishes to survey. Its recent impact on the field of archeology has been immense. LiDAR scans in Guatemala have revolutionized our understanding of the ancient Maya civilization, for example. The LiDAR is able to strip away the rain forest to reveal the full extent of Mayan cities as foundations of old buildings, pyramids, and roads are then clearly revealed and mapped. Scholars must now write new textbooks because they have vastly underestimated the scope and population of Mesoamerica. If applied to the Blair Mountain Battlefield, LiDAR could reveal every single entrenchment on the ridgelines, every pathway, and reveal discoveries in a matter of days that would take years with only archeologists on the ground. McDaniel and the others listened intently. When I finished, McDaniel said that it seemed like a reasonable and valid request. He said he would look into it, but made no commitment.

We discussed the National Guard base last. I pointed out that I had nothing against a military base. However, if the companies wished to blast part of the battlefield in order to build a 7,000-foot runway for the National Guard, they should be willing to make a significant compromise. The FOBM board had given me the authority to offer a compromise; we would drop all opposition to the National Guard base if the companies allowed for a full archeological survey of Camp Branch before blasting, guaranteed to leave the rest of the battlefield untouched, and either donated or sold their remaining lands. We would not oppose underground mining on the battlefield, but the surface must be untouched.

When I finished this proposal, McDaniel stood up and began pacing the room slowly. Nobody spoke for what seemed like a very long time. McDaniel eventually returned to his seat. He told me that he would discuss this with the executives from the other companies, after which we could have a follow-up meeting. I shook hands with them all and left.

No one at FOBM took this compromise offer lightly. After much discussion, we concluded that Alpha only needed to blast about fifty acres of the battlefield in order to build the needed runway for the base. If they limited blasting to this area, over 1,200 acres of the battlefield would be permanently preserved. We knew that we would take a lot of heat from the environmental community if this compromise came through, but we were willing to take it. The companies could still mine most of the coal reserves underground, which would mean they would actually hire more workers than if they used MTR, the National Guard would get their base, and we would get an archeological study and guaranteed protection for the rest of the site. Everybody would win. I left hoping that I had convinced them to give up the fight and resolve the controversy at Blair Mountain, but I still remembered those boulders by the side of the road on the last day of our protest in 2011. Nothing could be taken for granted.

Six days after my meeting at the Coal Association headquarters, a federal grand jury indicted Don Blankenship on four counts of mine safety and security crimes in connection with the 2010 Upper Big Branch disaster, which killed twenty-nine miners. The mine explosion, referred to as "industrial homicide" by the UMWA, had been the subject of congressional hearings and a regulatory investigation, both of which concluded that Massey Energy had failed to follow safety standards and laws. The district attorney's office in West Virginia, led by Booth Goodwin and Steve Ruby, began climbing up the corporate ladder with a series of convictions. In 2011 and 2012, Massey's security chief, a mine foreman at Upper Big Branch, and a mine superintendent were all convicted of crimes relating to the mine disaster. These crimes included destroying evidence, lying to investigators, and a conspiracy to violate safety laws. Goodwin and Ruby had revealed a corporate culture that consistently ignored safety regulations for the sake of production. When Massey official David Hughart entered into a plea bargain and testified that Blankenship conspired to violate mine safety laws, the district attorney's office finally had a testimony linking the dangerous conditions in the mines to the CEO. Blankenship was indicted in Charleston on November 13, 2014, and released on a $5 million bond.[3]

The notion of a coal company CEO being held accountable for mining deaths appeared to be a watershed moment. With the coal industry facing a dramatic financial downturn and a major CEO awaiting trial, we felt that this momentum could benefit our quest. In early December, representatives from each of the groups on the state LUMP case met with WVDEP reps and members of the governor's staff to reach a preliminary agreement on declaring the Northwest Flank unsuitable for surface mining. The attendees included Diane Beatty, from the Ohio Valley Environmental Coalition; Cindy Rank, representing the West Virginia Highlands Conservancy; Bill Price, with the Sierra Club; Raamie Barker, the governor's senior advisor; Mari-Lynn Evans; Barbara Rasmussen; and myself. Harold Ward at WVDEP; Jason Wandling, WVDEP's attorney; and Aaron Isherwood, representing Sierra's legal team, joined us by conference call. In this meeting, our groups agreed to drop the LUMP case in exchange for WVDEP declaring the Northwest Flank off limits to surface mining. The governor's office agreed to approve the settlement. Much of the meeting revolved around publicity and messaging. Sierra and the other groups wanted to coordinate a PR message with the state government and they talked about what language to use. Discussing the PR did not interest me until the settlement had signatures. FOBM wanted the agreement finalized so that we could concentrate on the permitted areas of the battlefield and reach an agreement with Arch and Alpha. Nonetheless, the meeting went smoothly and the work FOBM had done in arranging this agreement appeared to have reached fruition. From this point, things would be turned over to the lawyers to produce a written settlement that could then be signed by all the parties involved.

The year concluded with one additional gain. On December 29, the SMB issued its final ruling on our September 8, 2014, hearing. On the disappointing side, the SMB did not hold Aracoma Coal accountable for the surface disturbances we found at Camp Branch. The ruling concluded that these disturbances involved timbering and not mining and, thus, were beyond the regulatory scope of the SMB or WVDEP. They also ruled that we produced insufficient evidence to prove that the areas destroyed were of archeological or historical significance. The entrenchments Kenny documented could have been, according the ruling, "naturally occurring phenomena." However, the ruling went on to conclude that "If Aracoma would mine in the buffer zone, additional archeological surveys (e.g. a Phase II or Phase III study) would be appropriate."[4]

The State Historic Preservation Office (SHPO) categorizes archeological surveys into three phases. A Phase I survey is merely a partial examination of a site that looks for general historical or archeological evidence. SHPO accepted the cultural resource surveys conducted by Aracoma as Phase I surveys. Phase II and Phase III surveys are much more comprehensive and detailed, and require excavation and examination. FOBM had been arguing all along that such surveys must be applied to the battlefield and now we finally had a ruling that at least mandated further surveys before mining could be considered. This ruling related to the programmatic agreement because the companies had argued that the cultural resource surveys already conducted were sufficient. The SMB agreed with our assessment.

Thus, 2014 ended with a good deal of momentum. We had stopped the coal industry at Camp Branch, putting the construction of the 7,000-foot runway for the National Guard on hold. We had reached a verbal agreement with the governor's office and WVDEP to declare 560 acres (the Northwest Flank) of the battlefield unsuitable for surface mining. We had secured a mandate for more extensive archeological study of the battlefield as a prerequisite for mining and a new round of negotiations had begun with the industry. Perhaps the scales now tipped in our favor.

## • BLAIR TWO-STEP •

In early January 2015, our attorneys, Aaron Isherwood, Peter Morgan, and Derek Teaney, submitted a written narrative of the LUMP agreement to Jason Wandling, the WVDEP counsel. On January 20, Wandling emailed our representatives and told them he was submitting the request for approval and would get back with them shortly.

Ten days passed without a word from Wandling. The FOBM members and I grew concerned. More than a month had passed since our meeting at the capitol. Because Harold

Ward, the director of Mining and Reclamation at WVDEP, and I had already hashed through the details months earlier, I felt the delay unnecessary. On January 30, I emailed Harold and asked if we should be concerned. On February 2, Harold responded to my email and wrote, "I am completely out of the loop on this since turning it over to legal." Four days later, on a Friday, Isherwood received an email from Wandling telling them that he planned to have a meeting with Harold on the following Monday and he would have an update for us shortly thereafter. For the next two months, we received no communication from WVDEP. Isherwood and our legal team repeatedly sent emails and called. They were repeatedly ignored. On April 17, Aaron had sent me an email confessing his worry that the governor was balking but said he would send yet another email. On April 20, Wandling finally responded with the explanation that he had been unexpectedly out of town and needed to catch up on a backload of work. Two days later, he emailed again and said he scheduled another meeting with the Division of Mining and Reclamation. Two weeks later, Isherwood informed me that our attorneys had arranged a call with Wandling and WVDEP on May 14.

All of us at FOBM had grown skeptical and deeply frustrated by the process. Yet, we elected to be patient. Kenny and I did not have much choice since we were spending most of our spare time preparing for the grand opening of the Mine Wars Museum on May 16. Between teaching full time, writing the exhibit narratives, and all of the other prep work I was doing for the museum, I could only donate an occasional moment on the phone with Isherwood or periodically send an email to check on the situation. However, the museum's grand opening also afforded us an opportunity. Earlier that spring, I wrote a letter inviting UMWA president Cecil Roberts to speak at the grand opening and he accepted. If I could meet privately with

President Roberts, perhaps I could convince him to put the UMWA's weight behind our agreement and help finalize the process. I enlisted the aid of Charles "Hawkeye" Dixon, an officer with UMWA Local 1440 in Matewan and one of our museum founders, and he agreed to set up a private meeting with Roberts during the grand opening event.

Two days before the museum opened, our lawyers finally spoke with Wandling over the phone. Wandling informed them that the state would approve the settlement, but we needed to submit a new LUMP petition to WVDEP. The original LUMP petition, submitted in 2011, asked for protection of the entire battlefield. The new petition, focusing exclusively on the Northwest Flank, should be prepared. Once we submitted the new petition, the state would process it with the intention of granting it. The original petition was over 100 pages. I asked Isherwood if WVDEP would accept a revised petition that singled out the Northwest Flank as opposed to a completely new one. He said he would check with Wandling and get back to me.

As mentioned in the previous chapter, the grand opening of the Mine Wars Museum was an enormous success. Yet, I was too absorbed in trying to move forward with the LUMP settlement to fully enjoy and reflect upon all the hard work put into the museum. As promised, Hawkeye Dixon arranged for Cecil Roberts and me to have a few minutes alone at the Local 1440 Union Hall down the street from our museum. Roberts was born and raised on Cabin Creek and is a descendant of Bill Blizzard, generalissimo of the miners at Blair Mountain. He served a tour of duty in Vietnam and, afterward, became a coal miner. He rose to prominence in the UMWA alongside Richard Trumka, who is the current president of the AFL-CIO. Roberts worked as an organizer in the Miners for Democracy movement, which restored district elections to the union in the 1970s. Elections for district officers had ended when John L. Lewis forced Frank Keeney to resign in 1924, and it is only fitting that a Cabin Creek miner would play a key role in restoring elections to the union. Roberts himself became president of the UMWA in 1995, successfully negotiated wage increases for coal miners, and built a reputation as Don Blankenship's most hated rival. With a number of coal bankruptcies on the horizon, Roberts would lead his union into a new battle over pension funds and healthcare for retired workers. That battle would last until December 2019, when Roberts, alongside Joe Manchin, would secure pensions for 92,000 miners nationwide and healthcare for some 13,000 families.[5] At age 68, with grey hair and a goatee, Roberts's charismatic speeches resembled those of a zealous country preacher. Folks at the museum's grand opening treated him like a celebrity. After giving the museum's dedication speech, he signed autographs and took selfies with miners and their families.

I briefed President Roberts on the current situation with Blair Mountain and our efforts to finalize the LUMP settlement. He told me the UMWA would gladly support the settlement and said he would personally call Governor Tomblin and speak to him on our behalf. Phil Smith, the UMWA's main publicist, would be our contact person and would keep us up to speed. I thanked President Roberts. We shook hands and then proceeded with the day's events. The meeting encouraged me, and I hoped the UMWA could give us the push we needed.

Roberts remained true to his word. On May 27, he called Governor Tomblin. According to Phil Smith, who briefed me on the call, Roberts told Tomblin that the UMWA wanted to see the settlement finalized and for the Northwest Flank to be declared unsuitable for mining. I felt it was an important moment. For nearly twenty years, the UMWA had vocally supported surface mining, and to see them actively lobbying on our behalf represented tremendous progress. One week later, Isherwood emailed me and told me that he heard from Wandling. WVDEP would accept a revised LUMP petition as I requested instead of a completely new petition. This would save us a lot of time and work. Kenny and I prepared the revised petition in June. We included updated archeological information conducted by Harvard Ayers and Kenny King on the Northwest Flank. In 2013, the National Geographic Channel show *Diggers* filmed Harvard and Kenny as they explored new areas around Crooked Creek Gap. We provided links to filmed footage of their work and seven photos of the new sites found by Harvard and Kenny. According to WVDEP's regulations, new information concerning a historic site must accompany a new petition. We included this recent information along with declarations of fact concerning the study and the Northwest Flank by Kenny and me. We also provided appropriate maps and a new written request for the unsuitable declaration concerning the Northwest Flank. Sierra's legal team then completed a polished form of the settlement and sent everything to WVDEP on June 24. At that point, the state had everything they requested to finalize the settlement.

Yet, the state continued to delay. Wandling did not acknowledge that WVDEP had begun reviewing our materials until July 13. Isherwood attempted to get more specifics and a timeline from WVDEP but kept getting the cold shoulder. By July 24, Isherwood, a veteran of years of environmental litigation, emailed me and noted that the state's behavior rivaled "the most bizarre experience of my professional career." Wandling finally contacted Isherwood on August 6. He informed Isherwood that the state was still on board to approve the settlement, but WVDEP may need to hold a public hearing if they declared the Northwest Flank unsuitable for mining. Harold Ward called me the following week and gave me a little more insight into the state's position. Harold wanted me to meet with Greg Wooten of NRP and John McDaniel of Arch before the state signed off on the LUMP settlement. Harold explained that the state and the coal executives favored a comprehensive settlement over the battlefield, and he believed it could happen. Because of recent coal bankruptcies and looming bankruptcy of other companies, Harold believed the industry may want to "pick their battles" and might be willing to buckle at Blair Mountain. I reminded Harold of my meeting with McDaniel and Rainey in 2014. In spite of their promises to move forward on a compromise, nothing had occurred since then. Harold insisted that circumstances had changed and the industry should be more willing to resolve Blair Mountain than ever before. After a discussion with everyone else at FOBM, I called Harold back two days later and agreed to his proposal to meet with Wooten and McDaniel.

Although Harold promoted yet another meeting with the industry and a comprehensive settlement, the months passed and the governor's office and industry executives continued to dance around our overtures for resolution. By September 1, Harold emailed me to say that both Wooten and McDaniel were on board for a meeting. Meanwhile, Wandling informed Isherwood and the legal team that WVDEP had reviewed our draft of the settlement and our revised petition. Although WVDEP found both the settlement and the revised petition acceptable, Wandling indicated to our legal team that they would not finalize the agreement until I met with the industry, hoping for a broader resolution.

As autumn progressed, all eyes turned to the trial of Don

Blankenship. The trial began on October 1 and stretched all the way to the first week of December. The prosecution effectively presented evidence that Blankenship microman-aged his coal operations and favored production over safety. Blankenship's memos to his coal underlings showed that he did not want to spend money on expensive bolts that would secure the ceilings of mine shafts, criticized his engineers for spending too much time on proper ventilation, and threat-ened to fire anyone who questioned the unsafe conditions in his mines.[6] The evidence appeared overwhelming and, yet, the jury deliberated for nine days. Apparently, one juror held up the deliberations. Rumors spread throughout the coal-fields that this juror had either been bribed or threatened by Blankenship. Although I have seen no evidence to support the claim, many still believe it. Finally, on December 3, the jury reached its verdict and found Blankenship guilty of con-spiracy to willfully violate mine health and safety standards.[7]

About three hours after the jury rendered their verdict in the Blankenship trial, Harold Ward called me. I had just given my last final of the semester and was driving home from campus when the phone rang. Harold asked if I would be willing to meet with Greg Wooten the next day. I found it odd that, after so many months of trying, Harold finally secured the long-promised meeting within hours of Blankenship's conviction. Nonetheless, I told him I would meet with Wooten. Harold informed me that Wooten wanted to meet at 1:00 p.m. in the lobby of Charleston's Embassy Suites Hotel—the same hotel where Blankenship was staying for the duration of the trial. I asked Harold if he would be there. He informed me that he would not; only Wooten would be there. Harold wished me luck and said, "I hope you two can work something out."

It seemed evident that the state wished to wash its hands clean of any proactive role in resolving preservation and protection of the battlefield. Our proposal regarding the Northwest Flank enabled WVDEP to protect over a third of the battlefield without interfering with any mining permits or directly dealing with the coal companies. No one could argue that WVDEP killed jobs with this action. There were no jobs to be killed, no mining operations to halt with this deal. And yet they still would not finalize the settlement because, I suspect, they feared backlash from the industry. I found it frustrating that in our efforts to sidestep directly dealing with coal executives and minimize the political risk for the state, they simply steered us back to the table with the very executives whose best offer to date had been a programmatic agreement and a measly promise to leave eight and a half acres at Blair untouched.

The Embassy Suites Hotel sits right across from the Charleston Town Center Mall in the middle of downtown. There is a sports bar connected to hotel and this is where Wooten and I went after meeting in the lobby on December 4. We grabbed a table, ordered coffee, and sized each other up for over an hour. Wooten has been a prominent resident of Logan County all of his life. He is no outsider. Wooten and his family attend a local church. His daughters graduated from Logan High School and Wooten paid the school's expenses for at least one of their proms. He is a Republican, and yet he chums around with Joe Manchin at events like the Greenbrier Classic golf tournament. He has known Governor Earl Ray Tomblin and his family for decades and could get a private audience with the governor anytime he wished. As I have mentioned before, he is tall. When we met, he leaned back in his seat much of the time—not in a laid-back manner, but with the air of someone comfortable with wielding power and giving orders.

"What's in it for us?" he asked, after several minutes of

small talk. "If I give you the Northwest Flank, what does my company get in return?"

According to Wooten, the state would only make the deal on the Northwest Flank with his approval. Furthermore, Wooten, or the companies he claimed to speak for, wanted something. I told him the same thing I told McDaniel and Rainey when I met with them the year before; we would be willing to compromise on Camp Branch, enabling the 7,000-foot runway to proceed if they gave up the rest. I reminded him that Alpha Natural Resources had filed for bankruptcy in August and, based on its stock market performance, Arch Coal would soon follow suit. As they restructured their holdings, it would behoove them to shed some of the fat, so to speak. The Blair Battlefield was the perfect place to do so. Wooten wavered on any commitment but said that we needed to have another meeting with all the relevant parties. I agreed on the condition that we held the meeting in a timely fashion. "Harold Ward has spent six months trying to get you to meet with me," I said. "I don't want to wait half a year for more talks." I told him that FOBM and the other groups wanted a speedy resolution. Wooten agreed to move quickly and, by December 7, Greg Wooten, John McDaniel, and Kevin Craig had agreed to meet with me at Jackson Kelly's offices in Charleston on January 6, 2016, at 10:00 a.m.

I did not want to go to this meeting alone. After speaking with everyone at FOBM and Isherwood at Sierra Club, we thought that Betsy Merritt would be the perfect choice to join me. Betsy was an attorney for the National Trust for Historic Preservation. FOBM had been cultivating a relation-ship with the National Trust for over a year and, although we had never met in person, Betsy and I had been on numerous conference calls together. Her preservation record is exten-sive and impressive. Most recently, Betsy had worked with preservationists and Princeton University to help achieve an agreement on the Princeton Battlefield. Her legal expertise and experience would be a huge asset.

Betsy flew into Charleston from Washington, DC, the night before our meeting on January 6. We had already talked through what we wanted and what to expect and both of us felt prepared. I met her at her hotel an hour before our scheduled meeting, and we proceeded to Laidley Tower, the tallest building in Charleston and the home offices of Jackson Kelly. We took an elevator to one of the top floors where Wooten, John McDaniel, Kevin Craig, and their Jackson Kelly attorney, Robert McLusky, awaited us in a conference room.

The meeting lasted for nearly three hours. I did most of the talking on our end as Betsy took extensive and detailed notes.[8] They asked about FOBM's vision for a park at Blair and I went into about a fifteen-minute sales pitch on the economic and educational potential of a historic park in the area. Wooten responded that Hatfield-McCoy ATV trails were already planned for the area after mining occurred, so they could still make money through tourism without a historic park.

"What are the implications for our ability to extract our reserves?" Wooten asked. I spoke about the significance of landscape. A park at Blair Mountain would not be appealing to anyone if half the mountain is blown away. Adkins Fork, of course, is the permit which overlapped onto Blair Mountain proper. I asked, "What would Arch need to give up Adkins Fork?"

"Bankruptcy," Wooten replied. He went on to speak of his distrust for the environmental groups. "How can we ensure that you have the commitment of everyone else to go along with a resolution?" McLusky mentioned that Alpha had offered to donate 244 acres on Blair and the enviros had balked. What would keep them from balking now? Wooten added that there were natural gas interests on the battlefield as well. Would the enviros allow drilling for gas? I told him I did not know.

Kevin Craig echoed Wooten's skepticism. He said, "The enviros just want to stop mining and kill coal. They are using the history just as an excuse to keep coal in the ground."

McLusky abruptly interjected and unexpectedly changed the focus to the Mine Wars Museum. Why did we need to protect Blair if we already had a museum in Matewan? McDaniel and McLusky then went on to say that our museum was full of artifacts that Kenny King stole from company lands. I told them that the artifacts on display at the Mine Wars Museum came from Crook Creek Gap and were not extracted from company lands.

We returned to discussing Adkins Fork. I mentioned that they could donate the land and get a tax write-off. Wooten responded that a tax write-off would not work for them and was not enough of an incentive. He also mentioned that the Adkins Fork Permit, on Blair Mountain proper, has the most coal reserves on the battlefield and was worth more money than the rest of the acreage combined. "Plus," he added, "in order to accommodate tourists at Blair Mountain, you have to level out some land for parking. There's no place for even tour buses to pull off the road. It is better to incorporate a park into a post-mining plan than leave the mountain untouched."

McClusky interjected that there were parts of Blair Mountain they could be persuaded to preserve. McDaniel and Wooten both agreed that they wanted a complete resolution, not a piecemeal resolution. They agreed that the state would not agree to a settlement on the Northwest Flank without a greenlight from them.

"You let us mine and then we'll give you all the post-rec-lamation lands," Wooten said.

McDaniel shook his head and said the landowners would "shoot us over this." He looked at me and asked, "What could you live with?"

I replied no mining on Adkins Fork.

McDaniel offered that they could give us other lands along Route 17 which were a part of the Miners' March in 1921. He said that there was the potential for some compromise. Wooten then threw out the possibility of preserving 1,000 acres.

Talk eventually veered toward the National Guard base. Wooten said that the National Guard would participate in the resolution process and offer some of their resources to help with a historic park. Wooten said that, in addition to a park, "you could sell tickets to watch the planes take off and land."

I asked them how much they would individually profit from the National Guard base. Wooten claimed that they would not profit at all.

"Why did you agree to build them a runway then?" I asked.

"For God and country," Wooten said.

I found myself at a loss for words. Betsy paused in her note-taking and looked up in disbelief. McLusky sat just to my right at the conference table and I noticed him looking down at his notepad and grinning. Wooten did not grin at all. He just stared right at me.

The talk then drifted to the upcoming presidential election. How would the political landscape influence a settlement?

"What will you do if Hillary Clinton is elected?" I asked. "Mountaintop removal could be halted altogether if we get another four to eight years of Democratic control."

They shrugged it off. Craig said that if Hillary won the election it would not induce them to abandon their coal reserves on the battlefield. "We're not worried about Hillary," McDaniel added. "We can tie up any new regulations in litigation for years."

By the time we approached the three-hour mark, we realized that we would reach no resolution on that day. McLusky said he would draw up a new settlement which would be an improvement from the eight and a half acres and preservation plan offered in the programmatic agreement. Once he finished a draft of the new settlement, he would send it to us and we could perhaps then work toward fine-tuning the details until we reached an agreement everyone could live with. We all consented that this seemed the best way to proceed and ended the meeting. McLusky promised to be prompt in drafting a new proposal.

Thirty minutes later, Betsy and I sat at a booth at an Outback restaurant. I felt exhausted and asked Betsy for her thoughts.

"We made real progress today," she said. "We have a better understanding for who they are and what they want. But there is still a long road ahead."

## • ARBITRARY AND CAPRICIOUS •

As coal in Appalachia reaches its end, more and more people have turned to look back at its beginning. Recalling the story of Blair Mountain and the Mine Wars offers perspective on these times as well as guidance. The Second Battle of Blair Mountain is a part of a larger war over history and memory in America, and our efforts have helped reinsert the history into the present collective consciousness. Keeping Blair in the public conversation, in fact, became a crucial way of continuing the preservation fight. Our efforts at FOBM and with the Mine Wars Museum provided a firm foundation upon which to build, but we were still limited in number and capabilities. Fortunately, we were not alone. Others, such as historian James Green and filmmaker Randall MacLowry, carried the torch in ways we could not. Green, a prominent labor historian from the University of Massachusetts, published his comprehensive study of the Mine Wars, *The Devil Is Here in These Hills,* in 2015. Impressed with the story, McLowery directed a two-hour documentary on the Mine Wars based largely off Green's work. The film included all the main historians of the subject: David Corbin, James Green, Rebecca Bailey, John Hennen, Paul Rakes, and my doctoral advisor, Ron Lewis, among others. Taking its cue from the book, the storyline focused on my great-grandfather as the central figure.

*American Experience: Mine Wars* premiered on PBS to a national audience twenty days after Betsy Merritt and I met with the coal executives in Charleston. Before the premiere, I sent an email to Greg Wooten, John McDaniel, General James Hoyer, and WVDEP Director Randy Huffman reminding them of the film and inviting them to watch. None of them responded with a review, but of course, I was not asking for nor expecting a friendly critique. I wanted them to understand that the existence of the film represented a renewal of interest in a past they may deem uncomfortable or worthy of destruction. They could blow up a battlefield or be complicit in such, but they could not destroy the history. Efforts of people like James Green and Randall MacLowry prove this. These acts also demonstrate that telling genuine history is an act of preservation. Today the film is widely used in West Virginia classrooms and it gives me comfort that a new generation of mountaineers will learn a story absent from my own educational experience.

Watching the film invigorated me. At once, I felt the pride

of knowing the Mine Wars had reached a national audience in documentary form for the first time while feeling the perpetual weight of the struggle in which we at FOBM found ourselves. The history and our efforts to protect it became nearly indistinguishable in my mind. MacLowry interviewed me for the film in 2014, exactly one week after my meeting at the Coal Association headquarters. I shared my knowledge of Frank Keeney while the events of our fight swirled in my head. Watching the premier in 2016 served as a pressing reminder that we had unfinished business with the coal industry. Although the conflict confronting FOBM did not compare with the difficulties the miners and my great-grandfather endured, it was nonetheless a continuation. The film greeted me like a cup of water handed to a marathon runner as he plods along.

And plod along we did. Three weeks after *American Experience: Mine Wars* premiered, I emailed Wooten and McDaniel again and asked for an update on the counterproposal settlement they promised. Neither of them responded. On April 5, I emailed them once more. This time, Wooten responded, "Charles, as I'm sure you are aware, the mining industry continues to be assailed on every front. Since our meeting, Arch has filed for bankruptcy, Alpha continues to work through its Chapter 11, and that's just the tip of the iceberg when one looks at the challenges of our industry." At our January 6 meeting, I asked Wooten what it would take for Arch Coal to give up the Adkins Fork Permit. He told me "bankruptcy." Four months later, bankruptcy had arrived and nothing had changed. FOBM had met with industry executives on numerous occasions, offered a compromise that would enable the 7,000-foot runway to be built for the military, and been repeatedly met with hollow promises. As a negotiated settlement appeared unrealistic, we pondered how to proceed.

Six days after Wooten sent me the email, an answer arrived when I received a call from Aaron Isherwood.

"We won the National Register lawsuit," he declared as soon as I said hello.

Vindication. After six years of litigation, we finally won the delisting case. To recap, on September 9, 2010, FOBM, Sierra Club, the National Trust for Historic Preservation, the Ohio Valley Environmental Coalition, the West Virginia Highlands Conservancy, and the West Virginia Labor History Association all joined forces and filed a federal lawsuit against the Department of Interior for their erroneous delisting of the battlefield. The DC Federal District Court initially ruled that our organizations lacked standing to file the lawsuit, as none of us were landowners. We appealed the ruling and won a decision in the District Court of Appeals in 2014. The Court of Appeals validated the standing of our organizations and remanded the decision back to the District Court for a ruling. Two years later, on April 11, 2016, Federal Judge Reggie B. Walton ruled in our favor and vacated the 2009 delisting of the Blair Mountain Battlefield from the National Register.

In addition to the victory in our favor, Judge Walton's ruling also revealed interesting details concerning the delisting of the battlefield. As explained in chapter one, Jackson Kelly, representing Massey Energy, Arch Coal, and Natural Resource Partners, submitted a second landowner list to the State Historic Preservation Office (SHPO) after the battlefield nomination had already been forwarded to the Keeper's office. On the Jackson Kelly list, the majority of landowners objected to the listing of the battlefield. Susan Pierce, the director of SHPO, in communicating with the Keeper's office, initially questioned the validity of the Jackson Kelly list, favoring instead the original landowner list previously forwarded to the Keeper. However, according to the court ruling, Randal Reid-Smith, Commissioner of the West Virginia Department of Arts, Culture, and History and Susan Pierce's boss, overruled Pierce and sent a letter to the Keeper's office in favor of Jackson Kelly's list.[9]

The court ruling revealed further discrepancies. After Jackson Kelly submitted their list, FOBM, under an initiative from Harvard Ayers, hired West Virginia attorney John Kennedy Bailey to research the land titles on the battlefield. Bailey's research discovered inaccuracies on the Jackson Kelly list. Most notably, two supposed landowners who signed affidavits objecting to the listing of the battlefield, August Phillips and Corbet Craddock, were already dead. FOBM submitted Bailey's research to SHPO and asked for a review. Paul Loether, of the Keeper's office, wrote SHPO and advised them to give Kennedy's work serious consideration. SHPO, however, refused, stating that they were no longer under any obligation to consider more information regarding the battlefield. Without SHPO's cooperation in properly processing the information, the Keeper delisted the battlefield.[10]

In Judge Walton's words, SHPO and the Keeper's actions "contain very little, if any, indicia of reasoned decision making. In terms of deliberation, the Agencies did not adequately scrutinize Bailey's research. This inadequacy included failing to meaningfully address his assertion that Phillips and Craddock had died."[11] Walton further observed that SHPO and the Keeper's Office lacked transparency in their ruling and failed to give any good reasoning as to why they accepted the Jackson Kelly list over the original list in the nomination. In short, "the Keeper failed to fulfill its duty to examine the relevant evidence and draw reasoned conclusions from it."[12] Walton concluded by ruling that the Keeper's decision to delist the battlefield was "arbitrary and capricious." Judge Walton

vacated the delisting and remanded the decision back to the
Keeper of the National Register.[13]

This brought us one step closer. We took the position that
the original listing should stand, meaning that Blair Mountain
had belonged on the National Register since 2009. WVDEP
and other state agencies should be legally required to enforce
the Historic Preservation Act.

The court victory further exposed the blatant corruption
presiding over the decision to delist. After the coal industry
submitted their landowner list and made their preferences
known, Commissioner Randal Reid-Smith directly intervened and overruled the director of SHPO, who approved the
National Register nomination. Joe Manchin, then serving as
governor, personally appointed Reid-Smith as commissioner
and, although court documents do not claim it, I cannot
imagine Reid-Smith writing a letter overruling his own staff's
conclusions without the governor's approval. Personal experience in West Virginia politics leads me to speculate that
someone in the coal industry called the governor, the governor
then called the commissioner; the commissioner then altered
the legitimate conclusions of SHPO to suit the interests of
the coal industry.

Who, then, possibly influenced Manchin and why? It could
have been Don Blankenship, who served as CEO of Massey
Energy at the time and would have been involved in plans for
the National Guard base at Camp Branch. But Bill Rainey,
as head of the West Virginia Coal Association and a chief
lobbyist for the industry, could also easily have been the one
to reach out to the governor. Or perhaps Greg Wooten personally intervened. He and Joe Manchin have appeared in
Facebook pictures together, enjoying a golf tournament at the
Greenbrier Resort. Additionally, Natural Resource Partners
was one of the companies represented by Jackson Kelly on

the issue. Perhaps all of them intervened. Did they want Blair delisted because they hated the idea of a monument to organized labor and wanted to cover up the history? Was it because they wanted to build a National Guard base? As revealed in chapter three, discussions between the industry and the military were underway precisely when the battlefield was delisted. Building a military installation and using patriotism as an excuse to destroy unwanted history is a clever plan, if indeed that was their intent. Did they simply want the money they could get from the coal? It is unlikely we will ever know the full range of motives. In a general sense, one can reasonably surmise that greed, pride, and hubris serve as underlying motivating factors. The inescapable fact is that a few key power players in West Virginia played a decisive role in fraudulently delisting a national historic property protected under the law so that it could be destroyed.

We could not immediately celebrate. Isherwood cautioned me that the Department of Interior might appeal Judge Walton's decision. FOBM postponed any action on the ruling until we knew for certain what Interior would do. Apparently, they were unsure of what to do themselves. On June 10, Interior filed a Notice of Appeal on Judge Walton's decision, but on July 26, they dropped the appeal. With the court victory now on firm ground, we acted swiftly. I emailed Greg Wooten and John McDaniel and asked, now that the federal case was over, if they would be willing to revisit our negotiations. Neither of them responded. On behalf of FOBM, I also sent emails to Harold Ward at WVDEP and Roger Calhoun at the Office of Surface Mining Reclamation and Enforcement (OSMRE) to request a meeting to discuss the impact the court ruling would have on their regulatory obligations. Although we had met with the ACOE numerous times in the past, the ruling would have no impact on their regulatory status. The ACOE does not distinguish between properties eligible for listing on the National Register and those on the National Register, so a meeting with them would be a waste of time. We needed to meet with WVDEP because their obligation changes for properties listed on the register. We needed OSMRE—the federal oversight agency—to be present in order to ensure WVDEP did not try to weasel their way out of those new obligations.

In a new addition to our list of agencies to pester, we contacted the West Virginia Division of Forestry. So far, the industry and the agencies had managed to sidestep any responsibility for the disturbances on Camp Branch by claiming timbering as the culprit. We wanted to close this loophole. Charles Dye served as the head of Forestry in 2016 and I emailed him, explained our situation, and requested a meeting. I emailed WVDEP, OSMRE, and the Division of Forestry all on the same day and, interestingly, they all responded exactly five days later and within an hour of one another. WVDEP and OSMRE agreed to meet with FOBM on August 26. The Division of Forestry scheduled a meeting with us on September 12.

By 2016, all of us at FOBM were seasoned veterans of regulatory agency meetings. We knew we needed to articulate in writing what we wanted WVDEP to do and we chose to do so by requesting an informal review. According to the regulations, a citizen or citizen's group that demonstrates a vested interest may request an informal review from WVDEP concerning potential regulation violations or permit issues. The avenue of an informal review request provided the best method of holding WVDEP accountable for their obligations regarding the battlefield. I spent several days trying to build my version of a legal case and eventually produced a letter we could present at the meeting. The final version requests that WVDEP order modifications to all three surface mining permits to prohibit mining within 1,000 feet of the battle-field acreage and for the Northwest Flank to be immediately declared unsuitable for surface mining. Such measures, if taken, would provide permanent protection from mountain-top removal.

Joe Stanley and I presented this informal review request to WVDEP and OSMRE in the August 26 meeting. OSMRE's regional director, Roger Calhoun, attended, along with one of his assistants. About ten representatives from WVDEP were present. Harold Ward could not make the meeting, but sent his deputy, Lewis Halstead, to head up the WVDEP reps. We handed copies of the request to everyone and went over it point by point. Joe and I could not help but notice the contrast between this and previous meetings with the agencies. In the early meetings after the protest march, most of the reps sat stone faced with their arms crossed. One could feel the tension in the room. By 2016, we knew most of the reps by name and had established a rapport with them. As we went over the letter, the reps scribbled notes and asked us questions. I joked to them that they took more notes than my students did. I kept an eye on Roger Calhoun throughout the discussion. Calhoun nodded his head with each regulatory point we raised as though he agreed. This was important, as OSMRE oversaw WVDEP's enforcement. At the conclusion, we all shook hands. The WVDEP reps told us they would begin work on the request right away and we left feeling confident.

Next in line came the Division of Forestry. Myers and Kenny joined me for this meeting, which took place at the Division's headquarters in Charleston. We were pleased to find the Forestry reps affable and welcoming. Of the seem-ingly endless number of meetings I have attended regarding Blair Mountain, this one occurred minus any of the usual tension. Charles Dye, director of the Division of Forestry, and his staff were open and helpful. They projected a map onto the wall and briefed us on the current timber operations in the vicinity of the battlefield. We were glad to learn that no current operations intruded with a thousand feet of the battle-field. Unfortunately, Mr. Dye elaborated on his department's severe limitations. In West Virginia, a private landowner does not have to apply for a permit to begin a timber operation on his or her own property. Unlike a proposed coal mine, where multiple regulatory agencies must approve before mining can begin, timbering can begin at the owner's leisure with no environmental review at all. The owner is required to notify the Division of Forestry and register their operation once it has begun, but Forestry cannot prevent an operation from starting on private property.

Dye further explained that if an owner fails to register with Forestry, they can be fined or have their operation sus-pended. The Division can also regulate operations where there are known endangered flora or fauna. We asked Dye about the National Historic Preservation Act. He said he had never dealt with the Preservation Act in all his years in Forestry. We informed him that state agencies must enforce the Preservation Act for a historic property listed on the National Register, privately owned or not. We offered the details of Judge Walton's decision to vacate Blair's delisting. This meant that the March 2009 listing is now valid again, according to our position. Frye did not dispute our conclu-sions. He confessed to being a bit of history buff himself and agreed that if they learned of timber operations on the battle-field area, they would contact SHPO, after which they would evaluate the operation.

Based on the surprising lack of state regulations on timber-ing, this meeting went about as well as we could have hoped.

No one disputed our positions and the leverage gained by winning the lawsuit appeared to change the tune of the regulators. Once again, however, another roadblock materialized. On September 30, Stephanie Toothman, then acting Keeper of the National Register, sent me an email. WVDEP and OSMRE had apparently been in contact with the Keeper as a result of our informal review request and asked for confirmation on Blair's status on the National Register. The Keeper informed them and FOBM that even though Judge Walton vacated the delisting, they still refused to list Blair Mountain on the National Register. They had hired a private contractor to search the land deeds, go over the submitted landowner lists and render a new decision on the battlefield. After reading the email, I called Lewis Halstead at WVDEP and he confirmed what I suspected. WVDEP would not enforce the Preservation Act without verification from the Keeper. In light of this information, I asked him if he would put our informal review request on hold until the Keeper rendered the final decision. Halstead agreed. Final victory eluded us once more.

## • GHOSTS OF BLAIR MOUNTAIN •

As the year drew on, my office phone began ringing more often. Journalists from all over the country, and some from Europe and Asia, called me regarding the upcoming presidential election. More specifically, they wanted to know why West Virginians seemed so enthusiastic about Donald Trump. Although West Virginia's five electoral votes played an insignificant role in the 2016 election, journalists nonetheless sought out voters from my home in hopes of explaining Trump's unlikely popularity. Most journalists overlooked the fact that Trump's appeal fit into a larger movement of rising conservative nationalism, antiglobalization, and authoritarianism influencing politics around the world. Trump's ideals and rhetoric echoed from Brexit to Brazil. Largely ignoring these global trends, the American media looked to rural Appalachia for a simplistic explanation.

That West Virginians supported the Republican nominee surprised no one. A number of factors contributed to Trump's popularity in West Virginia: the prevalence of the Mind Guard System and its impact on shaping the worldview of West Virginians, local Democratic corruption, the successful use of identity politics by the RNC and right-wing media, fear and loathing of perceived liberal elites in academia and Hollywood, racist xenophobia, and the decline of unionism. To this, add the fact that Hillary Clinton was an unpopular candidate and the Democrats were overconfident. The Clinton campaign largely ignored Wisconsin, Michigan, and rural Pennsylvania, taking the Rust Belt for granted, just as Gore took West Virginia for granted in 2000. It cost them both dearly.

As someone who taught in the coalfields, I had a front row seat to the entire phenomenon, and I had seen it all before. West Virginians who knew nothing of Blair Mountain and lived in the Mind Guard System were primed for Trump. The Trump rallies I watched on television closely resembled the coal rallies conducted by Don Blankenship. Both types of rallies were emotionally driven, hypernationalistic, authoritarian spectacles. The rallies I witnessed in Appalachia fostered a cult of personality around King Coal; the rallies I witnessed in the 2016 presidential campaign conjured a cult of personality around a reality television star.

In the end, Trump carried every county in the state. Meanwhile, Jim Justice, a coal operator, owner of the Greenbrier Resort, and richest man in West Virginia, won the governor's race. Justice promoted himself as a regional

Trump. As a political outsider and successful businessman, he seemed to fit the part. He frequently bragged about his close relationship with the Trump family and, naturally, promised to make coal great again. Both candidates vowed to deregulate the industry and gut the regulator agencies. Trump and Justice's victory in 2016 speaks volumes about the profound impact of collective historical ignorance. If West Virginians had learned anything at all from Blair Mountain, the Mine Wars, the industrial disasters, or the P. T. Barnum industrialist-politicians throughout our state's history, then big businessmen like Trump and Justice would have never stood a chance of winning. Obviously, our road to save Blair Mountain became longer and rockier with Trump in the White House and Justice in Charleston.

A few days after the election, I traveled to New York City for the premiere of *Blood on the Mountain*. Mari-Lynn Evans and Jordan Freeman directed and produced this sweeping documentary about King Coal's impact and influence in West Virginia. I think of the film as Appalachia's *Apocalypse Now*. Told in a nonlinear, nearly abstract fashion, the film spans a century of coal company rule from a torrent of angles. Subjects such as Blair Mountain, black lung, union murders, Don Blankenship, mine disasters, and corrupt politics assault the viewer with no narration—only captured moments on film accompanied by interviews. It is intended to shock the uninitiated. Before one can process a coal slurry plant larger than the Hoover Dam, the film jumps to a mine explosion, and then to the murder of union leaders and their families, all separate events beneath the umbrella of coal. The film premiered at the Landmark Sunshine Theatre in Manhattan on November 14.

For me, the film felt like looking at an old high school yearbook. I knew all the faces. Terri and Wilma Steele, who

were FOBM members for a time and worked to create the
Mine Wars Museum, lent their voices. Hawkeye Dixon,
another Mine Wars Museum founder, spoke about Don
Blankenship and the fall of the union. It is odd knowing
nearly everyone in a documentary, knowing the stories
behind their stories. Mari-Lynn interviewed me for the film
in 2013, right in the midst of our tussle over Camp Branch.
The film includes footage of the Camp Branch Surface Mine
permit renewal hearing in 2013, but the viewer is not given
an explanation for what is on the screen. The film simply
spotlights the mayhem and asks, "What do you make of
this?"

The New Yorkers did not seem to know what to make of
it. Nick Mullins, who is a former coal miner turned activist
and writer, and I shared a panel after one of the screenings in
Manhattan. We advised the audience to remember this film
when reading or watching a story about "Trump Country."
The film would go on to be released on Netflix, win a
number of awards, and be nominated for an Emmy. Awards
and acclaim aside, Mari-Lynn and Jordan's most enduring
achievement is that the film is authentically West Virginian.
Mountaineers told their own stories of grim and grit and
the film preserved them. *Blood on the Mountain* revealed an
undercurrent of resistance in the mountains—an Appalachian
Reconquista, if you will.

Although we still lacked a resolution on Blair Mountain
and we rode against the prevailing political winds, our work
produced its own monuments. *Blood on the Mountain* and
the continued success of the Mine Wars Museum testified
to this. A month after the election, UMWA Local 1440
invited the entire museum board to their annual Christmas
Dinner in Matewan and declared us honorary members of
the United Mine Workers of America. This was no small

act. President Cecil Roberts personally endorsed the resolution voted on by Local 1440. As we accepted the honor, I naturally thought about Frank Keeney. He helped build the union in West Virginia, but after Blair Mountain and the subsequent treason trials, UMWA president John L. Lewis forced my great-grandfather to resign as district president. Keeney remained outside the UMWA for the rest of his life. During the Depression, as Keeney formed his own union, the UMWA attacked and slandered him. They dubbed Keeney a false prophet of unionism and ostracized him. Eighty years later, a new UMWA president made his great grandson an honorary member. I cannot speak for what it means to the other museum board members. For me, it was another cup of water in the marathon.

Both new state and national administrations made it clear they favored industrial expansion over environmental and preservationist concerns. FOBM adjusted our strategy accordingly. I learned that Randy Huffman would be stepping down as the director of WVDEP in January 2017 and I made one final attempt to finalize the LUMP settlement. The effort only lasted a few phone calls. Huffman politely listened to my last-ditch sales pitch but, ultimately, he and the state backed out of the verbal agreement to declare the Northwest Flank unsuitable for surface mining. Governor Jim Justice appointed Austin Caperton, a former coal executive, as the new head of WVDEP and declared the coal industry would stop hearing the word "no" from the state agency. "No matter what the request may be," Justice said of the industry, "the first words out of [WVDEP's] mouths should be we're going to try with all in us to do what you want to do." Two weeks into his new job, Caperton fired Wendy Radcliff, WVDEP's environmental advocate who had been sympathetic to FOBM and our efforts.[14] Harold Ward called me, said that he felt bad that the Northwest Flank deal fell through, and suggested that "maybe we should look again at approaching the Army Corps of Engineers."

Things did not look good. No one at FOBM felt optimistic about the ACOE; working with them in the past had been like cutting a ribeye with a spork. In addition, we realized that the coal industry, emboldened by Trump and Justice's victories, had no interest in furthering negotiations on the battlefield, so we looked to other avenues and continued to keep Blair Mountain in the public consciousness. The very presence of the Mine Wars Museum and the numerous events we held there obviously helped. Working on the museum's journal allowed me an avenue with which to both expand upon the prevailing historic narrative and keep the issue fresh in people's minds. Betsy Merritt, of the National Trust for Historic Preservation, recommended me to write an article on our preservation work in the Trust's *Forum Journal*. The opportunity enabled me to tell our story and, for the first time, reveal the drama behind Camp Branch and the proposed National Guard base. Historian Benjamin Sawyer and Bob Crawford, bass player for the Avett Brothers Band, invited me to tell our story on their history podcast, *The Road to Now*. Independent reporter Matt Orfalea interviewed me via Skype and made a YouTube video about our efforts, including a narrative about the National Guard base. The Cultural Landscape Foundation, based out of Washington, DC, also promoted our efforts. Although we appeared stuck in the mud, we continued to build support and let the industry know that we were not going anywhere.

Eventually our struggle caught the attention of freelance writer Ron Soodalter, who wrote an in-depth narrative of the Second Battle of Blair Mountain for *The Progressive*. Ron interviewed most of us at FOBM and reached out to

Wooten and McDaniel, who refused to speak with him. Ron did gain an audience with General James Hoyer, with whom Mary Anne Maul and I had met twice regarding the National Guard base. Late in the evening on November 28, 2017, Ron emailed me with some shocking news. I immediately called him to verify what I had read. "It's true," he said. "General Hoyer assured me that the National Guard no longer has plans to build the 7,000-foot runway. He said I could quote him on it."

This was gigantic news. The National Guard had been conducting training exercises on the 4,000-foot runway for some time, but they had abandoned plans for the second runway. Alpha Natural Resources originally planned to blast Camp Branch Area B, which intruded onto the battlefield, in order to provide the material for this second runway. If the National Guard no longer wanted the runway, Alpha had no reason to blast on the battlefield. Hoyer did not specify when or why the military had changed its plans. In our 2016 meeting with the coal executives, plans for the 7,000-foot runway were still very much on the table for "God and country," as Greg Wooten exclaimed. To this day, we do not have a definitive answer, but I cannot imagine that the military would have scrapped plans for the 7,000-foot runway without our intervention. Since 2013, everyone at FOBM felt that Camp Branch was the key to saving Blair Mountain. If we were correct, perhaps victory was within reach.

We did not celebrate yet. The Keeper continued to delay on a new ruling for the battlefield. For a time, we worried that the military might intervene behind the scenes so that they might expand the facility at Camp Branch. Ron Soodalter's findings managed to allay these fears, but we refused to rest on our laurels. Should the Keeper rule against us, we needed contingency plans. The success of the Kanawha Forest

Coalition in stopping a mountaintop removal permit near Charleston inspired a new strategy as our discussions with the legal team at the Sierra Club expanded to include flora and fauna on the battlefield. If we could document the existence of endangered or rare species of plants and animals, as the Kanawha Forest Coalition had, we could prevent further disturbances in the area regardless of the Keeper's ruling. Aside from his work as an amateur archeologist, Kenny King is also a talented photographer. For years, he has habitually photographed flowers while on the battlefield. We began searching his collection in the hopes of finding documentation of endangered regional plants such as the Running Buffalo Clover, the Harperella, and the Virginia Spiraea. Kenny made additional trips to the battlefield in search of rare and endangered flowers. We documented the presence of the rare yellow-fringed orchid, but because the state listed the flower as rare and not formally endangered, it could not initiate legal action. On the fauna side of the equation, we kept an eye out for examples of the rare Cerulean Warbler and evidence of the endangered long-eared bat. If we could find hibernacula or roost trees used by the long-eared bat, we could, according to Aaron Isherwood, curb any potential mining or timbering in the area. None of us at FOBM had much time to spend probing the forests around Blair for endangered plants and animals, but we put a plan of action in place if the Keeper's final order went against us. I recalled John McDaniel's words from our meeting in 2016, "We can hold new regulations up in courts for years." If the Keeper ruled against us, we could find ways—endangered plants, habitat, something—to hold them up in court until the value of the coal was not worth the effort.

As the wait continued, the spirit of Blair Mountain, and the miners who fought there, haunted the hills of West Virginia in ways even we could not predict. On Thursday, February 22, 2018, the Mine Wars Museum reserved a booth for History Day at the State Capitol. Kenny King and I had attended History Day in 2012 representing FOBM, and, as I described earlier, politicians avoided us like the plague. The Mine Wars Museum, however, received a much warmer welcome as the name did not have the same political connotation as FOBM. The museum has maintained a presence at History Day every year since 2016. Lou Martin and I represented the museum our first year; Catherine Moore and I handled the second. On the third year Katey Lauer and Lou planned to be there for the full day whereas I would meet them early in the morning to help set up our displays, after which I would leave to go teach class. About an hour before the Capitol building opened to the public, I met up with Lou and Katey on the Capitol grounds. Usually, many reenactment groups arrived early on History Day, toting displays and wearing their historic outfits. While it is somewhat amusing to stand in the security line at the entrance to the Capitol with men and women dressed in Civil War uniforms and colonial garb, it can also take a while to get inside and get everything set up in a timely fashion. Which is why we arrived an hour early. We were completely unprepared for the size of the crowd that awaited us.

Hundreds of striking teachers and school service personnel had already formed a significant line, which stretched for about fifty yards, at the entrance to the Capitol. We set up our display amid a swarm of teachers packing the area between the Senate and House Chambers. Polly, one of my two sisters and a high school Spanish teacher, arrived at our station with my niece and bought a couple of bandanas to wear.

"I'm Frank Keeney's great-granddaughter." She said, "So I have to wear a bandana."

She was not alone. By midday, thousands of teachers

filled the Capitol complex, holding signs, wearing matching T-shirts, and conducting coordinated chants. Dozens of them wore red bandanas. Katey and Lou sat at our station and watched as the spirit of Blair Mountain reemerged in front of their very eyes.

The strike itself lasted for thirteen days. Ultimately, the state agreed to a 5-percent wage increase for teachers and school personnel and Governor Justice appointed a task force to revise the West Virginia Public Employees Insurance Agency (PEIA) and address the high premiums. The victory in West Virginia inspired teachers in Oklahoma, Arizona, Kentucky, and Los Angeles to launch their own strikes. For those equipped with knowledge of West Virginia history, it came as no surprise that a resurgence in the American union movement would originate in the same place where the Battle of Blair Mountain occurred. Katie Endicott, a teacher from Mingo County understood this. "We know how to stand with courage because we have watched our parents, grandparents, and great-grandparents stand on the picket line," she said. "The willingness to stand is a part of our DNA; it is in our very blood."[15] Teacher Mark Salfia added, "West Virginia labor has a long and proud history of fighting for what is right. . . . We stood united fighting for the future of West Virginia just as our ancestors had done at Blair Mountain."[16]

The teachers' strike was a continuation of the tangible undercurrent resisting prevailing narratives about West Virginia. No matter what the textbooks say, what memes appear on social media, how much outsiders oversimplify, or what the Coal Association spouts, the red bandana continues to resurface. As long as people remember Blair Mountain, there will be those who will wear the bandana and march their own roads. The history is a well from which future activists may draw. I like to think that FOBM's preservation work and the Mine Wars Museum's success kept the history in the conversation enough to provide a spark of inspiration for the teachers in 2018.

Three months after the teacher's strike, the Keeper issued its final decision on the battlefield. In its ten-page decision, made public on June 29, the Keeper's Office described its methodology in determining the status of Blair Mountain. First, Deidre McCarthy, chief of the National Park Service Cultural Resource Geospatial Information System (GIS) Facility, identified all the parcels of land ownership that overlapped onto the 1,669 battlefield acreage at the time of the 2009 nomination. McCarthy found that her list matched SHPO's list of land parcels originally submitted to the Keeper. They determined that there were sixty-two land parcels on the battlefield. The Keeper's Office then contracted Zeigler & Zeigler L.C., a West Virginia law firm based out of Hinton, who specialized in real estate law and land records to identify the owners of these parcels that overlapped on the battle-field. The goal was to sift through the contradictions between the landowner and objection lists submitted by SHPO and Jackson Kelly. The research uncovered a number of discrep-ancies. Not only did the Keeper's research verify that dead people were on the objector list, they identified twenty-one other objectors who were not even landowners on the battle-field. Ultimately, the Keeper concluded that there were eighty-three owners on the battlefield and only twenty-eight valid objections. With the vast majority of landowners in approval, the Keeper placed the Blair Mountain Battlefield back on the National Register of Historic Places.[17]

Later that night, FOBM held a conference call in which we congratulated one another on finishing the fight. There were no parades, no big parties. The local media covered the victory, but aside from a couple of stories, the national media, fixated on the latest presidential tweets and scandals, barely took notice. It did not matter. We set out to prevent the blasting of the battlefield by the coal industry and the relisting meant that we achieved our original goal, saving around twelve miles of mountaintop ridgelines.

Many factors contributed to our victory. Early work proved to be crucial, from archeological studies by Kenny King, Harvard Ayers, and Brandon Nida to the 2011 protest march, which invigorated the preservation movement. Local groups such as the Ohio Valley Environmental Coalition, Keepers of the Mountains, the West Virginia Highlands Commission, and the West Virginia Labor History Association contributed heavily by joining us on lawsuits and supporting the 2011 march. Regarding FOBM, in 2012 we adopted three long-term strategies for winning at Blair Mountain:

1. **Identity Reclamation:** Take control of the public narrative and win the support of the local population.
2. **Become Citizen Regulators:** Learn the system and use it to our advantage.
3. **Political Maneuvering:** Get in the room with the power players and find a solution.

It is worth taking a moment to reflect upon these strategies and their outcomes.

First, we successfully took control of the narrative. When my tenure at Southern began in 2009, the coal industry dominated the cultural, socioeconomic, and political narrative in the coalfields. No one spoke of Blair Mountain in Logan. Although the coal industry influence remains strong, the movement to save Blair Mountain has effectively inserted Mine Wars history into the local and national consciousness.

People now travel across the country to visit the Mine Wars Museum. Even Joe Manchin, who would not publicly mention Blair Mountain for years, visited the Mine Wars Museum in 2016. His website featured a picture of him in front of the exhibits. To his credit, Manchin has recently become supportive of preserving the battlefield and even has voiced opposition for mountaintop removal mining.[18] Political candidates such as Paula Jean Swearengin, Richard Ojeda, and 2020 gubernatorial candidate Stephen Smith have all adopted the red bandana as a symbol and evoked the history of Blair Mountain in their political campaigns.

Filmmakers, artists, writers, and musicians have produced new works inspired by the history. West Virginia poets such as Crystal Good and V. C. McCabe have included Blair Mountain and the Mine Wars in their works. New novels by Topper Sherwood and Kimberly Collins have added to the growing fictional books surrounding Blair Mountain. *Storming Heaven: The Musical*, based off Denise Giardina's 1987 Mine Wars novel, debuted in 2019. Catherine Moore has authored a new book about the Mine Wars. Striking teachers reference the history and connect it to their own fight. National journalists refer to Blair Mountain more often in their coverage of labor and Appalachia. In 2020, the history gained even more national attention as our museum expanded to a new, much larger building across the street from our original location. We hope to add a public archive, library, and local art gallery in our new facility. Additionally, the Mine Wars Museum and other groups are gearing up to commemorate the Battle of Blair Mountain Centennial on Labor Day Weekend 2021.[19]

The efforts of the coal industry to destroy the battlefield inadvertently and ironically placed a greater spotlight on the history. We did not break the Mind Guard System, but we certainly gave it a black eye and a bloody nose. More people in the coalfields know about the Mine Wars than ever before and, thus, understand the need to preserve the places connected to the history. In 2009, a surface miner and student escorted me to my car on campus because he feared for my safety. Eight years later, strangers occasionally approached me and offer words of encouragement as I filled my tank at a gas station or when I stopped at Tudor's Biscuit World. Some of them have Trump and Friends of Coal bumper stickers on their trucks. We won this battle for local hearts and minds because we focused exclusively on the history and connected it to regional identity and labor. This strategy took years to materialize and patience to realize, but it worked—History. Labor. Culture.

We used the system to our advantage to win at Camp Branch. Our successful effort to stop surface mining on Area B of Camp Branch protected less than fifty acres of the battlefield, but it prevented Aracoma Coal from building a 7,000-foot runway for the Air National Guard. A significant amount of circumstantial evidence pointed to a link between plans for the base and the delisting of the battlefield. It is unlikely we will ever know all the details, but I find it difficult to believe that the National Guard would have abandoned plans for the runway without our efforts. If Aracoma Coal had blasted at Camp Branch and built the base according to their original plans, all bets would have been off concerning the rest of the battlefield.

We won at Camp Branch because we became citizen regulators. We learned the regulations, successfully documented infractions, and held the government regulators accountable for their failure to regulate the companies. We used the Freedom of Information Act to get all documents from every regulatory agency and copies of all the permits. We found a paper trail of the military base plans as well as proof that Aracoma Coal had violated the permit conditions and that the agencies had not enforced those conditions. We put together a scrappy win before the Surface Mine Board (SMB) and documented permit violations on Area B. Our efforts resulted in a federal investigation by the Office of Surface Mining Reclamation and Enforcement (OSMRE). The SMB acknowledged the necessity for more thorough archeological studies and it forced the West Virginial Department of Environmental Protection (WVDEP) to restrict mining to 1,000 feet from the battlefield. Camp Branch was a turning point in the Second Battle of Blair Mountain.

We also won support within the regulatory agencies. Over the course of eight years, FOBM repeatedly met and corresponded with six separate federal and state agencies, as well with politicians, corporate executives, and generals. Our understanding of local politics and culture enabled us to navigate our way forward and establish working relationships. We gained support from individuals within these agencies who anonymously gave us information and helped us behind the scenes. When the Keeper relisted the battlefield, several individuals at these agencies called me and offered their personal congratulations. To the present day, regulators call me and keep me abreast of any permit changes or industrial activity near the battlefield. As of 2019, Arch Coal had completed underground mining operations at Blair Mountain and had relocated their surface mining equipment to other areas of the state. Officials at WVDEP have assured me that they will not allow surface mining on the battlefield.

Legal victories also proved crucial. Although grassroots, local organizations led the way in saving the battlefield, we would not have been successful without legal support from the Sierra Club, the National Trust for Historic Preservation, and the United Mine Workers of America (UMWA). FOBM could be a pebble in the industry's shoe before the SMB, but

to win federal cases, we needed aid from the national organizations. They possessed the funds and legal teams necessary to win the National Register lawsuit. Aaron Isherwood
and the rest of the lawyers representing Sierra, the National
Trust, and the UMWA were wise enough to let us take the
lead on the local level and generous enough to give us the
legal backing needed to win. Over several years, we nurtured
good working relationships with individuals in these organizations in order to construct a formidable alliance. To have
an industrial union and the nation's largest environmental
organization on the same side of an issue is significant. More
such alliances will be necessary for political and economic
progress in the future.

Not all of our efforts bore fruit, of course. One of our
goals was to "get in the room" with the appropriate players
in order to reach a settlement. Although we did get in the
room, our efforts to negotiate creative solutions, such as
our proposal with the Northwest Flank, ultimately proved
unsuccessful. These efforts failed because corporate executives would not compromise and because political leadership overruled the agencies on the LUMP settlement, but we
nonetheless won the support of many men and women who
work as regulators and inspectors. Such support allows us
to continue to monitor potential timbering or gas drilling
threats to the battlefield.

Finally, we weathered internal storms. Stress, industry
intimidation, ideological differences, slow progress, and
a host of other factors can cause grassroots organizations
to fall apart. FOBM nearly collapsed beneath the weight
of what we tried to achieve, but we managed to perse-
vere. Although many individuals came and went throughout the course of our fight to save the battlefield, everyone

contributed to FOBM's success and each has earned a right to say that he or she helped win the Second Battle of Blair Mountain. I think people should be grateful for the history they helped preserve.

My family has fought the coal industry for over a hundred years. It is a legacy I cannot escape and it still follows me everywhere. The driveway where I park my car to visit my parents is the same one Frank Keeney walked up on his weekend visits to Alum Creek. A few blocks from where I now live in Charleston, I can see the building where Frank Keeney owned his nightclub. At Haddad Riverfront Park, where he parked cars in his old age, the city offers its Live on the Levee concerts to the public during the summer. I cannot go to one of these concerts without thinking of him. Certainly, with each step I took in the fight to save the Blair Battlefield, I felt Frank Keeney's shadow over my shoulder.

Something happened, though, as the Second Battle of Blair Mountain progressed. The history that weighed on me for so many years transformed from a shadow to a ray of light. It became a source of strength, pride, defiance, endurance, and victory. It is a ray of light passed from parent to child, like the man who took his son out of elementary school to meet Frank Keeney. It is passed from teacher to student. Not only with words in the classroom, but with deeds on the picket line. These rays of light continue to be passed from musician to listener, poet to reader, curator to visitor. In the end, I found that the real shadow was not the weight of the past, but the absence of it in the public consciousness.

I did not step out of Frank Keeney's shadow. Others pulled me out. From Kenny King, who took a metal detector onto Blair in 1991, to everyone who ever served in Friends of Blair Mountain, to lawyers who argued our cases, to the local environmental groups who supported us, to the protestors who marched, and to the team who worked to build the Mine Wars Museum. They saved Blair Mountain. They made it a light instead of a shadow. Thanks to them, the light will continue to shine.

# Appalachian Anthropocene

*The company still owns the land.*
—Denise Giardina

*You can't save these people. You can't save people who
don't want to be saved.*
—Joe Stanley

It bears repeating once more; Blair Mountain is not only
who we were, it is who we are. A glance around the
globe proves the point. Mine wars still wage in places like
Asturias, in northern Spain, where coal miners were fighting
their own conflict with companies and the state as recently
as 2012. Striking miners used handmade rockets to fire upon
riot police in yet another bloody mountain labor conflict.
In Colombia, fourteen union leaders were assassinated in
2018 alone. Exxon Mobile still employs twenty-first-century
versions of mine guards in Indonesia and Africa, who sometimes drive locals from their homes at gunpoint to make

way for drilling. Some of these locals are then forced into labor. Little children in Zimbabwe, Tanzania, and South Africa mine the earth for gems in company camps. The US Department of Labor estimates that currently around 152 million children work in forced labor around the world.[1] In this sense, the Battle of Blair Mountain did not end. It simply changed locations. As long as humans can get rich from digging things out of the ground, they will continue to do so. Wherever they do, there will be conflict, and someone will later try to cover it up. It makes one wonder how many undiscovered Blair Mountains have happened throughout world history. If we learn the lessons, perhaps there will be fewer in the generations to come.

Blair Mountain's future will likely be a reflection of the state's, and perhaps the nation's, destiny. Much depends upon our addiction to fossil fuels. Although mountaintop removal no longer threatens the battlefield, there are few legal protections from drilling and timbering. The landowners could choose to leave the acreage alone, it could become a park, or it could still be ravaged with drills, axes, and bulldozers. I can confidently state that everyone who worked to save Blair Mountain did so because we all want a better future for the region. We all realized that the economic and educational benefits of saving the place outweigh its value in coal, timber, and gas profits. If nothing else, the work of FOBM in saving the battlefield from mountaintop removal has demonstrated that preservation can be more valuable than extraction. Building is better than destroying. After the battlefield returned to the National Register, FOBM reached out to executives to see if they would be willing to reconsider selling company property on the battlefield. To date, they are not. Nonetheless, the history has found a welcome home in

Matewan where the Mine Wars Museum continues to grow alongside the reach of the story.

While West Virginians must continue to learn from coal's past, they must also come to grips with the fact that it is not our future. Our fight to save the battlefield coincided with a dramatic downturn in the coal industry. To many coal miners and their families, this downturn signified the success of President Barack Obama's "War on Coal" and the negative impact of federal environmental regulations on the industry. Oversimplified political rhetoric masked the truth that King Coal's reign over energy production in the United States nears an end. Throughout much of the previous century, coal produced over 50 percent of the electricity in the United States. Proponents of coal could rightfully say, "Coal keeps the lights on." By 2020, however, coal only produced 23.5 percent of the nation's electricity. These numbers will inevitably drop further in coming years as coal is replaced by renewable energy sources, nuclear energy, and natural gas.[2]

The natural gas boom coincided with King Coal's bust. As of April 2020, natural gas produced 38.4 percent of the nation's electricity while renewables climbed to 17.5 percent of the market.[3] The so-called Shale Revolution, which largely involved mass application of hydraulic fracturing—or fracking—meant that natural gas quickly became a cheaper way to produce electricity. By 2015, natural gas equaled coal as the main producer of electricity in the United States. Between 2010 and 2020, over 280 coal-fired power plants shut down or were scheduled for decommission. The downturn has been so dramatic and the changes in the market so substantial that Charles Patton, the executive vice president of external affairs for Appalachian Electric Power (AEP), declared that coal-fired power plants have, at best, a limited future. AEP announced that it has no plans to build new coal-fired power plants and will shut down much of its current thermal coal consumption in the coming years. "Technology causes you to look at the world differently," Patton observed. "You can't get stuck in the past or with the status quo. We've learned that and we are moving forward."[4]

The signs of the ascendency of natural gas are quite evident in West Virginia. Much of the state sits above the gigantic Marcellus Shale, which holds tremendous natural gas reserves. Energy corporations have taken notice and new drilling operations sprang up all across the state. By 2019, natural gas employed nearly as many people in West Virginia as coal. Meanwhile, overall gas production has more than tripled in the last decade. State leaders see the potential for gas to lead to a boom in chemical manufacturing, which could possibly create thousands of blue-collar jobs in the state. Governor Jim Justice has even attempted to lure the Chinese government into investing nearly $80 billion in natural gas infrastructure in West Virginia, despite indications in 2019 that natural gas extraction has far outstripped global demand.[5]

Skeptical observers justifiably believe that history is repeating itself in West Virginia. Journalist Ken Ward Jr. pointed out that natural gas development has proceeded along the same lines as the coal industry did over a century before. There is very little regulation of the industry within the state, WVDEP is severely limited in its ability to deny drilling permits, tax breaks are given to companies, and the tax money collected is not set aside for local education or infrastructure. State residents have dealt with property violations as gas companies have surveyed private property without consent of the owners. Gas companies who drill on private property with consent have found legal loopholes enabling them to pay fewer royalties to the landowners. Little regard is given to the impact of drilling on local water supplies or levels of methane leaked into the atmosphere. The proposed Mountain Valley Pipeline, which is intended to transport natural gas across a large portion of the state, was approved by WVDEP without a completed review on the environmental impacts. The Forest Service and Army Corps of Engineers, meanwhile, have either dropped studies before they were completed or actively changed their regulations to allow the pipeline to be constructed.[6] Such early indications make it appear as though West Virginia will continue to be stuck in an extraction economy that produces wealth for companies and few benefits for mountaineers. Echoing the familiar Mind Guard narrative, proponents of natural gas argue that West Virginians should be grateful for the jobs provided, rather than the companies being grateful for the resources we have. King Coal may have met his match, but it may only mean West Virginians are exchanging one fossil fuel king for another. If these criticisms hold true, the hopes so many are putting in natural gas may blow up in our collective faces.

In truth, the manner and ease with which natural gas companies are able to sweep into the state is only possible because West Virginians failed to learn the lessons of Blair Mountain. Scholars have seen this story before; unregulated extraction, local landowners left out, the servitude of elected officials, the language used to justify their actions, and the promises of jobs as ransom. Tragically, buried history may have buried the future of West Virginia.

Natural gas is not the only culprit in this story. There are several other factors contributing to the fall of King Coal in Appalachia. Coal reserves in the region are declining. A 2018 study published by the Appalachian Regional Commission puts it bluntly, "After aggressive mining in Central Appalachia for more than a century, the remaining coal is more expensive to extract, compared to other coal-producing regions, because it tends to be deeper in the ground and/or seams tend to be thinner."[7] More expensive extraction obviously cuts into the profitability of the industry and its ability to compete in the open market.

As mentioned earlier, renewable energy continues to gobble up a larger share of the electric production market. Between 2009 and 2015, the cost of building a new solar plant dropped by 80 percent. By 2018, solar power provided 374,000 jobs, over four times as many jobs as the coal industry, and nearly three times as many jobs as coal, oil, and natural gas plants combined.[8] Wind power also rose in prominence and currently employs more than 100,000 people in the United States, also surpassing coal employment.[9] By 2019, renewable energy employed over 555,000 people in the United States, compared to less than 54,000 jobs in the coal industry.[10] Certainly, as the technology for renewables continues to improve, solar and wind power will become more cost efficient, will be a better source of job creation, and will inevitably eat up a larger share of the energy market. If renewable power provides more jobs than coal and natural gas while contributing less than 20 percent of the energy supply, think of how many hundreds of thousands more jobs can be created with a more complete energy transition to renewables. Fossil fuel lobbyists who claim that the United States needs to stay with coal and natural gas to save jobs are spinning a ridiculous falsehood, one obviously apparent to anyone who can count. With proper investment, this energy transition could actually mean hope for coal country.

Not only would a transition to renewables create more jobs than fossil fuels, there is a moral argument for energy transition. Over 100,000 people have died from coal mining accidents in American history. Unknown thousands of miners have additionally died from black lung disease. To put it another way, more Americans have died mining coal than US combat deaths in the American Revolution, War of 1812, Mexican War, Spanish-American War, Korean War, Gulf War, Iraq War, and Afghanistan War combined.[11] As long as coal mining continues, miners will die from job accidents and black lung. Solar panel farms on former mountaintop removal sites could employ thousands of former coal miners who would no longer have any fear of black lung, mine collapses, explosions, and the boom and bust cycles of the industry. Indeed, why would anyone continue to support a form of electrical generation that inevitably kills some of its own workforce when we could transition to a type of energy production that kills no one?

The changing global market, specifically the demand for metallurgical coal used in making steel, put another nail in Appalachian coal's coffin. Although a trend more than a permanent condition, Asia's demand for steel diminished after 2012. The major coal corporations had expanded their assets in anticipation that China and India would become their golden goose. The global downturn in demand for metallurgic coal hit the industry at the worst possible moment. Although metallurgic coal demand has increased slightly since 2017, the industry is still at the mercy of the boom and bust cycles of the global market and can never be dependable as a steady form of employment. Although coal will continue to produce electricity in the Far East, Appalachian coal cannot compete with Western coal, whose companies can ship their product to the Pacific coast at a lower cost. Nor will Appalachian coal be able to compete with Australian, Indian, and Chinese coal companies and their own vast reserves.[12]

Environmental activism has also struck a blow, most specifically, the Sierra Club's Beyond Coal Campaign. Beyond

Coal has effectively challenged the coal industry with dozens of lawsuits. Most importantly, environmental groups have collectively won over the youth in America and Europe. Although the Mind Guard System still functions in the coalfields, younger people across Western civilization want a transition to forms of energy production that do not ruin the water, pollute the air, destroy the health of workers, and heat up the planet.

In similar fashion to the 1920s, the coal industry's overexpansion ultimately hurt its bottom line. As mentioned in chapter two, Peabody Energy, Alpha Natural Resources, and Arch Coal made massive acquisitions in 2011 and, as a result, accrued billions in debt. When the above factors combined to assault the industry, they did not have the financial reserves to absorb the blows and numerous companies declared bankruptcy. Like a kid fresh out of college weighed down by maxed-out credit cards and student loans, the industry stood no chance of weathering the economic storms.

Environmental regulations, although exaggerated for political purposes, have also damaged the industry. Most notably, the Mercury and Air Toxics Standards Rule, implemented by the Obama administration in 2015, made older coal-fired power plants more expensive to operate and less able to compete with other energy producers.[13] Without a doubt, Obama's proposed Clean Power Plan and new stream protection rules would encourage the demise of the coal industry, but the reason regulations are listed as last on this list instead of first is the simple fact that the Clean Power Plan and the new stream protection rules proposed to OSMRE never actually went into effect. The Supreme Court ruled that the EPA had overstepped its bounds with some aspects of the Clean Power Plan and the Trump administration killed the new stream protections before they could be implemented.[14]

It is possible that Obama's regulations influenced investors who began to turn their financial resources away from coal toward natural gas and renewables, but the regulations never became reality.

This drastic downturn in the industry immediately and tangibly impacted coal communities. Tax revenues for the state dropped considerably, leaving less funding for education and infrastructure. Mining jobs decreased. Although the company town system no longer exists in West Virginia, miners still face similar financial predicaments as their forefathers, leaving them woefully unprepared for the industry's collapse. Many miners today start work immediately out of high school; a few do not even wait until graduation and drop out early. Even though miners today make much more than in previous generations, the current system, in the absence of the company towns and stores, is still based on a credit lending system with a healthy dose of consumer culture. In the twenty-first-century coalfields, a miner takes the job and often marries young. It is common for high school sweethearts to marry a year or two after graduation and begin raising a family shortly thereafter. Of course, the young couple will need a home. After taking his new job, the miner is generously advanced credit at the local bank for a new mortgage and referred to a local dealership where he can buy himself a new pickup and a new SUV for his wife. SUVs, I found, are a status symbol in the coalfields. It is common for a miner to buy an SUV costing at least $40,000 for his wife and give her a Coal Miner's Wife sticker to put on the back. His new truck will also be at least $40,000. The young miner, lacking an education that could equip him to manage his finances, may also overextend with the purchase of new toys: a four-wheeler, a state-of-the-art tree stand for deer hunting, some new hunting rifles and gear, a big flat screen television with surround sound, and so on. In short, by the time he is twenty-one, our miner is a husband, father, homeowner, enormously in debt, and living paycheck to paycheck, just as his ancestors did. As coal companies go bankrupt and lay off workers, families find themselves mere weeks away from economic ruin.

Predictably, families have moved away from Appalachia. Enrollment at the college where I teach has dropped. Certainly, coal country has seen downturns before, but this is different. In the past, unemployed miners and their families depended on extended families, the union, and the local churches in their times of need. In central Appalachia, extended families have often provided an important safety net during bust cycles of the industry, but patterns of out-migration have scattered rural families and the safety net is simply not as large as it once was. Union members have traditionally looked out for one another during hard times and tough strikes, but the vast majority of union membership is retired and continually diminishing in number. Churches have also provided dependable and necessary charitable work in the region for generations. The congregation I attend gives away thousands each year in charity: from food baskets, to feeding the homeless and orphans, to school supplies for underprivileged kids, and other direct assistance to those who have fallen on difficult times. While the hillsides are still dotted with hundreds of church buildings, many of them today have significantly dwindling congregations. This is due, in part, to young people moving away after college and to those fleeing unemployment in the coal industry. It is also due to changes in social norms, as fewer Generation Xers and Millennials regularly attend churches. Thus, numerous congregations only entertain an elderly few. These churches do not have the energy or the resources to offer help as they once did.

The lack of such traditionally dependent safety nets certainly exacerbates an already difficult time in the coalfields. As a remedy, the Obama administration offered up the Power Plus plan, intended to pump government money into coal country for the purpose of retraining workers and building a post-coal economy. Hillary Clinton announced that she would expand on this policy. Whether or not these plans would have made a difference, we will never know, as Donald Trump defeated Clinton and killed the Power Plus plan. A few coal families truly believed they would not need the plans because Trump promised to bring back coal jobs. Many others were not delusional enough to deny reality; they just wanted coal jobs to be available long enough to get their kids to college. These families live life on a cliff. Theirs is the reality of potential death in the mines and the psychological burden accompanying such risk. They live in a constant state of debt with no savings. When you walk the tightrope in life, you cannot afford to think twenty steps ahead; you can only concentrate on the next step. Plans promising to retrain miners, who are married with children, for jobs that do not yet exist are not going to be welcomed, even if they are the best option. It is no surprise that miners do not want to go back to school for training in a new occupation. It is even less of a surprise that they cannot think ten years ahead to the impacts of climate change when they are thinking two weeks ahead to the next paycheck and the bills. But regardless of anyone's preferences, King Coal's days are numbered. The tragedy is that state and federally elected leaders have failed to prepare their constituents for this inevitability even though they knew it was coming.

Whether my fellow West Virginians like it or not, a journey through the wilderness is upon us. If there is to be a Promised Land at the end, we must build it ourselves. Thankfully, efforts to build a new Appalachia are underway. Community colleges, such as the one where I teach, have opened new technical programs to retrain coal miners. The UMWA offers scholarships to unemployed coal miners as well. I have been fortunate enough to teach a number of these miners and have seen them earn their degrees. Young Appalachians are also forging ahead with their own initiatives. Take Stephanie Tyree, for instance. A lawyer, activist, and participant in the 2011 protest, Stephanie became the director of the West Virginia Community Development Hub. Under her guidance, the Hub has helped develop numerous community economic projects around West Virginia such as the Turn This Town Around project and WV First, which connects small business owners around the state.[15]

Those searching for a new economy in Appalachia often look to former mine sites. Abandoned mountaintop removal sites amount to an astonishing 330,000 acres in West Virginia alone. Although very little of this property has been developed, organizations are emerging with a variety of ideas. Investment in solar panel farms could provide thousands of jobs, but solar energy is just one of many solutions. The group Cultivating Appalachia creatively hopes to promote lavender farms. Lavender grows well on the barren mine sites and could be harvested for oil to be used in soaps and other cosmetics. Project leaders estimate that such farms could annually generate around $10,000 an acre.[16] Still others favor hemp or medical marijuana cultivation, cash crops with enormous profit potential.

Unfortunately, inadequate reclamation practices and the failure of the state to require reliable surety bonds have created huge barriers to developing former surface mine sites. Coal companies have managed to skirt their financial responsibilities to clean up their abandoned mines by declaring bankruptcy, transferring their assets, and leaving state taxpayers to foot the bill. This corporate escape strategy has left Appalachian communities with continual chemical drainage that infects local water supplies. Major shareholders and high-level executives of these absentee corporations are shielded from the environmental damages and costs as they sacrifice the long-term health and economic development of West Virginia for their short-term economic benefit.[17]

The Reclaiming Appalachia Coalition is an exciting initiative meant to deal with this problem. The coalition is divided into five sister social enterprises. Reclaim Appalachia works specifically with abandoned mining lands for future development. Rediscover Appalachia aims to promote tourism and small craft businesses. Refresh Appalachia works to grow a vibrant local farm and food economy. Local farmers can register with the organization and make their produce available to order online and have it delivered to one of several distribution sites. Revitalize Appalachia coordinates community-based construction and reconstruction projects in abandoned and vacant buildings across the region. Rewire Appalachia promotes expansion of solar power, IT, and broadband in rural communities.[18]

Helpful legislation has been proposed. In 2017, a bipartisan group in both houses of the United States Congress introduced the Reclaim Act. This bill promises to generate $1 billion in funding for economic development on former mining sites. Although polls show that approximately 89 percent of voters in Appalachia support the bill, the National Mining Association and West Virginia Coal Association, among others, have heavily lobbied against it, since it would provide an economic alternative to coal mining in the region. The Trump administration, however, refused to support the legislation and the bill has yet to pass.[19]

Author Richard Martin suggests a GI Bill for coal miners.[20]

Fearing a return to the Great Depression after World War II, the federal government passed legislation to provide education and accessible mortgages for returning service members. Historians credit the GI Bill as being one of the more successful pieces of economic legislation in the twentieth century, as it greatly helped expand the middle class and build a postwar economy. In similar fashion to US soldiers, coal miners have risked their lives and many have paid the ultimate price for the prosperity of other Americans. A GI Bill revised and retuned for miners could lessen the blow energy transition will levy on thousands of families in West Virginia and elsewhere and help build a post-coal economy.

Historian Stephen Stoll went as far as drafting his own piece of legislation for Appalachia. The proposed Commons Communities Act calls for the creation of a series of commons communities organized by the US Department of Agriculture. These commons would be designed for a specified population and managed by the residents. Corporations would not be allowed to own property on these commons. Stoll suggests that income taxes on the top 1 percent of household incomes and an industrial abandonment tax, placed on fossil fuel and manufacturing corporations that have left the region, will pay for social services and education within these commons. Stoll himself admits that the idea needs further development and that significant obstacles to passage and implementation of such an act exist or, as I have told my students many times, every football play ever devised works perfectly on the chalkboard. Regardless of its practicality, Stoll's idea is correct in identifying the need for more regional economic autonomy and local control over land and resources. Such autonomy, if properly applied, could enable regions to better withstand economic recessions and climate disruption.[21]

Yet another promising strategy is to learn from successful

ventures in other mountain and extraction regions around
the world. Tom Hansell's documentary and companion
book, *After Coal: Stories of Survival in Appalachia and Wales*,
searches for answers in this way. Hansell chronicles efforts
to build an international dialogue with events such as the
Global Mountain Regions Conference. He explores Welch
community regeneration in their deindustrialized coalfields
and notes that the most successful projects are often bottom
up and grassroots in origin. Indigenous businesses and local
entrepreneurialism are needed to rebuild dilapidated industrial regions. As Hansell's work demonstrates, participation
from the federal government is also helpful. The Welch government supports a program called Communities First. This
program funds community regeneration projects without
dictating the destiny of former coal towns. Regeneration in
Wales is also aided by the fact that many former mining sites
are public lands managed by the Forest Commission.[22] Most
former mining sites in Appalachia, by contrast, are still privately owned by absentee corporations that have little stake
in building regional infrastructure.

Attempts at political reform are underway. Candidates such
as Paula Jean Swearengin and Richard Ojeda openly challenge
absentee corporations and the local good-old-boy system.
Stephen Smith, 2020 West Virginia gubernatorial candidate,
has launched an effort to bring about no less than a political paradigm shift in West Virginia. His campaign slogan,
"West Virginia Can't Wait," aspires to break the state free of
fossil fuel and outside corporate control, rebuild unions, and
champion socially progressive ideals. Smith often evokes the
Mine Wars in his rhetoric and boasts an agenda that he calls
"the boldest state platform in modern American history."[23]
Katey Lauer, his campaign manager, has set about creating
a grassroots organizational infrastructure for nearly seventy

state candidates. If successful, their ambitious agenda could certainly upset the political balance of power in the state.

Appalachia will need many solutions if it is to overcome the considerable obstacles of the twenty-first century. West Virginia is one of the few states to lose population in recent years. Young people are not staying. The opioid crisis has ravaged the region. There is no piece of legislation that can rebuild a broken home and drugs have broken many in the mountains. Many mountains themselves are also broken. Corrupt politicians and compromised regulatory agencies have allowed coal companies to get away with destroying water, air, and infrastructure while leaving no funds for the cleanup. Many creative ideas now circulate regarding former mountaintop removal sites, but as Denise Giardina put it in the last line of her novel *Storming Heaven*, "The company still owns the land." As long as they do, development cannot reach its potential in a way that benefits locals. Meanwhile the federal government, which could be a significant source of funding and regeneration for Appalachia, is $23 trillion in debt. It is uncertain how a government in such a massive financial hole can be a reliable funding source in the future. But perhaps the largest impediments to a sustainable future in Appalachia are the combined juggernauts of global over-consumption and climate change.

As the population of earth approaches eight billion people, climate change and global overconsumption will likely reshape the geopolitical landscape of the entire planet in the coming decades. Industrial agriculture will face near-term threats, migrations will increase, regional conflicts for resources will become the norm, and reactionary nationalism will continue to rear its ugly head. Furthermore, the 2020 COVID-19 pandemic has exposed perilous vulnerabilities in our global-ized neoliberal world—our overdependence on world food and trade supply chains, our lack of any semblance of regional economic self-sufficiency, deficiencies in infrastructure. The list goes on. If climate change and global overconsumption continue unabated, the 2020 pandemic will serve as a mere preamble for what the twenty-first century has in store. Thus, any plans for a sustainable economy in the region must take into account the changing world around us. Unless industrialized nations dramatically alter the ways they function, we may soon find that adaptability is a far more realistic goal than sustainability.

My experience with the Blair Mountain Battlefield taught me that industrialists will fight tooth and nail to delay any real action on climate change for as long as possible, no matter the consequences. Even if the political will exists to enact giant legislation such as the proposed Green New Deal, fossil fuel corporations will challenge it in court. Even if they lose, they can delay implementation for years. Unfortunately, we do not have many years to burn. Such realization has led scholars such as Dr. Jem Bendell, professor of Sustainability Leadership and founder of the Institute for Leadership and Sustainability at the University of Cumbria, to conclude that building a sustainable future is now an impossibility. Bendell has coined the term *Deep Adaptation* to describe how societies must prepare themselves for agricultural collapse, mass migrations, wars over vital resources, and crumbling economic systems.[24] This is not to suggest that everyone should build a bunker in preparation for the apocalypse, but those working to shape the future must do so with their eyes open to reality. Regions must become more economically and agriculturally autonomous so that we can be better prepared to adapt. Unfortunately, many West Virginians I know dismissively roll their eyes at the very mention of climate change. Call it a Stockholm Syndrome, a Mind Guard System, a canary in a cage, or whatever you

wish, psychological barriers must be broken if we are to successfully navigate the Anthropocene.

I would like to think that everyone's work to save Blair
Mountain has broken a few of those barriers and taken us a
few steps in the right direction. Earlier in this book, I have
referred to Blair Mountain as a sacred landscape. To understand Blair Mountain as sacred is more than simply placing
value on the history, it represents a needed reversion to a preindustrial mentality that views the natural world as something
more than a road to material wealth. The love of money is the
root of all evil, not the love of mountains. If our civilization
truly begins to view places such as Blair Mountain in a more
reverent and sacred light, we may yet find a better road ahead.

## • LESSONS FROM THE ROAD •

If activism were easy and fun, everyone would do it. In the
course of our efforts to save the Blair Mountain Battlefield,
Friends of Blair Mountain (FOBM) took on three multi-
billion-dollar corporations, a state government, and the military-industrial complex. We won with no fundraising, little
use of the internet, and without resorting to civil disobedience as a tactic. Conventional knowledge suggests that activists need all of these things to achieve their aims. The success
of FOBM defies such wisdom. We proved that it is possible
to achieve victory in a different, albeit less glamorous, way.
This is not to claim that we were perfect, or made every correct decision. My hope is that other activists, and potential
activists, can read our story and find our tactics and strategy,
our successes and failures, useful in their own crusades. In
that spirit, I have compiled a list of advice for the budding
activist. If I had a time machine and could visit myself ten

years ago, below is the list I would present to myself. Take it for what you will:

· Achieving your goal will be harder than you think and take longer than you anticipate and, no, you are not the exception.

· You are running a marathon, not a sprint. Adjust your strategies and mentality accordingly.

· Protests have their place but successful activism is much more than protests.

· Expend energy on strategies capable of producing tangible gains.

· Build alliances.

· Pragmatism is more crucial to success than idealism.

· Surround yourself with people who are dependable and levelheaded.

· Avoid those who talk big and deliver little. You will inevitably interact with many who do.

· Do not seek or expect glory for your activism. Try to distance yourself from those who do.

· Most of your friends and family will not understand what you are doing and why you are doing it. You will not be able to explain it to them. You must learn to be at peace with this.

· The majority of people you know will not share your passion, even if they agree with your stance. This does not mean that you do not attempt to spread the fire inside you, but it means many people will simply not care as much as you do. You must learn to be at peace with this. If you do not, it will drive you insane.

- The longer your activism endures, the more you will be tempted with self-righteousness. Resist it.

- When dealing with your companions, remember that it is easy to tear down and difficult to build up. Strive to do that which is difficult.

- Resist too much emotionalism. This is not to curb your passions, but to direct them. If emotional highs are the wind in your sails, you will not weather the storms.

- Be patient and resolute. Endure.

- Whenever possible, treat those who oppose you as adversaries, but not as enemies. If you hate those who oppose you, your emotions may get the better of you, causing you to act rashly or foolishly. Hate impedes your road to success.

- When dealing with politicians, regulators, or executives, do your best to always be polite and professional, especially when you least want to be.

- Learn from those who oppose you—how they use the system to their advantage. Learn their methods. It will help you win.

- Develop a strong work ethic.

- Do not boast about your work ethic. Let it stand on its own as an example.

- If you are underestimated, count it as a blessing. It may even be a good idea to encourage others to underestimate you. Let them feel superior. Use their arrogance and miscalculation against them.

- Continue to be patient and resolute. Endure a little more.

- Trust no one.

· The previous line is actually a joke. I am just a fan of the *X-Files* and thought it would look cool on the list.

· Keep your sense of humor. It is a lifeline.

· Document everything.

· Constantly discuss strategy.

· Having the moral high ground is wonderful, but it in no way ensures victory.

· Prepare to be hated by people who claim to be on your side.

· Your personal relationships, and perhaps your career, will suffer as a result of the path you have chosen. Deal with it. Do not let it make you bitter. Count the cost before you begin and know that your personal life may be a casualty of the war you wage.

· Listen to everyone and everything.

· Have faith.

· If I have not mentioned it before, be patient and resolute. Endure to the end.

Lastly, I encourage you to find your own Blair Mountain. Wherever you live, look around. Surely there is something that can be improved: a school policy to change, a better county commission, a building to be restored, a place to be remembered and cherished. The fight to save Blair Mountain educated me on the importance of local and state politics and the need to restore America from the bottom up. Instead of placing hopes on would-be messiahs in Washington, reengage in the world immediately outside your door. You may find another Blair Mountain right in front of you. Once you do, step onto the road and do not look back.

# Acknowledgments

>>>>> <<<<<

**A**cademics are typically not much on faith, but without my faith in God, I could not have been successful or even managed to keep my sanity over the previous ten years. Thanks go out to my close friends and family for their unwavering love and support. Special thanks to everyone who served in Friends of Blair Mountain, the Mine Wars Museum crew, every lawyer who has given us representation, the Sierra Club, the Ohio Valley Environmental Coalition, the West Virginia Highlands Conservancy, the National Trust for Historic Preservation, the West Virginia Labor History Association, and the United Mine Workers of America for their indispensable contributions. Shawn Sowards, Bill Clough, Lillie Teeters, Lou Martin, and Ron Soodalter reviewed early versions of this manuscript and provided valuable insight. Big thanks go out to the brilliant Paul Corbit Brown who generously allowed me to use his photographs in this book. I greatly appreciate Derek Krissoff and the staff at West Virginia University Press for working with me and giving this story a platform. Elizabeth Catte also provided strong editorial assistance, helping me whittle the original draft down to a manageable size. I am eternally grateful for you all. *Montani semper liberi.*

# Glossary

**Army Corp of Engineers (ACOE):** A federal agency within the Department of Defense that primarily oversees dams, canals, and the protection of US waterways. Under the Clean Water Act, the ACOE issues and regulates 404 permits for development projects, such as surface coal mining, that may have adverse impacts on waterways.

**Blair Mountain Battlefield Nomination Area (BMBNA):** Stretching for over twelves miles of ridgelines in Logan County, West Virginia, the nomination area refers to the specific 1,669 acres of the battlefield as described in its official nomination for inclusion in the National Register of Historic Places.

**Battlefield Buffer Zone:** Sometimes referred to as the *view shed*, this is a 1,000-foot boundary around the entirety of the Blair Mountain Battlefield Nomination Area. Development projects that intrude within the 1,000-foot boundary can be subject to review by state or federal regulatory agencies.

**Clean Water Act:** Passed in 1972, this legislation governs water pollution in the United States and empowers the Army Corps

of Engineers to issue permits and regulate projects that may
have adverse impacts on waterways.

**Friends of Blair Mountain (FOBM):** Created in 2010, this
nonprofit organization works to protect and preserve the Blair
Mountain Battlefield.

**Friends of Coal:** Created in 2002, this group functions as the
public face of the coal industry in West Virginia. They work
to improve the image of the industry by creating television
and radio ads, conducting educational programs, influencing
school curriculum, and sponsoring numerous regional sporting events ranging from college football games to high school
cheerleading competitions.

**Keeper of the National Register:** This official serves in the
National Park Service and oversees the National Register of
Historic Places. The Keeper's Office maintains the National
Register and evaluates properties nominated for inclusion on
the list. The Keeper has the final authority to approve or deny
nominations based on the regulatory process established in the
National Historic Preservation Act.

**Lands Unsuitable for Mining Petition (LUMP):** This type of
petition seeks to protect sites of significant historic or environmental value from surface mining. State departments of environmental protection evaluate such petitions and have the authority
to protect certain acreage by declaring it unsuitable for surface
mining. In 2011, FOBM and other groups submitted a LUMP
to the West Virginia Department of Environmental Protection.

**National Historic Preservation Act (NHPA):** Originally
passed in 1966, this legislation is the most significant historic

preservation law in the United States. The Preservation Act created the Advisory Council on Historic Preservation, the National Register of Historic Places, State Historic Preservation Offices, and the Section 106 Review Process. The law intends to provide some protection for historic and archeological sites, specifically sites listed on the National Register.

**National Register of Historic Places:** This is an official list of properties and sites in the US deemed worthy of preservation. The Keeper's Office, within the National Park Service, oversees the National Register. A variety of factors determine a property's eligibility for inclusion on the National Register, including its historic or cultural value and the integrity of the site. Properties on the National Register are eligible for grants, loans, and tax incentives for the purpose of preservation or restoration. Properties can also gain a measure of protection through the Section 106 Review Process or through state laws, which vary from state to state.

**Office of Surface Mining Reclamation and Enforcement (OSMRE):** A federal agency within the Department of Interior created by the Surface Mining Control and Reclamation Act in 1977. OSMRE has its headquarters in Washington and three regional offices, one of which is located in Charleston, West Virginia. This agency sets federal regulatory standards on surface mining and has the authority to inspect mining sites. However, its primary function is to oversee state departments of environmental protection. If the state agencies are not properly enforcing the law, OSMRE investigates and intervenes.

**Section 106 Review:** Established by the National Historic Preservation Act, a Section 106 Review requires regulatory agencies to consider the effects of any development projects, such as mining, on properties eligible for listing on the National Register. In a 106 Review, the State Historic Preservation Office works with companies and other groups that have a vested interest in the site to assess any potential adverse impacts a project may have and work to mitigate damages. At times, mitigation between companies and activist groups takes the form of a programmatic agreement, where the companies agree to meet certain terms before the project begins.

**State Historic Preservation Office (SHPO):** Under the National Historic Preservation Act, each state is required to create a State Historic Preservation Office. This office oversees nominations of sites for inclusion in the National Register, coordinates Section 106 Reviews, and assesses potential damage to historic sites from projects such as mining. SHPO often submits recommendations to regulatory agencies and companies but does not have the independent authority to deny mining and construction permits. The head of SHPO is a political appointee chosen by the governor.

**Surface Mine Board (SMB):** Within the West Virginia Department of Environmental Protection, the Surface Mine Board hears legal appeals regarding mining permits and regulatory infractions. The board is comprised of seven members, all appointed by the governor, and has the authority to revoke permits, deny permits, and cite companies for breaking regulations.

**Surface Mining Control and Reclamation Act (SMCRA):** Passed in 1977, this law regulates surface mining and reclamation of surface mines. The law requires coal companies to obtain a permit before surface mining and to post a bond sufficient to cover the cost of reclaiming a mined surface area, and it prohibits mining in national parks and other designated areas. The law created the Office of Surface Mining Reclamation and Enforcement (OSMRE) that sets regulatory standards individual states must either meet or exceed.

**West Virginia Coal Association:** Founded in 1915 with its headquarters in Charleston, West Virginia, this organization works to advance the interests of the coal industry on a state and federal level. Nearly every coal producer in the state is a member of the Coal Association. The Coal Association's efforts focus on lobbying for advantageous legislation and endorsing political candidates. They are an extremely effective organization and, in the past, have demonstrated the ability to block legislation or get legislation passed. It is difficult for any politician in West Virginia to win an election without their endorsement.

**West Virginia Department of Environmental Protection (WVDEP):** Created in 1991, WVDEP controls the state's environmental regulatory programs. Regarding coal mining, WVDEP sets state guidelines, issues surface and underground mining permits, inspects mines, and directly handles enforcement. Federal oversight of surface mining is provided through the Office of Surface Mining Reclamation and Enforcement (OSMRE). The director of WVDEP is a political appointee chosen by the governor.

# Notes

## PREFACE
..........

1.  Raymond Chafin, *Just Good Politics: The Life of Raymond Chafin*
    (Pittsburgh: University of Pittsburgh Press, 1996), 1.

## CHAPTER ONE. FIGHTING FOR A BATTLEFIELD
...................................................

1.  Petri J. Raivo, "Politics of Memory: Historical Battlefields and Sense of
    Place," *Nordia Geographical Publications* (2015 Yearbook 44:4): 97,
    http://www.worldcat.org/title/politics-of-memory-historical-battlefields
    -and-sense-of-place/oclc/729076608.
2.  Scholars do not agree on the exact numbers of who participated in the
    armed march. Corbin argues that 15,000 to 20,000 is a safe estimate. In
    recent years, 10,000 has become the standard number used, although no
    new evidence has emerged to give us precise numbers. See David Alan
    Corbin, *Life, Work, and Rebellion in the Coal Fields: The Southern West
    Virginia Miners, 1880–1922* (Chicago: University of Illinois Press, 1981),
    218–224.
3.  Technical Report Number 2: The Battle of Blair Mountain, Cultural
    Resource Survey and Recording Project, West Virginia University,
    Institute for the History of Technology and Industrial Archaeology,
    January 16, 1992, 142.
4.  Bryan T. McNeal, *Combatting Mountaintop Removal: New Directions*

*in the Fight Against Big Coal* (Chicago: University of Illinois Press, 2011), 19–21.

5. For details on the Preservation Act, see "National Historic Preservation Act of 1966," NPS.gov, https://www.nps.gov/history/local-law/nhpa1966 .htm, accessed on April 19, 2020.

6. Harvard Ayers, "Blair Mountain Exposed: What the History Books Won't Tell Us," *Blair Mountain Journal* 1, no. 1 (Fall 2013): 5–8.

7. Miners must apply to get benefits and coverage if they contact black lung disease. For a good look at how Jackson Kelly has worked to keep miners from those benefits, see Chris Hamby, "Coal Industry's Go-To Law Firm Withheld Evidence of Black Lung, at Expense of Sick Miners," *Center for Public Integrity,* October 29, 2013, https:// publicintegrity.org/environment/coal-industrys-go-to-law-firm-withheld -evidence-of-black-lung-at-expense-of-sick-miners/. For a list of the Order of Vandalia Award winners, see "Roll of the Order of Vandalia," West Virginia University, https://vandalia.wvu.edu/roll-of-the-order-of -vandalia, accessed on December 10, 2019.

8. Legal briefs, Sierra Club, et al. v. Ken Salazar, et al., No. 10-1513-RBW, March 11, 2011, 1–3.

9. Sierra Club v. Salazar, 14–17; for news coverage of the delisting, see Jeff Biggers, "Mountaintop Removal Mayhem: Blair Mtn Scandal (Feds See Dead People), Coal Profits Soar, EPA Disses Scientists," *Huffington Post,* May 25, 2011, http://m.huffpost.com/us/entry/416028.

10. Howard B. Lee, *Bloodletting in Appalachia* (Morgantown: West Virginia University Press, 1969), 87–88.

11. C. Belmont Keeney, "A Republican for Labor: T. C. Townsend and the West Virginia Labor Movement, 1921–1932," *West Virginia History* 60 (2004–2006): 2–3.

12. The world's first coal-fired power plant debuted in Manhattan on September 4, 1882. It was invented by Thomas Edison. Jeff Goodell, *Big Coal: The Dirty Secret behind America's Energy Future* (Boston: Mariner, 2007), 102.

13. Information on my family history comes from Roscoe C. Keeney Jr., *2,597 Keeney Relatives* (Parsons: McClain Printing Company, 1978), 8–11, 65–66. For detailed information on Keeney and Mooney's role in Paint Creek and Cabin Creek, see C. Belmont Keeney, "Rank and File Rednecks: Radicalism and Union Leadership in the West Virginia Mine Wars," in Melinda Hicks and C. Belmont Keeney eds., *Defending the Homeland: Historical Perspectives on Radicalism, Terrorism, and State Responses* (Morgantown: West Virginia University Press, 2007): 18–27.

14. Quotes taken from Fred Mooney, *Struggle in the Coal Fields: The Autobiography of Fred Mooney* (Morgantown: West Virginia University Press, 1967), 46; Winthrop Lane, *Civil War in West Virginia* (New York: B. W. Huebsch Inc., 1921), 85; and Edmund Wilson, *The American*

*Jitters: A Year of the Slump* (New York: C. Scribner's Sons Inc., 1932), 150.

15. Robert Shogun, *The Battle of Blair Mountain: The Story of America's Largest Labor Uprising* (Cambridge, MA: Westview Press, 2004), 141.
16. Lane, *Civil War in West Virginia*, 85–86.
17. Malcolm Ross, *Machine Age in the Hills* (New York: MacMillan and Company, 1933), 155.
18. Ross, *Machine Age*, 155.
19. Keeney letter to local union, 1922, Kanawha County Coal Operators Association Collection, West Virginia State Archives, Charleston, West Virginia.
20. Ross, *Machine Age*, 157, 160–161.
21. For a more detailed look at Keeney's role in the organization of the Armed March on Logan and subsequent Battle of Blair Mountain, see Keeney, "Rank and File Rednecks," 29–37.
22. Lane, *Civil War in West Virginia*, 87.
23. *Hearings, The West Virginia Coal Fields*, 67th Congress, 1st Session, 1921, 198–199.
24. Jerry Bruce Thomas, *An Appalachian New Deal: West Virginia in the Great Depression* (Lexington: University Press of Kentucky, 1998), 8–11.
25. *Charleston Daily Mail*, April 22 and April 30, 1931; Mooney, *Struggle in the Coalfields*, 147; William Blizzard Jr., telephone interview by author, June 15, 2000; *United Mine Workers Journal*, September 1, 1930 to January 1, 1932. In virtually every issue of this journal during that time, a section was dedicated to denouncing Keeney and his union.
26. Edmund Wilson, "Frank Keeney's Coal Diggers," *The New Republic* (July 1931): 195–199.
27. Gordon L. Swartz III, "Walter Seacrist: A Songwriting Miner Remembers the Mine Wars," in Ken Sullivan, ed., *The Goldenseal Book of the West Virginia Mine Wars* (Charleston, WV: Pictorial Histories Publishing Company, 1991): 33–35.
28. *The Charleston Gazette*, August 5, 1931; *Huntington Herald-Dispatch*, August 12, 1931; Wilson, "Frank Keeney's Coal Diggers," 195–199.
29. David Alan Corbin, "Frank Keeney Is Our Leader and We Shall Not Be Moved: Rank and File Leadership in the West Virginia Coal Fields," in Gary Fink and Merl Reed, eds., *Essays in Southern Labor History: Selected Papers, Southern Labor History Conference* (Westport, CT: Greenwood Press, 1976): 144–145.
30. Ross, *Machine Age*, 157.
31. James and Geraldine K. Jackson Interview by author, Charleston, West Virginia, August 1993; Kathleen Keeney and Donna K. Lowry Interview by author, Alum Creek, West Virginia, August 1992.
32. C. Belmont Keeney, "A Union Man: The Life of C. Frank Keeney," unpublished masters' thesis, Marshall University, 2000, 56–61.

33. C. Belmont Keeney, "Still Fighting Blair Mountain," *Preservation Alliance of West Virginia Newsletter* 16, no. 2, November 2009.
34. Harvard Ayers to Chuck Keeney, email, November 9, 2010.


## CHAPTER TWO. MARCHING INTO BLAIR

................................................

1. Jordan Freeman, one of the directors of *Blood on the Mountain*, filmed my interview with Ken Hechler in 2012 during which we discussed his impressions of Nazis, Martin Luther King Jr., Truman, and others. See also Richard Goldstein, "Ken Hechler, West Virginia Populist and Coal Miners' Champion Dies at 102," *New York Times*, December 11, 2016.
2. Shirley Stewart Burns, *Bringing Down the Mountains: The Impact of Mountaintop Removal on Southern West Virginia Communities* (Morgantown: West Virginia University Press, 2007), 26–27.
3. Burns, *Bringing Down the Mountains*, 29–30.
4. Sean O'Leary and Ted Boettner, *The State of Working West Virginia: 2012*, West Virginia Center on Budget and Policy, September 2012, https://wvpolicy.org/wp-content/uploads/2018/5/SWWV2012_091912.pdf.
5. For a look at the labor environmental standoff over Dakota, see Chis White, "Labor Unions, Liberals, Come to Blows over Dakota Access Pipeline," *Daily Caller*, August 19, 2016, http://dailycaller.com/2016/09/19/liberals-labor-unions-come-to-blows-over-dakota-access-pipeline/.
6. Steve Mellon, "Murder of the Yablonskis," *Pittsburgh Post-Gazette*, April 26, 2013, https://newsinteractive.post-gazette.com/thedigs/2013/04/26/murder-of-the-yablonskis/.
7. Bryan T. McNeil, *Combatting Mountaintop Removal: New Directions in the Fight Against Big Coal* (Chicago: University of Illinois Press, 2011), 82–83.
8. Underground miners always carry extra water with them during a shift in the mines so that they have an emergency supply in case of a tunnel collapse or some other incident. During the heyday of unionism, if a miner poured out his extra water (usually in a bucket), the action signaled a walk out or strike. Production would immediately halt and the miners would leave the work site. It is well known throughout coal country that miners would do this during deer season. I personally observed it numerous times throughout my youth. The practice became so prominent that some coal operators would simply shut down their mines for a few days during the season to allow miners to hunt.
9. Laurence Leamer, *The Price of Justice: A True Story of Greed and Corruption* (New York: Times Books, 2013), 65–68.
10. Michael Shnayerson, *Coal River: How a Few Brave Americans Took on*

*a Powerful Company—and the Federal Government—to Save the Land They Love* (New York: Farrar, Straus, and Giroux, 2008), 19–25.

11. McNeil, *Combatting Mountaintop Removal*, 104–108.

12. Shannon Elizabeth Bell, *Fighting King Coal: The Challenges to Micromobilization in Central Appalachia* (London: MIT Press, 2016), 93–96.

13. For information on the Friends of Coal campaign, see https://www .friendsofcoal.org/.

14. Peter A. Galuszka, *Thunder on the Mountain: Death at Massey and the Dirty Secrets Behind Big Coal* (Morgantown: West Virginia University Press, 2014), 46–49, 181–182.

15. Shnayerson, *Coal River,* 118–120.

16. Joyce M. Barry, *Standing Our Ground: Women, Environmental Justice, and the Fight to End Mountaintop Removal* (Athens: Ohio University Press, 2012), 52–59.

17. John Alexander Williams, *Appalachia: A History* (Chapel Hill: University of North Carolina Press, 2002), 236. For use of the word *Red Neck* in conjunction with the Mine Wars, see Fred Mooney, *Struggle in the Coal Fields* (Morgantown: West Virginia University Press 1967), 15–38; Howard B. Lee, *Bloodletting in Appalachia* (Parsons, WV: McClain Printing Company, 1968), 94–106.

18. Patrick Huber and Kathleen Drowne, "Redneck: A New Discovery," *American Speech* 76, no. 4 (Winter 2001): 434–437; Fredrick A. Barkey, "Red Men and Rednecks: The Fraternal Lodge in the Coalfields," un-published presentation given to the author: 1–6.

19. Nancy Isenberg, *White Trash: The 400 Year Untold History of Class in America* (New York: Viking, 2016), 187–189.

20. Kurt Anderson, "The Protestor," *Time* 178, no. 25 (December 26, 2011): 54–89.

21. Michael Martinez, "EPA Revokes Permit for Hilltop Mining Project in West Virginia," CNN, January 13, 2011, http://www.cnn.com/2011 /US/01/13/west.virginia.epa.coal/index.html; Vic Svec, "Peabody Energy Completes Acquisition of Macarthur Coal," PR Newswire, December 20, 2011, https://www.prnewswire.com/news-releases/peabody-energy-nyse -btu-completes-acquisition-of-macarthur-coal-135915093.html.

22. Mayur Sontakke, "Why All Major Acquisitions in the US Coal Industry in 2011 Failed," *Market Realist,* December 3, 2014, http://marketrealist .com/2014/12/major-acquisitions-us-coal-industry-2011-failed/.

23. *Charleston Daily Mail,* July 7, 2011.

24. Lou Martin, "Marching to Blair Mountain and Beyond," *Blair Mountain Journal* (Fall 2012): 14.

25. David Alan Corbin, *Life, Work, and Rebellion in the Coal Fields: The Southern West Virginia Miners, 1880–1922* (Chicago: University of Illinois Press, 1981), 222.

26.  Corbin, *Life, Work, and Rebellion,* 221.
27.  Lon Savage, *Thunder in the Mountains* (Pittsburgh: University of Pittsburgh Press, 1991), 106–107.

## CHAPTER THREE. CAMP BRANCH

.......................................

1.   Testimony of Joe Stanley and Kenneth King, SMB Hearing Transcript, December 9, 2013, 58–61, 120–121 (hereafter cited as SMB Transcript).
2.   General Allen E. Tacket to John Jones and Greg Wooten, October 9, 2009, Freedom of Information Act (hereafter cited as FOIA).
3.   Greg Wooten to John Jones, November 4, 2009, FOIA.
4.   West Virginia State Code, Section 22-3-22, Subsection (d).
5.   Details about our internal disagreements, the issues surrounding the Blair Community Center and Museum, and the standoff between FOBM's board and its executive director are well documented in our board minutes from March 6 to April 15, 2012. Regina Hendrix, our board secretary at the time, recorded detailed notes from eight different conference calls regarding these matters. For purposes of brevity and to avoid pouring salt into old wounds, I left a few details out of the main narrative.
6.   One can find a full copy of the Clean Water Act at https://www.epa .gov/sites/production/files/2017-08/documents/federal-water-pollution -control-act-508full.pdf, accessed on September 14, 2017.
7.   SMCRA can be accessed online at https://www.gpo.gov/fdsys/pkg /USCODE-2011-title30/pdf/USCODE-2011-title30-chap25.pdf, accessed on September 14, 2017.
8.   A full copy of the Preservation Act, with amendments, can be found at "National Historic Preservation Act of 1966," NPS.gov, https://www .nps.gov/history/local-law/nhpa1966.htm, accessed on April 19, 2020.
9.   I have been told about the little black books kept by magistrates and county officials by a variety of sources, including state troopers. I'm probably in a few myself. For the perpetuation of these county fiefdoms in the latter half of the twentieth century, see Ronald Eller, *Uneven Ground: Appalachia Since 1945* (Lexington: University Press of Kentucky, 2008), 30–32.
10.  Eller, *Uneven Ground,* 245.
11.  Jared Diamond, *Collapse: How Societies Choose to Fail or Succeed* (New York: Penguin Books, 2005), 176–177, 275–276.
12.  One can watch the Marsh Fork Elementary protest in the Jordan Freeman's documentary film *Low Coal,* Evening Star Productions Inc., 2011.
13.  WVDEP Permit S-501390, Amendment No. 1, FOIA.
14.  Supplemental Information to Section 3.5 of the EID Camp Branch Surface Mine, Corps of Engineers, I.D. No. 199900448, FOIA.

15. There are several written accounts of Keeney's meeting with General Bandholtz. Perhaps the most thorough is found in Fred Mooney's biography. Mooney was with Keeney at the meeting. See Fred Mooney, *Struggle in the Coal Fields: The Autobiography of Fred Mooney* (Morgantown: West Virginia University Press, 1967), 91–92.
16. West Virginia State Code, Section 22-3-22, Subsection (d).
17. Roger Calhoun, Director, Charleston Field Office, OSMRE to Joe Stanley, November 19, 2013.
18. Information on the West Virginia Surface Mine Board can be found at "Surface Mine Board," West Virginia Department of Environmental Protection, http://www.dep.wv.gov/smb/Pages/default.aspx.
19. Testimony of Charles Belmont Keeney III, SMB Transcript, 26.
20. West Virginia Surface Mine Board, Order Denying Aracoma Coal Company's Motion to Intervene, Appeal No. 2013-07-SMB, January 22, 2014.
21. OSMRE began an investigation of Camp Branch after our site visit. The investigation looked into three areas: that the companies interfered with our ability to document the visit, whether or not the companies had illegally mined on Part B of Camp Branch, and whether historic preservation laws, according to the permit conditions, were being properly followed. The details are listed in this letter: Roger Calhoun to Joe Stanley, November 19, 2013.
22. Harold Ward to Joe Stanley and Friends of Blair Mountain, Informal Review, May 8, 2014. This letter summarizes the state's action in enforcing the 1,000-foot buffer zone as well as its reasoning for calling the disturbances "timbering."

**CHAPTER FOUR. THE NORTHWEST FLANK**

1. James Green, *The Devil Is Here in These Hills: West Virginia Coal Miners and Their Battle for Freedom* (New York: Atlantic Monthly Press, 2015), 274–275.
2. Michael M. Meador, "The Siege of Crooked Creek Gap," in Ken Sullivan, ed., *The Goldenseal Book of the West Virginia Mine Wars* (Charleston, WV: Pictorial Histories Publishing Company, 1991): 66–69.
3. Tom Clarke to Derek Teaney and Jessica Yarnell, July 5, 2011, FOIA.
4. Clark to Teaney and Yarnell.
5. "Logan, WV Surface Mine Turned into National Guard Training Facility," *The Logan Banner*, July 25, 2014.
6. Ginger Mullins to Charles Belmont Keeney, July 21, 2014.
7. Blair Mountain Memorandum of Agreement, Draft, July 21, 2014, 8. Hereafter cited as Blair Mountain MOA.
8. Blair Mountain MOA, 10.

9.   Blair Mountain MOA, 10–11.
10.  William M. Hunter, "Cultural Historic Survey for the Proposed Aracoma Coal Company Camp Branch Surface Mine Amendment No. 2, Logan County West Virginia," Cultural Resource Analysts Inc., July 29, 2014, i, 6–7.
11.  Charles B. Keeney to Ginger Mullins, Army Corps of Engineers, August 15, 2014.
12.  James E. Casto, "Elk River Chemical Spill," *West Virginia Encyclopedia*, June 11, 2018, http://www.wvencyclopedia.org/articles/2428.
13.  Elizabeth S. Merritt, Deputy Counsel National Trust for Historic Preservation, and Peter Morgan, Staff Attorney Sierra Club Environmental Law Program, to Ginger Mullins, Chief, Regulatory Division, US Army Corps of Engineers, August 27, 2014, 1.
14.  Merritt and Morgan to Mullins, 6.
15.  Laura P. Karr, Staff Attorney, UMWA, to Ms. Ginger Mullins, August 21, 2014, 2.
16.  Sierra Club, et al., Appellants v. Sally Jewell, in Her Official Capacity as Secretary of the US Department of Interior, et al., Appellees, Appeal from the United States District Court for the District of Columbia, August 26, 2014, No. 12–5383, 8.
17.  Harold Ward, Acting Director, WVDEP, to Joe Stanley and Friends of Blair Mountain, May 8, 2014, 3.
18.  Billy Joe Peyton to Charles Keeney, Harold Ward, Mark Schuerger, and Fran Ryan, September 6, 2014.
19.  Peyton to Keeney, Ward, Schuerger, and Ryan.
20.  Camp Branch Surface Mine Application, United States Army Corps of Engineers, #199900448, 2005, 148.
21.  Bradley W. Stephens, Friends of Blair Mountain, Inc., Initial Brief, Joe Stanley & Friends of Blair Mountain, Inc., v. West Virginia Department of Environmental Protection, Appellee, and Aracoma Coal Company, Inc., Intervenor, Appeal No. 2014-01-SMB, (Submitted on October 16, 2014), 2–3.
22.  Christopher M. Hunter, Intervener's Proposed Findings of Fact and Conclusion of Law, Joe Stanley & Friends of Blair Mountain, Inc., v. West Virginia Department of Environmental Protection, Appellee, and Aracoma Coal Company, Inc., Intervenor, Appeal No. 2014-01-SMB, (Submitted on October 16, 2014), 4.

**CHAPTER FIVE. IDENTITY RECLAMATION**

1.   Niall Ferguson, *Civilization: The West and the Rest* (New York: Penguin Books, 2011), 324.

2. David W. Blight, *Beyond the Battlefield, Race, Memory, and the American Civil War* (Boston: University of Massachusetts Press, 2002), 120–121.
3. John Gaventa, *Power and Powerlessness: Quiescence and Rebellion in an Appalachian Valley* (Urbana: University of Illinois Press, 1980), 252.
4. David Alan Corbin, *Life, Work, and Rebellion in the Coal Fields* (Chicago: University of Illinois Press, 1981), 61.
5. Gaventa, *Power and Powerlessness,* 61–63.
6. Gaventa, *Power and Powerlessness,* 61.
7. James Green, *The Devil Is Here in These Hills: West Virginia Coal Miners and Their Battle for Freedom* (New York: Atlantic Monthly Press, 2015), 143–144.
8. Lon Savage, *Thunder in the Mountains: The West Virginia Mine War* (Pittsburgh: University of Pittsburgh Press, 1990), 155–159.
9. John Hennen, *The Americanization of West Virginia: Creating a Modern Industrial State, 1916–1925* (Lexington: University of Kentucky Press, 1996), 97.
10. Hennen, *Americanization of West Virginia,* 98, 140.
11. Hennen, *Americanization of West Virginia,* 62.
12. Hennen, *Americanization of West Virginia,* 141.
13. P. H. Penna speech transcript, Logan County Coal Operators Association Collection, West Virginia State Archives, Charleston, West Virginia.
14. Phil Conley, "West Virginia War," *The New York Times,* August 27, 1922.
15. G. T. Swain, *The Blair Mountain War: Battle of the Rednecks,* reprint (1927; repr., Chapmanville, WV: Woodland Press, 2009), 2.
16. Swain, *Blair Mountain War,* 3.
17. Swain, *Blair Mountain War,* 9–10.
18. *Preston Republican,* March 18, 1923.
19. *Preston Republican.*
20. Phil Conley, *History of the West Virginia Coal Industry* (Charleston, WV: Education Foundation, Inc., 1960), 1.
21. Conley, *West Virginia Coal Industry,* Preface.
22. Marshall Buckalew, "Phil Conley," *The West Virginia Encyclopedia* (Charleston: West Virginia Humanities Council, 2006), 160.
23. Phil Conley, personal journal entry, December 30, 1933. Phil Conley Collection, West Virginia State Archives, Charleston, West Virginia.
24. Memorandum, John D. Newsome to Mrs. Kerr, February 6, 1940, 1, Phil Conley Collection.
25. Memorandum, Newsome to Kerr, 3.
26. Memorandum, Newsome to Kerr, 4; Martin G. Cherniack, "The Hawk's Nest Tunnel Disaster," *The West Virginia Encyclopedia* (Charleston, WV: West Virginia Humanities Council, 2006), 324–325.
27. Paul D. Casdorph, "Homer Adams Holt," *The West Virginia Encyclopedia,* 346.
28. Memorandum, Newsome to Kerr, 4.

29. *The New Republic*, November 29, 1939, 153.
30. Memorandum, Newsom to Kerr, 6.
31. Memorandum, Newsome to Kerr, 1–2.
32. Jerry Bruce Thomas, "The Nearly Perfect State: Governor Homer Adams Holt, the WPA Writers' Project, and the Making of West Virginia: A Guide to the Mountain State," *West Virginia History* 52 (1993): 91–108.
33. Senator Dwight Griswold to John Foster Dulles, January 28, 1953; Senator Robert A. Taft (Ohio) to John Foster Dulles, February 9, 1953; W. S. Hallahan to Phil Conley, December 20, 1954; Eric Hallbeck to Mr. Costi J. Eliasco, September 8, 1955, Conley Collection.
34. Phil Conley, *West Virginia Yesterday and Today* (Charleston: West Virginia Review Press, 1931); Phil Conley and Boyd Stutler, *West Virginia Yesterday and Today* (Charleston: Education Foundation of West Virginia, 1952); and Phil Conley and Boyd Stutler, *West Virginia Yesterday and Today* (Charleston: Education Foundation of West Virginia, 1966).
35. Conley, *West Virginia Yesterday and Today*, 1931 edition, 150. This edition was used in schools until the 1950s.
36. Conley, *West Virginia Yesterday and Today*, 150–151.
37. Otis K. Rice, *West Virginia: The State and Its People* (Parsons, WV: McClain Printing Company, 1972), 240.
38. Vicki Wood, *West Virginia: The History of an American State* (Atlanta: Clairmont Press, 2004).
39. David Alan Corbin's eighth-grade experience mirrored my own. See David Alan Corbin, ed., *Gun Thugs, Rednecks, and Radicals: A Documentary History of the West Virginia Mine Wars* (Oakland: PM Press, 2011), 1–2.
40. Corbin, *Gun Thugs, Rednecks, and Radicals*, 3–4.
41. Toby Wilkenson, *The Rise and Fall of Ancient Egypt* (New York: Random House, 2013), 40–43.
42. Jackson J. Spielvogel, *Hitler and Nazi Germany: A History* (Upper Saddle River, NJ: Prentice Hall, 1996), 171–174.
43. Spielvogel, *Hitler and Nazi Germany*, 808–809.
44. Joshua A. Fogel, ed., *The Nanjing Massacre in History and Historiography* (Berkeley: University of California Press, 2000), 92.
45. Hennen, *Americanization of West Virginia*, 38.
46. One can also watch videos of the Ladies Auxiliary conducting their presentations on the Friends of Coal website: http://www.friendsofcoal ladies.com/#!coalintheclassroom/c6l0. Accessed on June 14, 2016.
47. *The Greening of Planet Earth* is available to watch on YouTube: https://www.youtube.com/watch?v=ep5ptrPN6ns, accessed on June 14, 2016. This film was followed by the 1998 sequel, *The Greening of Planet Earth Continues*, which is also available on YouTube: https://www.youtube.com/watch?v=27XbnyWC5WM, accessed on June 15, 2016.

Although both films were funded by fossil fuel interests, they interestingly do not dispute global warming at all, but rather argue that global warming will increase crop yields worldwide and make the Earth a more lush, luxurious planet.

48. Bruce Gellerman, *Living on Earth: Coal in the Classroom*, radio broadcast, May 13, 2011, transcript, http://www.loe.org/shows/segments .html?programID=11-P13-00019&segmentID=3.

49. Website of Cedar Inc., http://www.cedarinc.org/, accessed on June 15, 2016.

50. Website of the West Virginia Coal Association, http://www.wvcoal.com /cedar.html, accessed on June 15, 2016.

51. Jie Jenny Zou, "Pipeline to the Classroom: How Big Oil Promotes Fossil Fuels to America's Children," *Guardian*, June 15, 2017.

52. Gellerman, *Coal in the Classroom.*

53. Eric Eyre, "WV House Oks Block on Science Standards Over Global Warming," *Charleston Gazette-Mail*, February 26, 2016, http://www .wvgazettemail.com/article/20160226/GZ01/160229560.

54. Jared Diamond, *Collapse: How Societies Choose to Fail or Succeed* (New York: Penguin Books, 2005), 432–433.

55. Richard Martin, *Coal Wars: The Future of Energy and the Fate of the Planet* (New York: Palgrave MacMillan, 2015), 65.

56. Operatives in the Baldwin Felts Detective Agency sent report letters to Albert and Lee Felts detailing the information they gleaned from their spying activities, including crawling under company houses in Mingo County. See the Felts Collection, Eastern Regional Coal Archives, Bluefield, West Virginia.

57. Application Blue Book, Adkins Fork Surface Mine, Permit # S-5005-03, West Virginia Department of Environmental Protection, 62.

58. Paul Nyden, "Historians Urge Creation of Blair Mountain Park," *Charleston Gazette,* June 25, 2012.

59. Nyden, "Historians Urge Creation of Park."

60. Nyden, "Historians Urge Creation of Park."

61. Deborah Weiner, "Script Was a Way of Life: Company Stores, Jewish Merchants, and the Coalfield Retail Economy," *Culture, Class, and Politics in Modern Appalachia: Essays in Honor of Ronald L. Lewis* in Jennifer Egolf, Ken Fones-Wolf, and Louis C. Martin, eds. (Morgantown: West Virginia University Press, 2009): 34–37.

## CHAPTER SIX. THE LONG ROAD

1. David Mistich and Ashton Marra, "Five Ways the West Virginia GOP Made History in the 2014 Election," November 5, 2014, http://wvpublic

.org/post/five-ways-west-virginia-gop-made-history-2014-election #stream/0.

2. Mistich and Marra, "Five Ways GOP Made History"; "West Virginia State Senate Elections, 2014," Ballotpedia, https://ballotpedia.org/West_ Virginia_State_Senate_elections,_2014, accessed on December 26, 2017; "West Virginia House of Delegates Elections, 2014," Ballotpedia, https:// ballotpedia.org/West_Virginia_House_of_Delegates_elections,_2014, accessed on December 26, 2017.

3. Blankenship Trial Timeline, *Charleston Gazette-Mail*, https://www .wvgazettemail.com/news/special_reports/blankenship_trial/, accessed on December 26, 2018.

4. West Virginia Surface Mine Board, Appeal No. 2014-01-SMB, Final Order, December 19, 2014.

5. Jonathan Greene, "Bill Protects Coal Miner Pension Benefits," *Richmond Register*, December 26, 2019, https://www.richmondregister.com/news /senate-oks-bill-to-protect-coal-miner-pension-benefits/article_6668926a -f7da-5401-a30d-a0bf2f40a849.html.

6. Ken Ward Jr., "Trial Testimony to Focus on Blankenship's Push for Coal Production," *Charleston Gazette-Mail*, October 5, 2015, https://www .wvgazettemail.com/news/trial-testimony-to-focus-on-blankenship-s -push-for-coal/article_d438da41-a6c2-572f-a74f-0f4039119a4c.html.

7. Dana Ford, "Former Massey Energy CEO Don Blankenship Found Guilty of Conspiracy," CNN, December 3, 2015, http://www.cnn .com/2015/12/03/us/west-virginia-don-blankenship-verdict-massey -energy/index.html; Kate Gutman, "Families React to Blankenship Verdict," *Charleston Gazette-Mail*, April 6, 2016, https://www.wvgazette mail.com/news/families-react-to-blankenship-verdict-i-hold-a-tombstone -you/article_78f6c498-90b3-5270-975f-6ed334a27aa4.html.

8. Nearly all of the meeting's details described in my narrative comes directly from Betsy Merritt's excellent and detailed notes, which she emailed to me on January 12, 2016.

9. Sierra Club, et al., v. Ken Salazar, et al., Memorandum Opinion, United States District Court for the District of Columbia, April 11, 2016, 15–16.

10. Sierra Club v. Salazar, Memorandum Opinion, 17–19.

11. Sierra Club v. Salazar, Memorandum Opinion, 39.

12. Sierra Club v. Salazar, Memorandum Opinion, 41.

13. Sierra Club v. Salazar, Memorandum Opinion, 46.

14. Ken Ward Jr., "Justice Says He's Going to Make DEP Stop Saying 'No' to Industry," *Charleston Gazette-Mail*, February 8, 2017.

15. Elizabeth Catte, Emily Hilliard, and Jessica Salfia, eds., *55 Strong: Inside the West Virginia Teachers' Strike* (Cleveland: Belt Publishing, 2018), 24.

16. *55 Strong*, 43.

17. Joy Beasley, Keeper of the National Register of Historic Places, Decision Memorandum, June 27, 2018, 5–10.

18. Stephen Lee and David Shultz, "Coal Backer Manchin Comes Out against Mountaintop Removal Mining," *Bloomberg Environment*, December 17, 2019, https://news.bloombergenvironment.com /environment-and-energy/coal-backer-manchin-comes-out-against -mountaintop-removal-mining.

19. New works of fiction and poetry regarding the Mine Wars include Topper Sherwood, *Carla Rising* (Martinsburg, WV: Appalachian Editions, 2015); Kimberly Collins, *Blood Creek: The Mingo Chronicles: Part I* (Williamson, WV: Blue Mingo Press, 2019); and V. C. McCabe, *Give the Bard a Tetanus Shot* (Milwaukee: Vegetarian Alcoholics Press, 2019). The West Virginia Public Theatre produced *Storming Heaven: The Musical* in 2019 as well. A quick Google search will reveal that Blair Mountain has been mentioned in numerous national and even international publications in recent years, such as *Jacobin Magazine*, *The Progressive*, and *The Guardian*.

## EPILOGUE. APPALACHIAN ANTHROPOCENE

1. Natalio Cosoy, "The Spanish Miners' Fight for Survival" BBC Mundo, September 3, 2014, https://www.bbc.com/news/business-29012977; Tula Connell, "Colombia Food Workers Union Denounces Leader's Murder," Sintraimarga, November 16, 2018; Steve Coll, *Private Empire: Exxon Mobile and American Power* (New York: Penguin Books, 2013); US Department of Labor Report, https://www.dol .gov/sites/default/files/documents/ilab/ListofGoods.pdf, accessed on November 18, 2018.

2. John W. Miller and Peg Brickley, "Arch Coal Files for Bankruptcy," *Wall Street Journal,* January 11, 2016, https://www.wsj.com/articles/arch -coal-files-for-bankruptcy-1452500976; Dana Varinsky, "Nearly Half of US Coal Is Produced by Companies That Have Declared Bankruptcy— and Trump Won't Fix That," *Business Insider,* December 9, 2016, http:// www.businessinsider.com/us-coal-bankruptcy-trump-2016-12. See also U.S. Energy Information Administration statistics, https://www.eia.gov /tools/faqs/faq.php?id=427&t=3, accessed on April 19, 2020.

3. US Energy Information Administration statistics, https://www.eia.gov /tools/faqs/faq.php?id=427&t=3, accessed on April 19, 2020.

4. Emma Foehringer Merchant, "Trump Can't Save Coal," *GreenTech Media,* February 19, 2018, https://www.greentechmedia.com/articles /read/trump-cant-save-coal#gs.FvzCFOE.

5. Ken Ward Jr., "The Coal Industry Extracted a Steep Price from West Virginia. Now Natural Gas Is Leading the State Down the Same Path," *ProPublica,* April 27, 2018, https://www.propublica.org/article/west -virginia-coal-industry-rise-of-natural-gas. For a 2019 assessment of

the gas industry see Clifford Krauss, "Natural Gas Boom Fizzles as U.S. Glut Sinks Profits," *The New York Times*, December 11, 2019, https://www.nytimes.com/2019/12/11/business/energy-environment/natural-gas-shale-chevron.html.

6.   Ward Jr., "Coal Industry Extracted a Steep Price"; Kate Mishkin, Ken Ward Jr., and Beena Raghavendran, "Regulators Change the Rules to Ease Pipeline Approval," *Charleston Gazette-Mail*, August 10, 2018, https://www.wvgazettemail.com/news/wv_troubled_transition/regulators-change-the-rules-to-ease-pipeline-approval/article_34473938-91e4-556e-bc36-12ecb4a1fb4e.html.

7.   Eric Bowen, John Deskins, and Brian Lego, *An Overview of the Coal Economy in Appalachia*, Appalachia Regional Commission Study, January 2018, 6, https://www.arc.gov/assets/research_reports/CIE1-OverviewofCoalEconomyinAppalachia.pdf.

8.   Kristin Korosec, "US Solar Jobs Jumped Almost 25% in the Past Year," *Fortune*, February 7, 2017, http://fortune.com/2017/02/07/us-solar-jobs-2016/; Varinsky, "Nearly Half of US Coal"; National Solar Job Census, https://www.thesolarfoundation.org/national/, accessed on October 31, 2018.

9.   Bureau of Labor Statistics, https://www.bls.gov/green/wind_energy/, accessed on October 31, 2018.

10.  For 2019 statistics, see the Environmental and Energy Study Institute website, https://www.eesi.org/papers/view/fact-sheet-jobs-in-renewable-energy-energy-efficiency-and-resilience-2019#3, accessed on December 16, 2019. For 2019 coal employment statistics, see the US Energy Information Administration Report, October 2019, https://www.eia.gov/coal/annual/pdf/acr.pdf.

11.  Coal mining fatality statistics can be found at the Mine Safety and Health Administration website, https://arlweb.msha.gov/stats/centurystats/coalstats.asp, accessed on December 16, 2019. The US Department of Veterans Affairs has statistics on American war casualties; see "America's Wars" (fact sheet), https://www.va.gov/opa/publications/factsheets/fs_americas_wars.pdf, accessed on December 16, 2019. There are no accurate statistics on black lung deaths, although estimates range in the tens of thousands.

12.  Bowen, Deskins, and Lego, *Overview of Coal Economy in Appalachia*, 6–10.

13.  Bowen, Deskins, and Lego, *Overview of Coal Economy in Appalachia*, 8.

14.  Lawrence Hurley and Valerie Volcovici, "US Supreme Court Blocks Obama's Clean Power Plan," *Scientific American*, February 9, 2016, https://www.scientificamerican.com/article/u-s-supreme-court-blocks-obama-s-clean-power-plan/; Brad Plummer, "Why Trump Just Killed a Rule Restricting Coal Companies from Dumping Waste into Streams,"

*Vox*, February 16, 2018, https://www.vox.com/2017/2/2/14488448
/stream-protection-rule.

15. For information on the WV Hub, see "What We're Doing," The Hub,
http://wvhub.org/what-were-doing/, accessed on November 1, 2018.

16. Josh Dean, "The Future of Mountaintop Removal Is Lavender,"
*Bloomberg Businessweek*, December 17, 2018, https://www.bloomberg
.com/news/articles/2018-12-17/the-future-of-mountaintop-removal-is
-lavender.

17. Peter Morgan, "West Virginia Admits That Its Bonding System Is on the
Verge of Collapse," Sierra Club blog, April 17, 2020, https://www.sierra
club.org/articles/2020/04/west-virginia-admits-its-coal-mine-reclamation
-bonding-system-brink-collapse. For more details on mining, bonds, and
bankruptcy, see Jared Diamond, *Collapse: How Societies Choose to Fail
or Succeed* (New York: Penguin Books, 2005), 455–458.

18. Each sister organization of the coalition has their own website. For more
information, see the Reclaiming Appalachia Coalition website: https://
reclaimingappalachia.org.

19. Mary Kuhlman, "Not Too Late for Congress to Help KY Coal
Communities," *Public News Service—KY*, December 17, 2018, https://
www.publicnewsservice.org/2018-12-17/livable-wages-working-families
/not-too-late-for-congress-to-help-ky-coal-communities/a64938-1.

20. Richard Martin, *Coal Wars: The Future of Energy and the Fate of the
Planet* (New York: Palgrave MacMillan, 2015), 252–253.

21. Steven Stoll, *Ramp Hollow: The Ordeal of Appalachia* (New York: Hill
and Wang: 2017), 272–276.

22. Tom Hansell, *After Coal: Stories of Survival in Appalachia and Wales*
(Morgantown: West Virginia University Press, 2018), 14–15, 75–76, and
85–122.

23. Stephen Smith's platform is available online at https://wvcantwait.com
/peoples-platform/, accessed on December 26, 2019.

24. Jem Bendell, "Deep Adaptation: A Map for Navigating Climate Tragedy,"
IFLAS Occasional Paper 2, July 27, 2018, https://www.lifeworth.com
/deepadaptation.pdf.

# Index

CPSIA information can be obtained
at www.ICGtesting.com
Printed in the USA
LVHW111604120921
697673LV00001B/89

9 781949 199857